P9-BVG-772

world: the problem of individual self-realization.

Among the contributors to this collection are:

ERIC BENTLEY

E. M. FORSTER

IRVING DEER

JOHN NORTHAM

DISCARD
HEADQUARTERS
WEST GEORGIA REGIONAL LIBRARY.

TWENTIETH CENTURY VIEWS

The aim of this series is to present the best in
contemporary critical opinion on major authors,
providing a twentieth century perspective on
their changing status in an era of profound
revaluation.

Maynard Mack, *Series Editor*
Yale University

I B S E N

A COLLECTION OF CRITICAL ESSAYS

Edited by

Rolf Fjelde

1965

Prentice-Hall, Inc.   A SPECTRUM BOOK   *Englewood Cliffs, N.J.*

Copyright © 1965 by Prentice-Hall, Inc., *Englewood Cliffs, New Jersey*. A SPEC-
TRUM BOOK. All rights reserved. No part of this book may be reproduced in
any form, by mimeograph or any other means, without permission in writing
from the publishers. *Library of Congress Catalog Card Number 65-23303*. Printed
in the United States of America—C. P 44881, C 44882

Contents

H-117402

IBSEN

Introduction

by Rolf Fjelde

Study Molière, study Shakespeare; but, above all things, the old
Greeks, and always the Greeks.

GOETHE

"Do you remember," inquired Ibsen from Rome of his compatriot,
rival, and ally in Norwegian letters, Björnson,

> do you remember "The Tragic Muse" that stands in the room outside the
> Rotunda in the Vatican? No statue that I have seen in Italy has taught me
> so much. I would say that it has revealed the essence of Greek tragedy to me.
> That indescribably sublime, calm joy in the expression of the face, that
> laurel crowned head with something supernaturally exuberant and bac-
> chantic about it, those eyes that look both inward and yet through and
> far beyond the outward object they are fixed on—that is Greek tragedy.

To anyone casually acquainted with Ibsen's reputation and works, these
words must seem out of character. A playwright is nothing if not mul-
tivocal; but among Ibsen's several well-recognized voices, this one is still
largely unfamiliar. It bears no trace of the angry, polemical tone of the
social reformer, the scourge of middle-class morality, the iconoclastic
thesis dramatist pulling down, like a white-maned Samson, the pillars of
a complacent and corrupt society—the definitive voice greeted by the
latter nineteenth century with such partisan revulsion or delight. Nor
does it accord with the dry, cool, classroom manner of the master theater
technician conducting tidy dramaturgic experiments in a laboratory of
advanced ethics—the definitive voice listened to by the second quarter
of the twentieth century with polite, antiquarian interest and then ignored through (as Eliot once wrote of Ben Jonson) a most perfect conspiracy of approval.[1] Rather, it speaks out of the heart of Ibsen's problem in his time, and thereby prophetically out of that continuing problem
in our own—and thus it is central to what Eric Bentley calls the third

---

[1] Even Brecht, representing pre-eminently the Marxist, anti-individualist position,
conceded that "I have nothing against Ibsen or Schnitzler. They are very good—for their
own time and their own class." Martin Esslin, *Brecht: The Man and His Work* (New
York: Anchor Books, 1961), p. 53.

phase of the world's attitude toward the founder of modern drama.

This problem has sometimes been described as one of vocation, of what Ibsen variously referred to in himself as a call, a mission, or a life-work—but this is to state it too narrowly. Reduced to the self-sufficing, Gyntian terms of professional competence, his own chosen vocation was to become an artist, or, more specifically, a dramatic poet. As such, in the course of "the study of dramatic art and literature, the principles, systems and history of which have been my chief concern," he would inevitably need to develop his understanding of the fountainhead of Western drama, Greek tragedy; and it is here, in the crystallization of that understanding, that the statue of "The Tragic Muse" seems to have played its invaluable catalytic role.

The theme of finding one's true vocation recurs throughout Ibsen's life and work, but its full importance is revealed only if seen as part of a larger problem: not merely a subjective quest for personal realization, but also an objective effort toward imaginative insight into the main tendencies of an age and a civilization. Again and again Ibsen's protagonists—Brand, Peer Gynt, Nora Helmer, Rosmer, Hedda Gabler, Solness—are shown as foundering on the dilemma of what to make of their lives in a society that is at least nominally open, the "little northern democracy" of Henry James's phrase; they do so as regularly and as symptomatically as, in a closed, if dissolving, late medieval society the Shakespearean tragic hero foundered on some transgression of fixed order and degree. Like "the heavens themselves, the planets and this center," the earth, Shakespeare's hero had his ordained place; it was given him *a priori* by the laws of nature and of nations, and the entire complex machinery of Shakespearean tragedy seems designed to demonstrate to him, at his own cost, that ignorance of the law is no excuse.

The Ibsen hero, on the other hand, neither knows his own place, nor has much reason to. The laws still exist, but their beautifully articulated order has broken apart; and he must discover or fail to discover, at his own cost, their various workings deep in his human nature. The method he employs in doing so, like the one the scientist uses in the arena of physical nature, is empirical and experimental—he closely observes himself, like Solness, and tests himself, like Hedda. In this condition of being thrown back on himself, he reflects the arrival, after a two hundred year time-lag, of a kind of Cartesian doubt in the field of the drama. For the pressing question of the self and what to make of it, of which the theme of vocation is the most obvious expression, is simply the inward dimension of the objective predicament confronting the late nineteenth century man whose spiritual biography is written into the plays from

Brand to *When We Dead Awaken*: namely, that at the very moment he needs it most, his cultural inheritance proves itself not enough to live on; that his age and his civilization no longer transmit to him the hard currency of an adequate schema of values; and that, morally and intellectually insolvent, he finds himself being propelled into political, economic, social, and hence psychological changes that are unprecedented in all the centuries since the emergence of the bourgeoisie on the historic scene.

If any one awareness underlies the third and most recent phase of Ibsen criticism, threatening to become "definitive" for our time, it is that Ibsen's solution to this larger problem—which permitted him the saving self-realization in his work denied so many of his characters—was considerably more radical, in the original meaning of the word, than has hitherto been appreciated. Born into a provincial milieu in an out-of-the-way corner of Europe, plunged into early poverty, deprived of an adequate education, presented with a hollow and outmoded national tradition whose praises he was expected to sing through the medium of an art at probably its lowest ebb in centuries, he had the intellect, the imagination, and the energy to turn these deficiencies into challenges; and the strengthening of talent that occurred through his progressive conquests of adversity served to carry him further and further in the consuming passion of his life, which was, in those several areas that concerned him most, to get to the root of things and build fresh and clean from a groundwork of truth.

Radical truth as the essential goal and guiding principle in life stands at the center of his achievement in the drama. F. W. Kaufmann makes abundantly clear, however, just how complex and protean Ibsen felt the demands of this truth to be. In its most powerful, immediately previous embodiment—in the theater of Goethe and Schiller—the concept of truth had been asserted with an absolute claim expressive of the idealism, ultimately Platonic, accompanying the belated arrival of the Renaissance in Germany rather than the scientific picture of the universe that even then had rendered the traditional idea of a moral world order obsolete.[2] From the time Ibsen becomes aware of this largest setting of the problem of the self and its vocation, in the clash of two all-encompassing systems and their respective criteria for truth—that is, roughly from the

[2] The background of this crisis in belief is lucidly presented in "The World as a Moral Order," Chapter 3 of W. T. Stace, *Religion and the Modern Mind,* in terms that I think duplicate Ibsen's understanding of the nineteenth century intellectual situation. The challenge of the scientific outlook would seem to have come, in his case, from biology through the impact of Darwinism.

time, in Rome, of his invocation of "The Tragic Muse" and of the writing of *Brand*—each of his plays represents an attempt to define some aspect of the "new truth" now called for. This truth, he sees, must be neither absolutist and hence inappropriate to the realities of a scientific age, nor superficially positivistic, reducing man to no more than the passive sum, or the fated victim, of heredity and environment, after the manner of the naturalism of Zola and the early Strindberg, with which Ibsen has sometimes mistakenly been identified.

Among those areas of concern that he returned to repeatedly in his major plays, I would single out four as meriting particular attention. In these, Ibsen's personal struggle to realize himself "in spirit and truth" coincided most productively with his efforts to effect "a revolution of the human mind," the renewal of a civilization burdened and bedeviled by ghosts of its past. The fact that these four areas receive the main share of attention in the essays that follow marks their authors as being, each in his own way, part of or contributive to the third and latest phase of Ibsen studies. There are, however, still other scholars and critics whose work must regrettably be omitted by reason of length or substantial overlappings of content. Nevertheless, the radical character of Ibsen's mind has been even yet so insufficiently appreciated (Robert Brustein's discussion in *The Theater of Revolt* is an exception) that, for all the penetration and at times brilliance of the best current researches into and evaluations of his writings, the third phase in Ibsen criticism may be said to have made only exploratory beginnings. Its most notable interpretations are pioneering rather than definitive, promising fulfillment in the work of decades to come. For future critics these essays, in aggregate, may be no more than the threshold of the truth about Ibsen, as well as of those larger truths, approached through him, about ourselves and the course of our civilization, for which, I would suggest, the passage on "The Tragic Muse" provides a convenient focus and revelatory clue.

To consider the four areas in order of ascending value, one could say, first, that Ibsen saw it as part of his mission or lifework to seek radical truth *artistically*. Fully half of the fifty-year span of his authorship is a record of continuous experimentation with form. Among the discards of his restless search are some of the finest masterpieces of the repertory, and yet the stylistic consistency of the plays that follow *Pillars of Society* leaves no doubt that only at this point did he feel he had arrived at that fit vehicle of truth in the theater he had been looking for. What is there, we may ask, about these plays, which seem to us so conservative in form, that would satisfy the aims of Ibsen's knowledgeable and uncompromising dramaturgy?

Rejecting the shallow boulevard theater of his day, Ibsen had necessarily to turn elsewhere for models. Halvdan Koht shows how indebted he was in his formative years to the powerful example of Shakespeare, and, in equally admirable detail, P. F. D. Tennant describes the scrupulous care with which he assimilated and mastered the physical stagecraft that was available to him, that stagecraft of painted flats and backdrops so appropriate to the two-dimensional melodramas of the reigning French mode, most particularly those of Scribe. And yet, as John Northam makes clear, neither Shakespeare nor Scribe—taking each as the prototype of a whole class of dramas—could give him the solution he was after. He could, and did, succeed in satisfying both himself and his audience by bringing the latter form closer to verisimilitude, but only at the expense of losing what the best of his earlier works had attained: "the poetry of life in the imagery of the theater." Northam's argument then conducts us through a play-by-play description of what it was Ibsen's genius to discover, namely, that the stagecraft of the theater of realism could be transformed into metaphors for the condition of modern man. The bold insight that gave him the stylistic solution to his later plays struck to the very root of the medium: all dramatic art, even the most literally realistic, could ultimately be seen as—to adapt Fergusson's phrase—an idea *in* a theater, an extended kinetic image shaped in the mind of the poet and accorded a credible density through precisely scored modulations of decor, costume, and lighting, along with the movement and speech of thematically deployed actors. It was as if, with each successive play, he was saying to his prosaic middle-class audience: "This then is what you believe in—hard, material fact; very well, I'll give it to you, in the fullest measure; but always in such a way that the meaning of the idea informs and dictates every apparent solidity that holds your eye." And so, after the lesson of the statue in the Vatican, he taught himself, and a few others, to see *through* the outward object. The implications of this approach are only beginning to be explored in Ibsen criticism.

If the eyes of Ibsen's tragic muse pierced through the outward object, it was as much of the essence that they should turn inward, probing for radical truth *psychologically*. Moreover, the two kinds of vision, though closely related, were kept separate, as opposed to the later, expressionistic plays of Strindberg, whose *fauve* landscapes, distorted portraits, and fantastic events make it clear that the tormented inner vision has overlaid and supplanted the objective world of fact. This condition of being sunk in oneself and seeking escape by projecting one's malaise upon the world is the germ of that age of unreason whose advent is prophesied in the Cairo madhouse in *Peer Gynt*; and its two epoch-shaping martyrs in the drama are Strindberg and Alfred Jarry. Ibsen's own psychological solution, more arduous and less sensational, was announced as early as the first essay he wrote for matriculation at the university, *On the Importance of Knowledge of Oneself:* it was to contain, comprehend, and master the trolls within—a lifetime struggle whose decisive battles and provisional victories were the plays themselves, encapsulating his insights into the roots of motive and conflict.

"Where have I been myself, whole and true?" Peer Gynt cries out at the end of his roundabout life of evasions. In the larger life of the plays, it is precisely the wholeness of self they imply, if only by privation, that is the source of their radical psychological truth. The world of Ibsen cannot be reduced to the will to pleasure of Freudian libido theory (though the hedonistic Peer Gynt could be described as a classic case history of crippling infantilism caused by an Oedipal fixation). It refuses to be confined to the Adlerian will to power (though that will permeates not merely the central character of *Hedda Gabler,* but the entire play, as has been persuasively argued by Jens Arup in an article too long to include here). Nor can it be condensed into harmony with the will to meaning of existentialist psychoanalysis (though Nora confronts her inauthentic existence in a traumatic crisis that ought to be clinically recognizable to Rollo May or Viktor Frankl). If, on the one hand, we find Leo Lowenthal stressing Ibsen's grasp of the social nature of personal conflicts, on the other hand we have Georg Groddeck referring those conflicts back instead to the powerful workings of an autonomous, apparently biogenic unconscious, in an interpretation rare among psychoanalytic literary studies in its respect for the poetic sovereignty of the text.

The limitations and contradictions of these varied approaches are indicative not of the failure of their practitioners, but of the richness of Ibsen's method, which fuses multiple meanings through ambiguity and paradox—as is effectively demonstrated in Irving Deer's examination of the first great triumph of that method in the titanic ironies of the dramatic poem, *Brand.* In that work and its immediate sequel, both so imbued with Kierkegaardian values, one senses that Ibsen's concrete insight as an artist puts him even more in touch than his Danish counterpart with the psychological truth of man's existence, with the fact that propositions arising out of the depths of the self can often only be expressed paradoxically, as both/and statements, rather than those either/or formulations that are logical necessities on the plane of the reason and will. The underlying inner conflict running through Ibsen's major plays could well be phrased figuratively as Peer Gynt versus the Boyg, i.e., the ego versus the objective self, the either/or realm of conscious choice versus the both/and realm of total being. The intuition of psychological whole-ness is at the root, for Ibsen, of what it means to have a self and be a self, which in turn is the proper end of man, the task of his self-realization.

The enemy of that task, and the source of outer conflict as it acts to occlude first the experience, then the memory of the whole self, is the social contract, which blurs the clear-sighted, authentically creative re-sponse to the situations of life in a miasma of compromise. As Northam rightly observes, "for a man of Ibsen's generation the great opponent of man was seen to be society . . . as a force working through a myriad of obscure agencies and trivial occasions." Ibsen's defensive reaction to that force drove him to a position verging on anarchism; and yet some re-sidual hope of finding a rationale for society, a redemptive purpose in the civilization that had shaped it, led him back through time to search for radical truth *historically*. The search drew him progressively away from the restrictive Norwegian literary nationalism, the edda and saga backgrounds, of the early plays into the history of Europe at large. It drew him south to Italy, into the study of Renaissance art and further back to the relics of the imperial Roman world. It impelled him toward the Greece he planned but was unable to visit—though the entire pas-sage on "The Tragic Muse" is a celebration of its influence on the shap-ing of his dramatic vision. And, finally, it brought him to consider ethical problems in terms of the contemporary viability of the long tradition of Christian faith, the life-giving marrow of European culture for more than a millennium. Through the theories of Hebbel and Hettner, Ibsen had learned to interpret the process of history as a dialectical drama of ideas; and now, at the midpoint of his development, he focused his atten-tion particularly upon those ideas formed out of the three main roots of Western civilization, the Greek, the Roman, and the Judeo-Christian.

The result of these trends of thought, the work upon which Ibsen lavished nine years of effort, regarding it afterward as generally under-estimated—in fact, as his masterpiece—was of course the immense ten-act double play, *Emperor and Galilean,* subtitled "a world-historical drama." Without necessarily granting it full honors as a masterpiece, one can agree with its creator that this work *is* all too often underestimated. Paulus Svendsen shows, through a wealth of specific references to the period of its composition, with what accuracy Ibsen seized a phenomenon having the subtlest and most profound implications for his time and our own, that of apostasy, and converted it into an action unfolding on two parallel historical planes: that of the Emperor Julian, at the moment of the formation of the Western synthesis, as well as, by inference, that of the modern messianic rebel, at the moment of its apparent dissolution and potential rebirth in that transvalued realm that Maximos calls the Third Empire. Without this enormous, flawed adventure into the philosophy of history, Ibsen would probably have become a half-forgotten satirist of nineteenth century Scandinavian society; with it behind him, he became—as Leo Lowenthal's observations suggest—diagnostician to an entire civilization.

Ibsen's return to primary sources was thus a rediscovery of basic Western values, or ideals, that often stood in startling dramatic contrast to the compromised versions of those ideals ordinarily assumed by society. At the summit of the scale of values, beyond the aesthetic and ethical stages delineated by Kierkegaard, lay the further reaches of religious experience, the ultimate ground of meaning expressed in and by the characters. Out of his effort to devise a language of symbols for otherwise incommunicable states of consciousness, and encouraged by his study of classical antiquity wherein the history of man merges with the figures of the gods, Ibsen fashioned what may yet prove his most productive contribution to the life of the drama: an approach to radical truth *mythically*. After a considerable period of trial and error he learned to model the deceptively naturalistic surfaces of his plays over an underlying archetypal structure much as Rubek, the sculptor in *When We Dead Awaken,* shaped the likenesses of his human portrait busts over the primitive, subsurface forms of animal heads.

This controlling core, with its own frequent ambiguity between archaic ritual patterns and exalted spiritual illumination, hidden like the sculptor's armature under the textured planes of the later works, would never have arrived at its mature development if Ibsen had not possessed right from the start the mythopoeic imagination, which, like "The Tragic Muse," seeks its meanings far beyond the outward object. His early method, however, was to make a coat of old mythologies and wear his tags of allusion on the surface of the text. By the time of *Peer Gynt,* this approach is called in question. In that most mythopoeic of all his plays, the Troll King complains that, though he knows himself to be real, he has faded in the popular mind to mere legend consigned to books; Peer Gynt replies that many have been in that way cursed. The play that follows, *The League of Youth,* seems to accept that conclusion and is in consequence literal-minded, mechanically contrived, and photographic in the extreme. But in *Emperor and Galilean* Ibsen returns to the issue; his hero Julian is made to ponder the role of myth: "Do you really think these tales of the gods have no great design and no vital purpose? Weren't these tales devised with the aim of leading the human spirit along a pleasant and easy path up to the mysterious mansions where the supreme god reigns—and thereby preparing men's souls for union with him? What else can they mean? Wasn't it for this reason that the ancient poets invented such tales . . . ?" And if the ancients, he might have added, why not the moderns? It was more than ten years before Ibsen worked out the implications of these two statements acknowledging, first, the skeptical temper of the modern mind and, second, the persisting relevance of myth. When he did, his solution allowed him to create the major innovation of a body of drama having mythic dimensions without explicit reliance on the traditional machinery of gods and demons. As George Steiner puts it in *The Death of Tragedy*:

> With the toy forest and imaginary hunt of old Ekdal in *The Wild Duck*, drama returns to a use of effective myth and symbolic action which had disappeared from the theater since the late plays of Shakespeare. In *Rosmersholm, The Lady from the Sea* and *Hedda Gabler*, Ibsen succeeded in doing what every major playwright had attempted after the end of the seventeenth century and what even Goethe and Wagner had not wholly accomplished: he created a new mythology and the theatrical conventions with which to express it. That is the foremost achievement of Ibsen's genius, and it is, as yet, not fully understood.[3]

His attainment in this area is most readily seen in a work like *Hedda Gabler*, where the mythological content is traditional and close to the surface of the text. Here, in what Caroline Mayerson suggests is a satyr play following after and mocking the lost scope of high tragedy, Eilert Lövborg stands as the surrogate of Dionysus, bringing new life to a sterile and claustrophobic society that finds no real need for it, scattering his talents as, in fantasy, he scatters his manuscript into the fjord, dying the death of the god, only to have ironic rebirth in the scraps of paper saved by Thea to be pieced together by George Tesman, the scholar-custodian of this latter Alexandrian age. Elsewhere, Ibsen invents his own images of the archetypes, exercising that mode of mythic imagination defined by Cassirer, in which the power of the conception derives from a sense of the basic solidarity of all life, whose vital principle is describable only in terms of action. Richard Schechner's article opens fresh, valid perspectives on those final plays where Ibsen, like Beethoven in the last quartets, is exploring entirely on his own, finding communion paradoxically only in the utmost solitude. (Schechner's assertion that the archetypal figures in Ibsen's late works become theatrically effective only in the end play of the series seems to me more dubious; how can one say, when judgment

[3] George Steiner, *The Death of Tragedy* (New York: Hill & Wang Dramabooks, 1963), p. 292.

to date has been chiefly based on inferior productions of inadequate translations?) The mythic elements in Ibsen's art would certainly appear to deserve more study in the future, both in individual plays and as recurrent motifs running through several successively, after the manner of Robert Raphael's promising approach to a more philosophical theme.

If, in this and other vital areas, the world of Ibsen, as it enters the third phase of its immortality, has begun to open "into deeper and deeper vistas in every direction, upward, outward, and downward," its expanding significance could be said to derive from a better understanding of what E. M. Forster, in the concluding essay of this collection, calls "Ibsen the romantic." We are possibly now far enough beyond its excesses to see that, in the romantic movement, the elements of the strange, the marvelous, the improbable, the unique were only the superficial aura. At times Ibsen's world emanates these qualities, but in substance he put his dark, tough-minded, impassioned intellect at the service of the romantic essence, as defined by W. T. Stace: "to the romantic, the world which we apprehend with our senses and our reason . . . the world of space and time, is only an appearance or manifestation of a deeper hidden spiritual reality which lies behind. This, I shall even risk saying, is the 'essence' of the romantic world-view." Unlikely as the comparison first seems, in his profound and contentious humanism Ibsen shares with Wordsworth a sense of something in man's nature far more deeply interfused. If initially it was the vehemence of his social criticism that won attention, it was that sense outraged by sanctimonious corruption that gave his work its cutting edge. If later he came to be studied as the master theater technician, it was because he was always, as Forster notes, "a poet, to whom creation and craftsmanship were one." And if today we see him in a far more comprehensive revolt against all those various distortions and reductions of feeling and value that mark our time even more than his; if, following Eric Bentley's suggestion, we are capable of appraising the damage done humanity by those who absolutely know what the world requires, in complicity with those who believe in nothing —the Brands and Peer Gynts of our century—then we have all the more cause to press beyond the unfashionable surfaces to the perennial roots of his art, there perhaps to gain a fleeting glimpse of the calm joy and the steadfast, inexhaustible vision of Ibsen's tragic muse.

Henrik Ibsen:
A Personal Statement

by Eric Bentley

The world's attitude to Ibsen has gone through two phases and is now, as I see it, entering upon a third. The first phase was that of the late nineteenth century, at which time one either expressed one's detestation of the dramatist's iconoclasm or one's enthusiastic acceptance of it. Either way, the Ibsen under consideration was the revolutionary; and one accepted or rejected him according as one was oneself a revolutionary or not.

The second phase of opinion came with the acceptance of Ibsen in the early twentieth century by society at large. A gain of this sort is always, at the same time, a loss. For general acceptance implies only a cessation of hostilities, not an active interest in an author; to be accepted is the first step toward being ignored. When the rear guard accepts an author, moreover, the advance guard drops him. Necessarily so, as the advance guard's function has been to scold the rear guard for paying no attention. Not so necessary, but quite natural, is the advance guard's tendency to turn against those it used to champion, perhaps even reviving arguments against them that had first been formulated by the rear guard. . . . In the nineteenth century, playwrights were warned against Ibsen by the diehard, older critics; in the twentieth century they began to be warned against him by the advanced young spirits. Bertolt Brecht's Epic Theater, beginning in the nineteen twenties, was, on the technical side, mainly a revolt against Ibsen, whose forms Brecht has described as rigid and narrow.

More important than technique, perhaps, was ideology. As the only fully elaborated Marxist theory of drama, Brecht's Epic Theater is the purest example of collectivism in twentieth-century dramatic writing, and

"Henrik Ibsen: A Personal Statement" by Eric Bentley. From *Columbia University Forum*, I (Winter 1957), 11-14. Copyright © 1957 by Columbia University; copyright assigned to Eric Bentley, 1958. Reprinted by permission of the author.

the extreme statement of his thought is to be found in the play *Die Massnahme* (published in English as *The Measures Taken* in *The Colorado Review*, Winter 1956-7) which celebrates the sacrifice of the individual to the group. In her book *Stalin and German Communism*, Ruth Fischer intimates that this play was suggested by the experiences of Gerhart Eisler as a Communist agent in China, and, by anticipation, it dramatizes the deaths of Radek and Bukharin, Rajk and Slansky, though not the subsequent admission, in 1956, that the confessions these men made were a pack of lies.

During the phase of history that produced Epic Theater, collectivistic thought spread far beyond the confines of the Communist movement, and, when I was in college in the nineteen thirties, the standard opinion was that Henrik Ibsen was *borné* and *petit bourgeois*—that he represented the end of individualism and not the beginning of the great new order. Only later did I learn that this view had been first expressed by Friedrich Engels himself and thereafter had been echoed by all Marxist critics from Mehring on.

And Marx and Engels were right, if their philosophy as a whole was right; it is a matter of that; while, equally, Ibsen will cease to seem *borné* and *petit bourgeois,* will become important again, to those who wish to stand *for* the individual and *against* what seems to them the hideous monolith of Soviet collectivism. To these the great individualists of the nineteenth century are still great, Ibsen among them. Great and exemplary—for they possess what we have lost but must at all costs recover.

They possessed, first and foremost, what Lionel Trilling and others have been calling the *mystique* of the self: their self-respect, and their belief in self-respect, went beyond opinion to sentiment, and beyond sentiment to faith. For them, there existed no Radeks and Bukharins—no people, that is, who could be asked to lie their lives away for an alleged collective good. In some much-quoted lines of verse, Henrik Ibsen once said that to live was to fight with the devils that infest the head and heart and to hold a Last Judgment over the self. The *mystique* of the self never found more pithy expression, nor the subject-matter of Ibsen's plays more precise definition. Even where Ibsen criticizes an individualist —as in *Brand* and *The Wild Duck*—he does so, not from any standpoint acceptable to a Marxist, but from that of another individualism. Brand's flaw, after all, is a defect in self-knowledge. Instead of living in harmony with his own nature, he attempts to live according to an abstract law which he must constantly foist on himself and others by arbitrary violence. This individualist becomes less of an individual all the time. By a supposed attachment to the *super*human, he has become *in*human.

Consider Mrs. Alving, the individualist as woman. We know that she reads the right books, though Ibsen leaves them unnamed so that each spectator can supply the titles of his own favorites. She belongs to the nineteenth-century Enlightenment. But we find out that she achieves enlightenment in general while keeping herself ignorant in particular of precisely those two or three things which it would do her most good to know: above all, of her complicity in the tragedy of Captain Alving. When she tells Oswald—at the end—that she shared the blame, because, in her prudishness, her fear of sexuality, she had not welcomed Alving's joy of life, she is also telling herself. Catastrophe in this story plays, as it were, the role of psychoanalysis, bringing to consciousness the guilty facts which the protagonist has so zealously kept under. Mrs. Alving, reader of books, has come to know many things; she has not come to know herself. She is not too much an individual, as Manders thinks, but too little.

My generation of undergraduates—that of the nineteen thirties—reserved its greatest contempt for the person who was "only interested in saving his soul" and was therefore neglecting the real task, that of changing the world. We didn't realize to what an appalling extent the motive force of our reforming zeal was fear of the self, a failure to face the self. We scoffed at the escapism of certain individualistic poets, and did not see that social collectivism could be the supreme escape, and conversely that there can be no healthy altruism which is not grounded in self-respect. Yet, if we hadn't been tipped off that Ibsen was *petit bourgeois,* we might have learned our lesson from him. For he saw that the altruism of a Gregers Werle was the outgrowth of a sick conscience; Gregers persecutes Hedwig because he is running away from himself.

With the disrespect for the self that has been so prevalent in our time goes, naturally, a disrespect for the whole inner life of man, as witness the overtone that the word *subjective* now carries. The *objective* is real, the *subjective* is unreal—in other words, you get at the truth by getting away from yourself. If anyone remarked of Neville Chamberlain in 1938 that at least his motives were good, there was always a young Marxist on hand to remark that we must not judge by motives but by objective facts. Here again, Ibsen belongs to the earlier tradition. He believes the motive itself to be an objective fact, and, in a strict sense, the primary fact—the one to start from. He would never have written a play about the rightness or wrongness of Chamberlain's policy, but he might well have written one about whether the man did indeed have good motives, whether his conscience was healthy. His plays are studies in *un*healthy conscience. Naturally, then, he seems not only old-fashioned but even wrongheaded to those who assume that life begins after integrity has been surrendered to a party, a class, or a state.

But I do not wish to focus my whole argument upon Communism because, in the present connection, Communism is only the extreme instance of a universal phenomenon—conformism parading as virtue. And in the West we encounter the danger less in the form of Communism than as a new attitude to life which David Riesman calls other-directedness, i.e., being oriented toward other people, not just in external matters, not just, as it were, when other people are looking, but in one's most intimate mental activity. Modern civilization lives under the sign of Mrs. Grundy.

Allowing for the inaccuracy of all such generalizations we may say that the spiky, individualistic Victorians were inner-directed. Trained under strong fathers in the discipline of self-reliance, they hearkened to the inner voice, and went their independent way. Whether we can ever get back to anything of the sort is a question going far beyond the scope of the present statement. But even Mr. Riesman (who seems to be a fatalist) permits himself some unmistakably nostalgic admiration, and, certainly, the stock of all the Victorian individualists has been rising as men have come to realize what a frightful mess the anti-individualists have been making of the world. Ibsen is a great exemplar of the inner-directed culture. *Peer Gynt,* though not quite a prophecy of other-directedness, is about the danger of self-disrespect, of having no sense of identity, of being a human onion, all layers and no center . . .

By this time, I may have given the impression that what Ibsen means to me is Conservatism, the Nineteenth Century, Darby and Joan, or even Songs My Mother Taught Me. Assuredly we have come to the point where Victorianism no longer suggests a narrow and enervating stuffiness but manliness, free intellect, abundant individuality—men like Henrik Ibsen rather than Pastor Manders. The great Victorians were rebels against Victorian*ism,* non-conformists one and all. In political theory, Henrik Ibsen leaned towards anarchism—of all *isms* the most remote from totalitarianism. His first audiences, as I have said, regarded him as primarily a rebel; and in the future, I think, he will be regarded as a rebel again.

Ibsen's plays are *about* rebels—from Catiline to Brand and Julian, and from Lona Hessel and Nora Helmer to Hedda Gabler and John Gabriel Borkman—and we should not need to be told by Ibsen himself (as we were) that he wrote only of what he had lived through, for re-belliousness is not only the subject of the plays but the motive force. Anti-clericalism (as in the portrait of Manders and of the Dean in *Brand*) and political satire (as in *The League of Youth* or the characterization of the Mayor in *Brand*) are merely the most obtrusive signs of a mentality that was critical through and through. As we retreat in horror, disgust, or mere boredom from the idea of the writer as Official Mouthpiece, we come back to the old liberal conception, most signally represented in this century by André Gide: the writer as questioner, dissenter, challenger, trouble-maker, at war with his age, yet by that token standing for the best in his age and helping the age to understand itself. In Ibsen, as in Gide, we who live in a time of fake radicalism are confronted by a real radical.

In speaking of fake radicalism, I again have more than Communism in mind—more even than politics. I am thinking, for example, of all playwrights who are considered daring, and whose courage is rather light-heartedly connected by critics with that of Ibsen and Strindberg. As people these playwrights are often much more Bohemian than Ibsen, and something much more quickly identifiable as Daring is smeared over the whole surface of their plays, which deal with assorted neuroses not even mentionable in the theatre of Ibsen's day. But Ibsen is supposed to have given Daring its start in *Ghosts*.

The mistake here is to imagine that the subject of *Ghosts* is syphilis. Lucky for Ibsen that it isn't, as the medical science of the play is now quite obsolete! His daring was not a matter of bringing up repellent subjects, though it included that. It consisted in his genuinely radical attitude to life in general. It is at the heart of his writing, not merely on its surface.

What is true in the sexual sphere applies also to politics. In our political plays today, we are given what is conventionally regarded as daring but what actually takes no courage at all to say—it is at best what used to be daring and is now calculated to produce cheers from a clique, class, or party rather than bad reviews in the press and rotten eggs from the gallery. An instance, oddly enough, is *An Enemy of the People* as freely adapted to the American stage in the mid-twentieth century by Arthur Miller. Ibsen's original, by contrast, though no profound piece of thought, and in my view one of his least vital plays, is genuinely daring, especially in its blunt challenge to the idea of majority rule. The reason the newer version is dull is that Mr. Miller was himself offended by Ibsen's daring, made excuses for him in a preface, and proceeded to censor offensive passages. The dangerous thoughts of the latter-day quasi-radical are all completely safe; Ibsen's plays were so subversive they frightened, at times, even their author.

One difference between the old radical and the new is that the former explored life while the latter lays down the law about it. *Die Massnahme* perfectly represents the newer procedure. Such a play is not drama of discussion or ideas, for the author isn't talking it over with you, he is telling you. Still less is it drama of exploration, for it is but an exemplification of an idea the author started out with.

Gerhart Hauptmann remarked once that the playwright must never re-word thoughts which he or his character has already thought: dramatic dialogue must only present thoughts in the process of being thought. Which is another way of saying that the playwright must not be directly didactic, for it is the didactic writer, out not to learn but to teach, who concentrates on finding effective form for thinking that was finished long ago. Didacticism seems not to have been a besetting temptation for Ibsen as it was for Brecht. It is an irony that the man considered the father of the drama of ideas makes so few explicit references to ideas in his plays.

Incidentally, *An Enemy of the People* is inferior Ibsen just because it is one of the few plays in which this author seems simply to be "telling us"—with upraised finger and an inclination to be very angry if we aren't good and do as we're "told." Generally, with Ibsen, we feel we are his companions in a search and therefore, in line with Hauptmann's principle, are not given summaries of what has been thought already but are present at the thinking. Mere summaries of experience (intellectual experience or otherwise) are without dramatic life. The pulse of the drama begins to beat at the moment the playwright begins to struggle with his experience. There is no better evidence for this truth than the life-work of Henrik Ibsen.

The principle invoked by Hauptmann enables us to understand the radical differences not only between Ibsen and Brecht but between Ibsen and the Ibsenites. The more the Ibsenites agreed with the Master, the worse the result was bound to be: for they were starting where he ended, namely, with his findings. It is of course open to writers who do this to improve on their Master in all the external qualities of literature—elegance, concision, clarity, and so on. For they are only paraphrasing. And it makes one realize that one values literature, ultimately, for other qualities than these. One will indeed suffer inelegance, inconcision, even unclarity with a good grace if only there is also a degree of inner movement, action, energy, conflict. . . .

There is a lesson in Ibsen for our so-called profession of playwrights today. The profession—by definition, perhaps—acquires a certain craft and then uses it. In other words, the professional writer works within the resources he has found himself to possess. Such-and-such worked very well last time; the presumption that it may work well again is enough to prompt a second use, and a third, and so on. Hence his youth is the professional writer's only creative period; there can indeed, on the terms just stated, be no development, but at best an increasing facility. Ibsen chose the path of constant development, accepting the risks, paying the price, and reaping the reward. The price is the forgoing of small perfection and easy success. Professional dramatic critics, out of something more than fellow feeling, will always tend to prefer the professional craftsman to the real artist: the merits of what the former has to offer are more easily recognized and measured, while the latter undoubtedly makes far more mistakes, and is not always improving. The pay-off comes at the end when the "mistake"—about which the critics have "rightly" been merciless—reveals itself as a needed part of a pattern. It has been said that all Shakespeare's plays taken together form one long play. Something of the kind can be said of the collected work of any real artist. Not the smallest fascination of Ibsen is the unity of his work, the profound meaning in the relation of play to play. To write both *Brand* and *Peer Gynt* is not just twice the job of writing one of the two; it is to force the reader to read the plays as thesis and antithesis in an artist's effort at synthesis. To follow up *Ghosts* with *An Enemy of the People* was more than an act of moral reprisal, and to follow up *An Enemy* with *The Wild Duck* was more than an act of self-correction: one thing leads to another in a drama which has *Catiline* for prologue and *When We Dead Awaken* for epilogue, the drama of Ibsen's whole *œuvre*.

Henrik Ibsen meant a lot to me when I first encountered theatre, literature, and adult life, and I return to him a couple of decades later when trying, as we do, to come to terms with the theatre, the literature, and the life around us, trying to locate the essential problems, discard impeding prejudices, correct obstructive errors, see through the facts to the meaning of the facts and, in all this, to accept the self that does the locating, discarding, correcting, and seeing, for, while the Bible tells us to love our neighbor as ourselves, Henrik Ibsen seems to remind us how unhelpful that injunction would be to people who did *not* love themselves.

Ibsen's Conception of Truth

by F. W. Kaufmann

Goethe's Iphigenie proclaims absolute truthfulness as the indispensable foundation for the establishment of humane relations between individuals and peoples. In order to save her integrity and to serve the cause of humanity, she is willing to risk her own life as well as the lives of her brother Orestes and his friend Pylades. Her desperate invocation of the gods, *"Rettet mich und rettet euer Bild in meiner Seele,"* is just one of the many instances which illustrate the fact that truth in this drama is measured in its relationship to some suprapersonal absolute from which it receives its sanction and its meaning, and some world order in which truthfulness may be a creative force incomparably superior to all physical force and opportunistic cleverness. Truthfulness in the setting of the *Iphigenie* drama means specifically to tell (and to act) the truth in the literal sense of the word; yet beyond that, truthfulness reflects the harmony of the total personality in word and action, and ultimately the harmony of the humane and the divine.

When, sixty years later, Grillparzer wrote his comedy *Weh dem, der lügt,* the classical faith in a moral world order in which ideal values support each other and triumph over the forces of evil had declined and with it the belief in the absolute value of truthfulness. To be sure, Bishop Gregor tries to save the ideal demand when he permits his nephew to be rescued from captivity only on the condition that Leon abstain from all deception. However, in the end he must confess that his ideal demand may come into conflict with other values, in this particular instance the values of freedom and life, and that compromises may be inescapable. He finally must admit that ideal truthfulness can be maintained only as a regulative principle, but cannot be carried out to its ultimate extent.

As the nineteenth century progressed, the transcendent frame of reference for truth disappeared almost completely. Science, in spite of its

"Ibsen's Conception of Truth" by F. W. Kaufmann. From *Germanic Review*, XXXII (April 1957), 83-92. Copyright © 1957 by Columbia University Press. Reprinted by permission of the author and Columbia University Press.

claim that human reason will ultimately be able to explain everything, substituted hypothetical systems, such as the evolutionary theory, for transcendence, and relativity for the former faith in the absolute. Scientific truth is not a fixed possession, but is always in process of being acquired. Correspondingly, moral standards and codes were subjected to question and criticism; libertinism and moral nihilism seemed to be the logical conclusion when the metaphysical sanction of these standards disappeared and the observance of the traditional codes depended entirely upon the pressure of conformity.

When Ibsen entered upon the scene of modern drama, he found it impossible to restore the idealistic demand of absolute truth, and he was too critical to accept the traditional code of ethics as an adequate instrument for the regulation of human relations. Ibsen's criticism therefore is directed both against abstract demands claiming absolute validity and all codes and social norms making similar claims for conformity. His aim is to establish "a new truth" which, in spite of the relativity of its content, imposes a much greater responsibility upon the individual than either the "ideal demand" or submission to the generally accepted codes and norms. This truth is more than a mere logical agreement of thought and fact; it is rooted much deeper, since it originates in the interpenetration of life and thought, and involves the total personality. Consciousness of truth in this organic sense can be derived neither from reason nor from emotional reaction alone. It has its source in the undefinable depth of the personality and only when this is realized may it be elucidated by reason; that which is emotionally perceived becomes true only when it has been so elucidated and manifests itself in meaningful action. Ultimately, such organic truth is to be found in the appropriate response to a given situation, based on an intelligent and sympathetic examination of all factors involved and carried out with the will to assume fullest responsibility for the decision. Ibsen's search for truth in both his letters and his plays points in this general direction, and although he never comes to either a clear formulation or a convincing embodiment of his idea of truth, it may be helpful to indicate the direction of his search in order better to comprehend his somewhat elusive term "truth" and its opposite, "life's lie." The problem of truth is most intimately related to Ibsen's struggle for self-realization which was described in an earlier issue of *Monatshefte*.[1] Just as Ibsen came very close to a final answer to that problem, but was prevented from giving it by a rationalistic residue, so it necessarily is with his conception of truth, because the authenticity which he

---

[1] *Monatshefte*, XLV(1953). For a general discussion of the problem of truth, see Karl Jaspers, *Philosophische Logik*, Vol. I, "Von der Wahrheit" (1947).

was seeking also accounts for his choice of truth in the existential sense of the word.

Some passages from Ibsen's letters will now be analyzed in order to clarify the issue in question. In his letter to Magdalene Thoresen of December 3, 1865, Ibsen states that his travels have given him the proper perspective "to see the hollowness behind the self-created lies of our so-called public life and the wretchedness of this whole personal phrase-mongering, which never is in want of words, yet never has the will and the strength or the sense of duty to do a great deed." To be sure, Ibsen refers to an incongruity between words and deeds, to a false identification of persons and their ideals; however, his attack is also directed against the shallowness of a "well-trained herd," the "self-satisfaction" of the Norwegian people, who are too honest "to commit a stupidity on a grand scale." In other words Ibsen finds the roots of untruth in the attempt to justify and to glorify the indifference with regard to the challenge of the time and to the fate of Denmark in particular, that is the failure to respond to the political situation in a way which, in his opinion, alone would be worthy of his nation.

During the Franco-Prussian War, Ibsen wrote to Georg Brandes on December 20, 1870, about the necessity of giving new content and life to old ideas: "Liberty, equality, fraternity are no longer the same things they were during the days of the guillotine of blessed memory. That is what the politicians do not want to understand, and therefore I hate them. People want only special revolutions, revolutions in external things, in politics, etc. . . . *What is important is the revolutionizing of the human mind . . .*" Here, as in the passage quoted above, Ibsen is protesting against the distortion of truth by outworn slogans. However, in this letter to Brandes another factor enters which is essential for Ibsen's conception of truth, and that is the factor of time. The slogans of the French Revolution may have truthfully expressed the aspirations of that time, but they have degenerated into false claims concealing petty selfish interests. To express the matter positively, such ideal slogans must be constantly revitalized in order to remain truths; and their truth must manifest itself in ever new decisions growing out of ever changing circumstances.

The idea that truth is nothing absolute, but in constant flux is most clearly expressed in Act IV of *An Enemy of the People,* where Ibsen attributes to Dr. Stockman the idea that "a normally constituted truth" lives no longer than twenty years at the most and then may hardly be called truth anymore. That the passage reflects Ibsen's own views is supported by a passage in a letter to Brandes, of June 12, 1883, in which

Ibsen concedes that they both must work for the dissemination of their views, yet Ibsen also defends his own position that an intellectual pioneer cannot expect to gather a majority behind him. He continues: "Within ten years the majority may have reached the position which Dr. Stockman held during the assembly. However in those ten years the doctor has not come to a standstill; he again will be ten years ahead of the majority. The majority, the masses, the multitude will never catch up with him; he can never have the majority for himself." In other words, truths remain truths only as long as the spirit is alive which first discovered the truth. When Ibsen ascribes a relative life-span and thus some merely objective validity to truth, one may argue in his favor that certain situations call for a similar response from all thinking individuals and that, while those conditions prevail, that particular response may be considered at least as potentially genuine and true, that is, as more than blind adoption of somebody else's opinion or imitation of his action. The ambiguity in the use of the term truth in this passage may perhaps be attributed to Ibsen's relationalistic heritage and a correspondingly slow absorption of the evolutionary idea with all its implications. The latter assumption is substantiated by the fact that Ibsen occasionally returns to the Hegelian pattern of a dialectical evolution, as e.g., in *Emperor and Galilean* and in a speech given in 1877 at a banquet in Stockholm, in which he expresses the conviction that the death of contemporary ideals will give rise to the realization of the Third Empire, in which classical beauty and Christian truth will find their synthesis. In any case, however, the passages which we have examined imply a belief in the necessity of a relentless struggle for truth and thus the realization that truth can never be possessed, but must always be in the process of acquisition. In his letter to Brandes of February 17, 1871, Ibsen expresses such a dynamic view with regard to freedom:

> I shall never consent to identify freedom with political liberty. What you call freedom I call liberties; and what I call freedom is nothing but a constant, active acquisition of the idea of freedom. He who possesses freedom as anything but as something to be striven for, possesses it as something dead and spiritless, for the idea of freedom has the peculiarity of constantly becoming broader during its acquisition, and if therefore somebody ceases fighting and says, "now I have it," he thereby shows that he has lost it.

Later on in the letter Ibsen applies the same relativity to morality and esthetic forms, and questions even the universal validity of mathematical truth. For the same reason he rejects in a letter to Caspari, of June 27, 1883, any claims of universal validity, except the one obligation "to realize myself in spirit and truth."

All these passages from his letters reveal Ibsen as a seeker of truth who knows that truth never is a possession, but a constant effort to find the appropriate response to every given situation which demands a decision, and that truth, once it is generalized and accepted as valid without re-examination in the light of the new situation, is already disintegrating and in danger of becoming a falsehood. He realizes that all human knowledge, judgment, and action can claim is a relative truth at best, since man is determined by motives which have their origin far back in the past and since the consequences of our judgment and actions are predictable only to a very limited extent. Therefore Ibsen could say of his production that every new work served the purpose of self-liberation and purification, "for one never stands above all co-responsibility and complicity in a society to which one belongs . . . Life means to fight the ghosts of dark powers within oneself; poetry—to sit in judgment over oneself." [2]

These general conclusions, derived mainly from Ibsen's letters, may be further substantiated by examples from his dramas. Little, if anything, needs to be said about those cases in which truth is deliberately distorted, since they are at best cases which serve the dramatic purpose of contrast-ing untruth with serious search for truth. By means of this technique Ibsen succeeds in supporting his major idea that truth is not a posses-sion, but a constant struggle against external and inward obstacles. Where the truth is attributed to a character in an oversimplified black-white contrast, it lacks the convincing effect of a truth sought and ac-quired in genuine struggle. For instance Dr. Stockman in *An Enemy of the People* fights for an unquestionable objective truth, but his lack of any understanding for the complexity of the situation and his fanatical intransigence almost cause his truth to appear as an undesirable nui-sance. On the other hand, a deceiver and scoundrel like Engstrand in *Ghosts* contributes by his actions as well as by his mere character to un-mask the fundamental untruth represented by Pastor Manders, and by contrast to enhance Mrs. Alving's honest, though futile, search for truth in words and deeds. The same function can be attributed to the poli-ticians in *Rosmersholm*. No matter how weak Rosmer's attempts to ac-tualize the truth in his life may seem, they gain at least significance when measured against the intrigues of the conservative Rector Kroll, who threatens him with public scandal unless he conceals his defection from the Church, and the request of the liberal Mortensgaard to remain a pastor because his party needs the influence of men in office in order to

morality turns into its opposite and nothing but deceit and
t remain.[4] If we try to formulate the general idea behind this
we find a further support for the conclusions drawn from
etters, namely that all truth which is accessible to man becomes
d when considered as absolutely valid. A moral code which
laim absolute validity would presuppose a vision encompassing
le field of actual and potential moral issues, an obvious impossi-
By pointing out the incompatibility of the specific demands of a
sen indicates another problem, namely that every choice involves
ction of other possibilities of perhaps equal moral importance, so
ilt is inescapable, a conclusion which should impose some humil-
n any searcher for truth. It is for this lack of humility that Ibsen
his pastor to stumble into the grotesquely paradoxical situation
ecclesiastical protector of commercialized vice.

ny proof were needed that Ibsen's fight for emancipation from
ional moral demands and the pressure of social norms is not to be
sed with moral anarchy, but rather a challenge to assume more per-
responsibility, one may refer to two plays, one written at the be-
g and the other at the end of his modern period. While Brand
ved it possible to acquire the absolute truth, Peer Gynt represents a
relativism in the extreme where it approaches nihilism. He rushes
one experience [to another], never exhausting the potentialities of
and never involving himself enough to experience the truth behind
transitory phenomenon. His world is a world of mere facts and inci-
ts, because he is incapable of giving his experiences any relevant
h by a serious effort to integrate them through personal involvement.
ause he cannot be true to himself, his life is one continuous series of
eptions and self-deceptions. The truth he should have lived is sym-
ized in Solveig, whose dramatic function corresponds to the *Deus*
ritatis in *Brand*. Solveig is the symbol of the self-transcending orienta-
n towards that integral oneness which alone is truth.

Peer Gynt may be considered a nineteenth-century caricature of Faust
ho deludes himself into the belief that his superficial and aimless activ-
es will contribute to his self-realization, the fool of a morality play in a
odernized version. Hedda Gabler, on the other hand, is a sophisticated
oman who has been neglected and never been understood in her youth,
nd who takes revenge for her frustrated emotional life by stimulating
e emotions of a man like Lövberg to an orgiastic pitch and then dis-
issing him in favor of the most philistine pedant for whom she cannot

[4] For further examples, see *Monatshefte, loc. cit.*

attract members and voters. For politicians and men like Engstrand or
Haakon Werle, men whose only concerns are public opinion and personal advantage, there exists no essential difference between truth and
untruth; both are used as it seems best to serve the purpose of the moment so that even objectively true statements lose their intrinsic value
and actually do not deserve to be called truth because the purpose is not
to establish any kind of authentic communication, but at best a superficial contact in which truth is part of the game and at worst a vicious
means to discredit and harm decent fellow-men.[3]

It may seem paradoxical at first that Ibsen attributes an almost equally
negative value to those who claim the possession of absolute truth, even
if they honestly believe in it. *Brand* still reflects Ibsen's search for absolute truth and his desire to establish universally valid demands, an
attempt which he later rejected as impossible. The young Norwegian
pastor gradually abandons all dogmatic fixation as a distortion of the
idea of transcendence. The more abstract his conception of the deity becomes, the less the traditional forms of worship satisfy him, and the more
rigorous become his moral demands upon himself as well as his parishion-
ers. He exaggerates those demands until they finally lose their solid
foundation in reality. His all-or-nothing position ends in an almost complete vacuum, since he has radically severed the connection between
existence and transcendence. With painful sarcasm Ibsen symbolizes this
separation of life and highest spiritual aspirations when Brand climbs
higher up to his "ice-church," while his followers desert him for a school
of herring. They had been able and willing to accept their pastor's leadership as long as he could offer them some concrete symbol of transcendence and some tangible form of worship, but when these vanish in the
empty space of the universe, the simple people fall back to the level of
material concerns from which Brand had tried to "save" them.

Brand's metaphysical error consists in the fact that he attributes absolute validity to one single aspect of human existence, that he tries to
universalize his own personal experience. For his image of the godhead
grew out of bitterness, hatred, and unrequited love. Therefore his deity
is a rigorous God who demands the abnegation of vital human drives,
the crippling of emotions. God exists for him only as *mysterium tremendum,* an enemy of life in a world which, as incarnate evil, stands in
almost dualistic opposition to God. This is the God whom Brand tries
to impose upon others as the one ultimate truth, a God whose image he
created out of a negative principle which could engender nothing but

[3] E.g., Rector Kroll's revelation to Rosmer about his wife.

death and suicide. Brand's search for absolute truth is doomed to failure, since transcendence must ultimately be universal oneness and harmony and therefore free of hatred. That is the reason why Brand's *mysterium tremendum* is refuted in the end by the *Deus Caritatis,* for only love which respects human existence and which is capable of selfless sacrifice can lead beyond mere existence towards transcendence. By pointing out Brand's failure to find the absolute truth, Ibsen places man's search for truth between the two poles of material existence without any higher orientation and a spirituality which evaporates into nothingness because it lacks its foundation in concrete life. In contrast to the *mysterium tremendum, Deus Caritatis* refers to an ultimate aim which, in its terminology as well as with regard to the situation in which the ideal is proclaimed, presupposes active search and striving and thereby a concrete dynamic relationship between the finite and the absolute.

In *Brand* the idea of moral perfection is still intimately connected with the quest for metaphysical truth. In Ibsen's social dramas the metaphysical question disappears entirely in favor of moral problems in more complex situations and therefore we find less concentration upon a single person and a single issue. Among the characters who most definitely remind us of Brand, Gregers Werle of *The Wild Duck* deserves special attention. Like Brand he is a fanatic for the truth, only much more self-centered, narrower, and above all no seeker of the truth himself. All he wants is to impose his "ideal demand" of absolute truthfulness in human relations upon others. It disturbs him that Hjalmar Ekdal lives in the illusion that Hedvig is his own child, while in reality she was conceived when Gina was the mistress of Haakon Werle, his own father. By revealing the truth to Hjalmar he applies his demand that the marital union should be based upon absolute truth to people for whom truth does not mean anything, since they are incapable of transforming such truth into an active incentive for their lives. With those people truth is nothing but dead knowledge which will soon be forgotten, for on a level which is hardly higher than that of domesticated animals there is no real difference between truth and illusion. In effect, truth under such circumstances is no more than an indifferent statement of facts; it is degraded to mere correctness, the agreement of facts and words. Furthermore, Gregers does not honestly seek an answer to this particular situation, but tries to apply a preconceived formula to it, and thereby deceives himself and drives an innocent girl into suicide. His failure of course does not justify Dr. Relling's position, according to which truth would be that which satisfies the human animal. He generalizes the inability of man to live with

the truth, and thus gives up human dig

More obvious is the falsehood of Torvald *A Doll's House.* To believe his words, untru donable crime which underlies all other crim that he concealed the truth about Nora's fathe He is too conceited to realize that truthfulness a social formality and that deception and frau him only when his honor and position are at s how indifferent he actually is with regard to tr involvement in public scandal is over. The fund mand of absolute truthfulness is that by taking yielding position with regard to truth, he prevent the forgery of the check in time, and that when vealed he is most eager to conceal it while at the arrogate for himself the right and the obligation further "crimes." Torvald's relation to truth is on and formality, restricted to that narrow sphere in v and the others are the defendants. He lives what Ibs while Nora's legal violation of the truth conceals n of which Torvald is at all capable, for by committi saved his life; at least she tried to find an adequate dilemma and was willing to assume the fullest respon

The most instructive example of absolute moral complete inadequacy Ibsen created in the figure of I *Ghosts.* As a pastor he claims to be in possession of *th* fore to be the final authority in matters of conscience. however he places himself in a highly ambiguous po himself with regard to that part of reality which cannot narrow formulas and is thus prevented from any access which are submitted to him for moral and spiritual advi books which he has not read nor would dare to read people like the Parisian artists without ever having seen Mrs. Alving back to her profligate husband without ex the horrible conditions in which she will have to live or th sequences of her return. Manders' inability and unwillingn to judge reality except through the eyes of codified moral sult in a continuous distortion of the vital truth. His et which rests on the specific commandments of the Decalogue, shattered since under the prevailing conditions, the pretence marriage, every single commandment is carried to the destr feel anything but contempt. A sophisticated lady who admits to herself that she has no talent for anything but boredom, she hates all norms as hypocritical while at the same time she poisons the lives of everyone, including herself, by her absolute disregard of the truth in all her personal relations.

Between the fool and the sophisticated lady stand such characters as Mrs. Alving and Rosmer, who are engaged in "the struggle which every serious-minded individual has to fight out for himself in order to establish a harmony between his life's conduct and his knowledge." [5] Reason is able to discover the inadequacies and the dangers of prejudices and social norms; yet the emotional bonds to the past and dependence upon public opinion are so strong that most individuals are incapable of living the truth which their reason has revealed to them. Mrs. Alving deceives the public by staying with her dissolute husband and by erecting the orphanage in his name. She deceives her son with deliberate lies about his father's virtues, thereby hastening his ruin. Rosmer deceives himself with regard to his wife's insanity and death, as well as to his relation with Rebecca. He deceives himself by claiming that his involvement in Beate's death disqualifies him from educating young people for spiritual nobility, when he ought to accept the challenge of his guilt by enhancing the value of his own life and ennobling that of others, a task for which the experience of guilt had more than adequately prepared him. He deceives himself and Rebecca when he insists that a voluntary death is the only possible atonement, while in reality it is an escape from the responsibility of atoning for his guilt as much as humanly possible by transforming it into an incentive to render the greatest service to fellow-men of which he is capable.

Examples in which the struggle for the harmony of life and knowledge is carried to a positive conclusion are rare in Ibsen and much less impressive than the negative and undecided cases discussed; and in these examples the fighting spirit is tempered by a tired resignation and the impression that the vital energy has been lost in the struggle. Thus Ellida Wangel in *Lady from the Sea* overcomes her vague longing for untamed nature in voluntary submission to the routine of married life with a husband whom she highly respects, but from whom she has none of that deep-rooted love for which one might prefer to reserve the word "truth" after all Ibsen's criticism of the "life's lie." The change from struggle to resignation is even more obvious in *Little Eyolf*, especially when one compares the corresponding issue in *Rosmersholm*. Unlike Rosmer,

[5] Letter to Björn Kristensen, Feb. 13, 1887.

Allmer accepts the obligation to educate "neglected and hated children" in atonement for his guilt, but the quest for truth all but disappears in his resignation.

Ibsen's last dramas may bear final witness to the fact that for him truth was not a social issue, but an eminently vital personal concern. In *The Master Builder* Solness torments himself with the question of whether he dedicated his whole art to the service of truth, or whether he betrayed that ideal by making concessions to the everyday needs of society; whether he expressed himself and his ideals in his creations or whether he tried to satisfy the masses with sham values. In *When We Dead Awaken* the artist Rubek confesses that he failed in his obligation to actualize the ideal in his life, and instead turned to the creation of monsters, or, if we interpret the symbol as Ibsen's self-confession, he first tried to find the truth in the abstract realm of the ideal demand and then lost himself in the portrayal of characters who were either satisfied in living their "life's lies" or vainly struggling for freedom in truth. The self-criticism of these last plays, however, illustrates again that Ibsen's conception of truth is as distant from abstract demands as it is from the chaotic concreteness of life.

In summary we may state that Ibsen's conception of truth is far more encompassing than what is ordinarily meant by the term; even the substitution of the term truthfulness is not sufficient to describe the whole complex of the problem. Although Ibsen's plays seem to be mainly concerned with the opposite of truth, the "life's lie," the ideal of truth is never quite absent; it is represented in the struggle of characters who even in their failure and because of their very failure point in the direction of that truth which, as the letters show, is for Ibsen the creative response to life, originating in concrete situations and transcending them without vanishing in the lifeless realm of the abstract.

Ibsen as a Stage Craftsman

by P. F. D. Tennant

It is a matter of considerable importance to remember that Ibsen's development as a dramatist was intimately connected with his practical association with the stage. His years of apprenticeship were spent first as salaried dramatist and instructor at the Bergen National Theater (1851-7) and then as "artistic director" of the Christiania Norwegian Theater (1857-62), while for a short period he was literary adviser to the Christiania Theater (1863). After leaving Norway in 1864 his connection with the stage was severed and, apart from schemes for the establishment of a new theater in Christiania, he no longer evinced any interest in the stage, though he was considerably influenced by the performances of the Meininger company, which he saw first in 1876 when Duke Georg invited him as his guest to attend a performance of his own play, *The Pretenders,* and decorated him with the Ernestine Order. Ibsen's most characteristic works, his social dramas, cannot fully be explained without reference to his particular experience of the stage in his early days, and it was this experience which stereotyped the dramatic form which he later adopted. Unlike his contemporary, Strindberg, he was uninterested in the practical innovations of the theater which occurred toward the end of the century, and his last plays were written with reference to the formal picture stage of his own experience with all its conventional resources of lighting and mechanism. The only instance of an experimental stage effect in Ibsen's later dramas is in his *John Gabriel Borkman,* in the last act of which Borkman takes a walk through the forest while the scenery moves past him. The following examination of his experience as a stage craftsman endeavors to assess the influence of the practical theater on his work as a dramatist.

"Ibsen as a Stage Craftsman" by P. F. D. Tennant. From *Modern Language Review,* XXXIV, No. 4 (October 1939), 557-568; later republished in *Ibsen's Dramatic Technique* by P. F. D. Tennant (London: Bowes & Bowes, 1948). Copyright 1939 by *Modern Language Review.* Reprinted by permission of the author, the Modern Humanities Research Association, and Messrs. Bowes & Bowes.

Ibsen wrote *Catiline,* practically speaking, without any knowledge of the stage. His next play, *The Warrior's Barrow,* was also written without much acquaintance with the practical side of the theater, but it procured him a free ticket to the performances of the Christiania Theater which he was otherwise too poor to frequent. He there became familiar with the current repertoire, and in his criticisms we find him paying considerable attention to the style of acting and the setting of the plays. But it is also obvious from these articles that Ibsen had not as yet "got behind the scenes." His chance came when Ole Bull summoned him to the Bergen National Theater in 1851. On November 6 he signed a contract to "assist the theater as dramatic author." This post as salaried dramatist was rather an anomaly in a theater of such small means, and in order to initiate Ibsen into the intricacies of the stage the management decided in February 1852 to give him a travelling grant for the purpose of studying European stages. On April 15 Ibsen left Bergen for Copenhagen in the company of the actors Johannes and Luise Brun, who were to study dancing and acting with Danish instructors. Ibsen was to produce a report of his studies and had been promised the position of stage-manager and producer in the theater on his return.

Ibsen installed himself in a room in Reverentsgade 205. He had a personal introduction from Judge Hansson in Bergen to the manager of the Royal Theater, the philosopher-critic-poet J. L. Heiberg, and was received very kindly. He was handed on to the care of the stage-manager of the theater, Thomas Overskou, who was most helpful. The season was then approaching its close, no new plays were being rehearsed, and Ibsen was advised to spend the first part of his time in the auditorium watching the finished products. He was given a free pass to all performances and this "little hard-bitten Norwegian with his watchful eyes," as Overskou called him, had excellent opportunities to witness a very extensive repertoire. He saw Phister play in Holberg, N. P. Nielsen in Oehlenschläger; he saw for the first time Michael Wiehe, whose performances he recalled many years afterwards, and, most important of all, he saw Höedt play his realistic version of Hamlet in direct opposition to the idealistic manner which was favored by J. L. Heiberg and the Germans. He saw Shakespeare's *Lear, Romeo and Juliet,* and *As You Like It,* saw plays by Scribe and admired their stage structure, and also plays by Hertz, Hostrup and Heiberg. Besides the Royal Theater there were two others in Copenhagen at the time, the Casino and the Royal Court Theater, both of which he visited. The latter Ibsen attended for a gala performance at which Hostrup's play, *Master and Apprentice,* was produced for the first time. This work probably influenced Ibsen's future production in its attack on the morals of journalism, while Hostrup's use of supernatural creatures may have played its part in the forming of the fantastic play Ibsen was writing at the time, his *Midsummer Eve.*

When the season was over Overskou at last took Ibsen behind the scenes at the Royal Theater. Of Ibsen's impressions we can only judge from a letter he wrote a few days before (May 30, 1852). "The theater's season ended last Friday," he writes. "Mr Overskou has promised to make me acquainted with the theater machinery etc., which was impossible during the season; however, the machinery at the Copenhagen theater is not of the best, and I hope in this respect that the German theaters will make a much more profitable study." Ibsen remained in Copenhagen another week studying the stage and procuring copies of plays, a costume book and musical scores for the Bergen theater. His choice of repertoire in Bergen was profoundly influenced by his stay in Copenhagen, in his productions of Scribe and of Scribe's Danish imitators, a repertoire well suited to the public with which he had to reckon at home.

Ibsen left Copenhagen on June 6 and arrived in Dresden on the 9th, where he stayed with a veterinary surgeon, Tröitzk, at Töpfergasse 13. He had letters of introduction to the Norwegian painter and art professor, J. C. Dahl, but on account of the latter's absence on holiday had to wait till the 16th before he met him. On June 24 he wrote: "He (Dahl) has now managed to procure me access behind the scenes at the theater, which I am certain will be of great value to me, since everything is in excellent condition." He had to pay for his admission to the performances, but in spite of straitened circumstances managed to see some sterling productions. He saw the Pole Bogumil Dawison play Hamlet, and he also saw Emil Devrient. Of other Shakespearean plays here he saw *A Midsummer Night's Dream* and *Richard III*. Hettner's book, *Das moderne Drama,* had just come out and here he was once more able to find support for his admiration of Scribe and Shakespeare. Hettner's book he had probably already read in Copenhagen, as the paper *Faedrelandet* advertised the opening of a new newspaper reading room in Silkegade where Hettner's *Das moderne Drama* and *Die romantische Schule* were displayed for the benefit of the readers.

In September Ibsen returned to Bergen. Here he took up his new post as stage-manager and producer. He was not independent, as he had hoped, but under the control of Hermann Laading, who was also given the same title, a situation which annoyed Ibsen and even resulted in making him challenge his superior to a duel. Whatever his official position may have been, Ibsen nevertheless both wrote and produced plays on his own. He was now able to put into practice the results of his studies abroad. His producer's note-book for the years 1852 to 1854 is preserved in the Bergen Museum, and this not only gives a very good idea of how he set to work but is also instructive in throwing light on his own dramatic technique.

For the period 1852-3 his method of preparation was as follows. In a broad column on the left side of the page he drew a painstaking diagram of the stage setting. In every case we find him using flats set behind one another, whether for indoor or outdoor scenery. These were of course painted in perspective to give an illusion of reality. The theater museum at Bergen has some amusing relics from this period which show with what skill the scene-painters could use their two dimensions. The diagrams were then filled in with the positions of the characters, whose movements were indicated by dotted lines. To the right of this diagram was a smaller column for cues and to the right of this again a broad column with notes indicating the movements and gestures of the characters. Pages without diagrams contained four columns, two for cues and two for notes on the movements of the actors. In 1853 the arrangement of his notes takes another form, more detailed and more practical for reference. Each page has four different columns, one for stage directions, one for positions, one for properties, and a fourth for notes. The column of stage directions is filled in either with written descriptions of the setting or diagrams, the latter often in two planes, vertical and horizontal, and frequently executed in color. The stage directions are divided into scenes according to exits and entrances in the French tradition, a convention which Ibsen used with his own plays at the time and only gave up when he wrote *Love's Comedy* in 1862. The directions are written and the diagrams are drawn with "right" and "left" as seen from the stage, in direct contradiction to his later custom and in conformity with the French models which he so closely followed in his own earlier plays. In a letter to August Lindberg (November 22, 1884) he wrote: "In reply to your question I hasten to inform you that *The Wild Duck*, like all my plays, is set from the auditorium and not from the stage. I set everything as I see it before me when writing." When Ibsen made this change it is impossible to say with any certainty, but it would seem to date from *The League of Youth*, which was written with the conscious intent to create a realistic illusion, or from *Ghosts*, where Ibsen declared his intention to be "to give the reader the impression that he was experiencing a piece of reality while reading." It is at any rate connected with the intention to write for the reader and not for the producer, an intention which is not obvious with Ibsen until he has left Norway and has severed his connection with the stage.

This producer's notebook, together with the plays Ibsen wrote on his return to Norway, show clearly what he learnt from his study tour. He had grasped the importance of the visual stage effect. Not only can we follow this in the diagrams and notes of his producer's book but also in the wealth of stage directions which now fill his plays. The contrast between *Catiline* and *Midsummer Eve,* the play he wrote during his tour, is very striking in this respect. The first act of *Catiline* is headed: "On the Flaminian highway outside Rome. A wooded slope. In the background rise the heights and walls of the town. It is evening." The setting of the first act of *Midsummer Eve* is described as follows: "Mrs Berg's garden, which is cut off from the highroad in the background by a fence with a gate. On the right the main building, erected in an attractive modern style; on the left farther up stage an old-fashioned timbered house." The stage directions in Catiline give only a hint of the locality, they give no indication of the distribution of the various sets about the stage. There could, however, be no doubt about the stage plan in *Midsummer Eve.* The setting here is bounded by foreground, background, and the right and left wings, which is not the case in *Catiline.* Ibsen has begun to set his plays in relation to a definite stage. The stage directions in *Catiline* and *The Warrior's Barrow,* with their sign-board curtness, are an inheritance from Shakespeare's editors, handed down via Schiller and Oehlenschläger. The extensive stage directions which we meet for the first time with Ibsen in *Midsummer Eve* are taken direct from the contemporary French drama of intrigue, which in this respect as in many others was a direct offshoot of the realistic English bourgeois drama of the eighteenth century.

The lavish settings and numerous changes of scene in Ibsen's Bergen plays would lead one to believe that the Bergen stage possessed extensive technical resources. This was by no means the case. The theater was built in 1800 in neo-classic style with a stage which was singularly ill equipped. In 1825 a Danish portrait painter was engaged to furnish the stage with modern machinery. This consisted of a variation of the apparatus which was employed in the eighteenth century court theaters, and as far as scene-shifting was concerned it was very efficient. The flats in the wings were mounted in grooves and connected to a central winch below the stage. Each flat had a group of two, three, or four grooves in which the successive sets could be mounted simultaneously. The winch could then in a very short time pull into position or withdraw any one of the sets.

The sets worked in combination with a backcloth which was quickly changed by folding or rolling. This expeditious method of scene-shifting, together with the scene-painter's proficiency in perspective painting, made practically speaking any scene possible. Ibsen's later demands for realism discarded two-dimensional perspective scenery and introduced three-dimensional scenery with walls and solid properties. The wagon or lift stage had by then not been invented, no one yet thought of using curtains, and it took much more time to change scenes of this kind. This latter consideration no doubt contributed to Ibsen's artistic economy in the unity of place which dominates in his early realistic plays.

Lighting was always of supreme importance to Ibsen in creating the atmosphere of a setting. In a letter to Schrøder with reference to the setting of *The Wild Duck* he wrote: "The lighting also has its significance; it is different for each act and is intended to correspond to the mood which gives each of the acts its special character." This symbolical use of light is characteristic of Ibsen even in his earliest works. In his preface to the second edition of his first work, *Catiline*, he dwells on the fact that the play was written at night and adds: "I believe that this is the unconscious reason for nearly all the action taking place at night." The play was undoubtedly written with a sense of the importance of the lighting in order to give it atmosphere, but certainly without regard for the technical possibilities. Not until Ibsen came to Dresden did he realize the possibilities of the lighting effects embodied in gas illumination. Oil lamps were used in Bergen until 1856, when gas was introduced in the theater. His appreciation of the importance of being able to control the strength of the lighting with gas illumination can be seen in *Midsummer Eve*, the play which he wrote abroad under the influence of his impressions there. The first act begins in the evening and a stage direction tells us that it "begins to get dark." In the second act "it is night; the moon is in the sky." The scene is then suddenly lit up by the opening of the fairy mound, a purely operatic stage effect, and the third act shows us the whole stage in bright daylight again. The play was a failure, and this no doubt was largely due to the fact that the theater machinery and lighting were not equal to Ibsen's demands. Anyhow, it is noticeable how Ibsen's next play, *Lady Inger*, follows the model of *Catiline* and passes in a crescendo of gloom, completely abandoning the effects of light contrasts which he developed to such an art later, and only indulging in such effects as would conform to the demands of realism on a lamp-lit stage. Ibsen, in his dual position of dramatist and stage-manager, would naturally advocate such a reform as the introduction of gas into the theater, and it appears not unlikely that he was responsible for its installation. Gas illumination was used in Bergen for the first time in 1856 and the theater was one of the first institutions to take advantage of it. *The Feast at Solhaug,* which was produced in January 1856, shows as yet no signs of the effect of the new illumination, but the next play, *Olaf Liljekrans,* is full of lighting effects, dusk, dawn and a midnight fire. The next play, *The Vikings at Helgeland,* with its full-blooded realism of setting, spares no opportunity for stage effect, and it is significant that Ibsen first sent his play to the Christiania Theater before producing it at his own, because he knew among other things that it possessed a very much better technical equipment. From now on Ibsen's stage directions never omit indications of lighting. Here, in the first act, the curtain rises on "thick snowy weather and storm." This is followed later by the stage direction: "The storm has ceased during the previous scene; the midday sun appears like a red disk on the horizon." The second act is by contrast illuminated by a log fire, the third is daylight, and the fourth act is lit by torches and the rising moon, which spreads an atmosphere of peace after the passing storm. Light is from now onwards used by Ibsen, not only to indicate the passage of time, but also as a symbolical accompaniment to the action. His early appreciation of the importance and possibility of light effects on the stage he owed to his visit to Dresden in 1852.

During his tour in Denmark and Germany, Ibsen became acquainted with contemporary stage machinery and lighting, together with the routine of producing. We have seen the fruit of his experiences in the detailed settings and stage directions of the plays he wrote at the time, which form a parallel to the painstaking plans in his producer's notebook. So far we have watched him exploiting the technical resources with which he became acquainted. If we now turn to the individualization of Ibsen's technique of setting and stage directions, we find here as everywhere a growing tendency toward a realistic illusion combined with an equally strong inclination to romantic symbolism. It is the latter which dominates in the later plays.

In *Catiline* and *The Warrior's Barrow* there is no conscious attempt at realistic setting. *The Ptarmigan of Justedal* and *Midsummer Eve* offer only vague indications of conventional sets and properties. The disposition of the various scenes is indicated, but not the nature of the individual objects. In the former we meet with a "wild but beautiful part of Justedalen," which only evokes a very vague picture. In the latter we know that the main building is "erected in an attractive modern style" while the building on the left is an "old-fashioned timbered house." This tells us nothing of the peculiarities of the two buildings, but is rather an indication for the property-man as to what sets are to be used. In *Lady*

Inger and *The Feast at Solhaug* we find a slight increase in detail, but
we are dealing with standard props all the time, "a magnificent room,"
"an old-fashioned carved high seat," and so forth. The same is the case
with *Olaf Liljekrans. The Vikings at Helgeland* is the first play with a
specifically realistic setting, and it is significant that it was written in the
year that Ibsen left Bergen and no longer had to reckon with the theater
stock of properties and sets. The setting of the first scene is as follows:
"A high shore which slopes steeply down to the sea in the background.
On the left a boat-house, on the right mountains and pine woods. The
masts of two warships can be seen down in the bay; far away on the
right, rocks and high islands; the sea is very rough, it is winter with thick
snowy weather and storm." The striking feature about this setting is not
so much the absence of standard props and scenery but the way in which
Ibsen sets an outdoor scene and overcomes false perspective. He uses a
high foreground which masks receding perspective, behind which the
backcloth can represent the middle and far distance without risk of showing up the actors out of proportion. The foreground is the only area of
the stage on which the actors appear and their size is then always in
proper relation to the scenery. This method of giving an illusion of reality to outdoor settings was in future always employed by Ibsen with only
two variations. The first was the high foreground which we meet again in
The Lady from the Sea, John Gabriel Borkman, and *When We Dead
Awaken,* the second the fenced-in garden where the fence has the function of masking the perspective, a setting which we remember as far back
as *Midsummer Eve,* and which recurs in *The Lady from the Sea, Little
Eyolf* and *When We Dead Awaken.*

One frequently hears of the stuffy atmosphere of Ibsen's plays, the
atmosphere which pervades the indoor settings of his modern tragedies.
From 1877, when *The Pillars of Society* was published, until 1886, the
date of the publication of *Rosmersholm,* all his plays were set indoors,
while the first three of these six take place in one and the same room.
After this date there is only one totally indoor play, *Hedda Gabler,* two
are set entirely out of doors (*The Lady from the Sea, When We Dead
Awaken*), and the remaining three have both outdoor and indoor settings.
The indoor setting is the direct result of Ibsen's conscious effort to create
a realistic illusion, while its abandonment coincides with his reversion
to romantic symbolism. Even more than in the case of the outdoor setting, the interior had to overcome the difficulties of perspective. As we
can see from Ibsen's diagrams for interior settings, the Bergen theater
used the type of scenery which was common at the time; that is to say,
that the side walls of a room were represented by transverse flies set

parallel behind one another as in the outdoor scenes, while the back wall was represented by a flapping backcloth perforated with doors and windows. The whole proscenium opening was used for rooms of all dimensions and the illusion of varying size was brought about by the false perspective of the scene-painter. In the setting of Ibsen's *Lady Inger,* for instance, the room in the first act would occupy as much stage space as the knight's hall in the third, though the latter might of course use a little deeper stage. In the impoverished theater at Bergen economy was everything as regards properties and scenery, and the painter was in consequence called upon to include in his settings flat pasteboard cupboards, chairs, and ornaments which the theater could not afford to procure in the solid. The effect of these settings as a peep-show panorama was often very illusory, but the impression was immediately destroyed by the movements of the actors. A reaction against this type of indoor setting began to make itself felt in Europe about this time. The study of the Elizabethan stage which had begun with Tieck led to various attempts at reconstruction, especially in the use of the little inner stage and the curtain background. Laube, in his historical productions, had already begun to simplify his scenery and had set his actors against a plain background, but the tendency of the day was for historical realism and against stylization, and here it was that the Meininger company seemed to have impressed Ibsen with their solid realistic scenery. Solid interior walls and ceilings for modern settings had already been introduced previously in France and England, and it may well be that Ibsen, during his residence in Germany, had seen imitations of this in modern plays. The settings of *Emperor and Galilean* are mostly outdoor ones and the few interiors show as yet no signs of modern realism. But when we come to *The Pillars of Society* it is a different matter. The earliest notes for this play date from 1870 and it was not finished until 1877, the year after Ibsen saw the first Meininger performances. As far as we can judge from the notes and sketches before 1876, the scene was removed in each act. The first act took place in Consul Bernick's morning-room, the second in the garden, the third on a road by the shore, and the fourth in a wood. After 1876 the setting immediately took shape and was restricted to Consul Bernick's morning-room for all the acts, while the directions give the most detailed description of the stage that Ibsen had hitherto indulged in. In this setting he has transferred the historical realism of the Meininger into modern surroundings, and has combined the interior with the fenced-in garden exterior to give a complete illusion of the "fourth wall." We have only to compare this scene with a corresponding scene in *The League of Youth,* its predecessor as a modern play, to see how Ibsen had individualized his technique. The second act of the latter play has the following setting: "The chamberlain's morning-room. Elegant furniture, a piano, flowers and rare plants. Entrance door in the background. On the left a door into the dining-room; on the right several glass doors opening into the garden." In this case we are still dealing with props and standard sets. In *The Pillars of Society* we find the following setting:

> A spacious morning-room in Consul Bernick's house. In the foreground on the left there is a door leading into the Consul's room; farther back on the same wall is a similar door. In the middle of the opposite wall is a fairly large entrance-door. The wall in the background is almost entirely composed of mirrors, with an open door leading out on to broad garden steps, over which is stretched an awning. At the bottom of the steps one can see part of the garden, which is enclosed by a fence with a little gate. On the other side of the fence, and parallel to it, runs a street which is flanked on the opposite side by small brightly painted wooden houses. It is summer and the sun is shining warmly. People pass by in the street from time to time; they stop and converse; they go and make purchases in a shop on the corner etc. . . .

Here there is no question of standard props or sets, the whole scene is an individual solid structure. We find Ibsen for the first time giving directions for a realistic setting and following the example of contemporary producers. The producers had hitherto looked to the past for their dramatists, and now Ibsen appeared and immediately carried them off their feet.

With *Pillars of Society* Ibsen inaugurates his series of modern indoor plays, and he becomes a master in electrifying these settings with dramatic potentiality. The dramatic importance of the ground plan and elevation of the houses in which his plays are set, together very often with the locality in which the houses stand, is very great in Ibsen's work. He transforms and adapts to his own use the secret stairs and trapdoors and sliding panels of romantic melodrama so that his doors and curtains and windows are equally pregnant with secrets in spite of their prosaic surroundings. Ibsen once spoke of himself as a builder, and there is no doubt that he had a supreme sense of the dramatic in architecture. We remember houses and parts of houses from Ibsen's plays as well as we know our own. His insistence on architecture begins with *A Doll's House*. The room in this case has four doors, each of them having its function, while two of them, the door to Helmer's study and the one into the hall, become the focus of dramatic tension, especially when Krogstad's letter is lying in the hall letter-box. In the course of the action we learn that the flat is on the first floor, we know where the kitchen and the nursery and Nora's bedroom are, and we hear the music from the fancy-dress party in the flat above. The effect of this technique is to give one a sense of tremendous dramatic activity focused on the one room visible on the stage, and also to give this one room an extension far beyond its real dimensions. This latter effect is increased by noises and talking off the stage. In *John Gabriel Borkman* a similar illusion of architectural solidity is brought about by the continuity of the four acts in which the action progresses without any time interval. At the end of the first act in Mrs. Borkman's room on the ground floor we hear music from Borkman's room above. The second act opens in Borkman's room where Frida Foldal is playing the piano, in the third Borkman comes downstairs and at the end rushes out of the hall door into the snow. The fourth act shows the outside of the house and Borkman walking out. The door to Borkman's room is also charged with dramatic tension. He is always waiting for the knock which will announce the arrival of the delegation which is to clear his reputation. A similar dramatic door we have in *The Master Builder,* when Solness says, "One of these days youth will come here knocking at the door," in response to which Hilde Wangel seals his fate by her prompt knocking. In *Rosmersholm* we find a genuine survival of romantic melodrama in the curtain behind which Rebekka overhears Rosmer's conversation with Mortensgaard.

Ibsen's appreciation of the dramatic value of a realistic setting is well illustrated in the case of *The Wild Duck.* In this case a study of the drafts of the play shows exactly with what care he worked out the details. The last four acts of the play pass in Hjalmar Ekdal's studio, and in the back wall we see the door which leads into the weird garret where the duck and the rabbits and pigeons are kept. In the second draft the stage directions describe the door as follows: "A large double door in the middle of the back wall constructed so that it can be pushed aside." When Ekdal insists on showing Gregers the attic, the directions state: "Ekdal and Hjalmar have gone to the back wall and each pushes aside the upper part of his half of the door." In the third act the same process is repeated: "Hjalmar and Ekdal open the upper part of the half-doors to the garret." Ekdal squeezes himself into the garret by opening the lower half of the doors slightly. Then Hjalmar "pulls a string; a piece of stretched fishing-net slides down in front of the door opening." In the play the door into the garret is constructed differently. Instead of being divided into four parts, which enables the upper half to be open while the lower remains shut, it is made of only two partitions, one on each side, which open and disclose the whole floor of the garret. It is a "broad double sliding door." In the second act Hjalmar and Ekdal disclose the whole attic in the moonlight, the animals being hidden in the shadow, whereas formerly the floor was not visible. In the third act Hjalmar and Ekdal again open each of the sliding doors and disclose the whole attic in the sunshine, together with its inhabitants. After this full glimpse, Hjalmar "pulls a string; from inside a curtain is lowered, the bottom part of which consists of a strip of old sailcloth, the upper of a piece of stretched fishing net. Thus the floor of the garret is no longer visible." In the earlier version the contents of the garret were seen by the actors alone and the duck still remained a formless figure for the audience. In the play the garret is fully revealed to the spectators with its bizarre display of animals and rubbish. The momentary glimpse of what is behind gives the sailcloth and the closed door a weird suggestive power which was absent when the duck remained unseen and unreal. This is only one instance of Ibsen's capacity for increasing the dramatic effect by a pure arrangement of scenery.

This constructive sense in Ibsen's indoor settings is equally strong in all his later plays and it is combined with great economy of material. His stages were set with regard to the function of the various units, the doors, windows, and pieces of furniture, and he cleared the stage of all the superfluous junk that was popular in the dazzling settings of French social dramas. His settings were inspired with a sympathy for the effect of milieu on the characters and often possess a *dramatic quality* independent of the characters themselves. Concentration and elimination were his principles in developing dialogue and character, and it was the same principles he applied to realistic settings; his dramatic sense was greatly aided by his painter's eye in their conception, and they form one of the characteristic features of Ibsen's drama.

Shakespeare and Ibsen

by Halvdan Koht

What did Shakespeare mean for Ibsen? Has he been an influence in the dramaturgy of Ibsen? Inevitably he has, since all modern drama has stood under the power of his genius. After he had been discovered by the European world in the second half of the eighteenth century, no dramatic author could escape his influence and his inspiration.

Therefore, it may seem strange that in the large number of works and studies regarding the great master of the nineteenth century drama, Henrik Ibsen, the name of Shakespeare only rarely occurs, and little of a positive nature is said about Shakespearean influence.[1]

The reason may be that this influence is only in a few cases directly traceable. But, perhaps, just for that reason it may be more profound and vital.

In a way, Ibsen himself has indicated that Shakespeare had a unique position in his mental world. He who so rarely ventured to stand forth as a speaker, let alone as a lecturer, once gave a formal lecture on Shakespeare. It happened on November 27, 1855. On that date, at a social-literary society meeting at Bergen, the so-called "Society of December 22" (founded in 1845), he spoke on "Shakespeare and His Influence on Nordic Art." [2] Nothing is reported on the contents of this lecture. No manuscript is preserved. Almost of necessity, by analogy, one's thoughts wander back to the speech the young Goethe delivered at the memorial celebration of Shakespeare which he arranged in 1771. That was, in fact, the proclamation of Shakespeare as the great prophet of a new epoch in European literary life. About his own discovery of Shakespeare, Goethe said:

> The first page I read of him made me his subject for life, and when
> I had finished his first play I stood like the blind-born whom on an instant

"Shakespeare and Ibsen" by Halvdan Koht. From *Journal of English and Germanic Philology*, XLIV, No. 1 (January 1945), 79-86. Reprinted by permission of the author and *JEGP*.

[1] That is the case also in my own *Life of Ibsen* (American edition, 1931).

[2] *Edda*, vol. x, Kristiania, 1919, p. 160 by Francis Bull.

a wonder-working hand makes seeing. I conceived, I vividly felt my existence infinitely enlarged; everything was new to me, as if previously unknown, and the unaccustomed light hurt my eyes.[3]

We dare not presume that Ibsen, in his lecture, expressed himself with
the same enthusiasm. He was not at that moment arriving immediately
from his first meeting with Shakespeare. He certainly spoke more deliberately and, according to the title of his lecture, on a more historical
note. We may conjecture that, regarding "influence on Nordic art," he
said something about the leader of Danish romanticism, Oehlenschläger.
He might have mentioned the greatest of all Norwegian poets, Henrik
Wergeland; but I doubt this because Ibsen had not much sympathy for
Wergeland and, also, because Wergeland was not a great dramatist but
essentially a poet (beside having many other qualities). But, doubtless,
Ibsen put forward a program; he must have explained the greatness of
Shakespeare, and I feel convinced that he concluded by asserting that
Shakespeare ought to exert a determining influence on future Norwegian
drama and theater. Ibsen himself had already undergone that influence,
and it had meant an epoch in his literary development.

When did Ibsen first meet Shakespeare? In his earliest attempt at dramatic authorship, *Catiline* (1848-1849), Shakespeare is not present except
by the intermedium of Schiller and Oehlenschläger, particularly through
Schiller's *Die Raüber*. The same holds true about his next drama, *The
Warrior's Barrow* (1850), where Oehlenschläger dominates. Only a couple
of years later did he come face to face with Shakespeare.

After Ole Bull, in 1851, had taken him to Bergen and made him a
stage-manager at the new theater there, Ibsen was sent the next year, with
some of the actors, to study theatrical art in Copenhagen and Dresden.
There, in the spring and summer of 1852, he had his first opportunities
to see Shakespeare's dramas on the stage, and there he experienced the
powerful impact of the master dramatist. In his first report from Copenhagen, May 16, 1852, he mentions[4] that he and his party had seen "*Hamlet* and other of Shakespeare's plays." He does not add a word about the
impression these plays made on him, but he puts them first in the list
of performances he had seen, even before those of his beloved Dano-
Norwegian dramatist Ludwig Holberg, and he prefaces the list by saying:
"As to the repertoire we have been very fortunate." The other Shakespearean plays which, during his visit in Copenhagen, were performed at
the Royal Theater were *King Lear, Romeo and Juliet,* and *As You Like*

---

[3] Goethe, *Sämtliche Werke*, Jubiläums-Ausgabe, vol. 36, Stuttgart und Berlin, 1907,
p. 4.
[4] Henrik Ibsen, *Samlede verker*, Hundreaarsutgave, vol. XVI, Oslo, 1940, p. 35.

It. In Dresden he saw *Midsummer Night's Dream, King Richard III,* and again *Hamlet*.

No doubt, of all these plays *Hamlet* impressed him most strongly. More than forty years later, he still recalled the two performances with great pleasure and said he had learned much from the comparison of the actors who had the leading part.[5] In 1857, in a detailed review of a new Norwegian drama performed at the Christiania Theater, he inserted an allusion to the same drama: "In *Hamlet* it is just the lack of active energy of the hero that determines the dramatic effect of the whole work." [6] When, in 1871, he sent his poetical greeting to the foremost actress of Denmark, Johanne Luise Heiberg, he mentioned among the parts she had impersonated only one from Shakespeare, "fair Ophelia," "flickering, gliding" across the stage.[7] That is *Hamlet* again.

Beside this drama, only two other Shakespeare plays are specifically referred to in Ibsen's writings. In *Peer Gynt* (1867) he humorously quotes *Richard III,* making his hero, left alone in the desert after having dreamt himself a king, exclaim: "My kingdom—well, half of it, say—for a horse!" Further there is *King Lear*. In a poem about the medieval royal hall in Bergen, *Haakon's Hall,* he compares its neglected, half-ruined state to King Lear, driven out by his daughters in the night and storm of the wild heath and covered with a fool's cap.[8] This poem probably was written in the year 1855, the same year in which he gave his lecture on Shakespeare. It gives another proof of the intensity with which the English master at that time was living in his mind.

The same year he had to stage a Shakespeare play at the theater at Bergen. It has sometimes been said that he showed his interest in Shakespeare by producing several of his plays there. But that is not correct. On the one hand, it was not he who decided the repertoire of this theater; he was not the director of it, he was no more than stage-manager and he could only propose. On the other hand, the Bergen theater had neither the material nor the artistic powers needed for the performance of Shakespearean dramas. During all the years Ibsen was working there, the theater performed only one of them, the comedy *As You Like It,* which he had seen in Copenhagen and which was acted in Bergen on September 30 and October 3, 1855. Even this play evidently was too much for the poor means at the disposal of the theater,[9] and the attempt to play

[5] Henrik Jaeger, *The Life of Henrik Ibsen,* London, 1890, pp. 69-70, and the same author, *Illustreret norsk literaturhistorie,* vol. II, 1, Kristiania, 1896, p. 569.

[6] Ibsen, *Samlede verker,* vol. XV, Oslo, 1930, p. 179.

[7] *Op. cit.,* vol. XIV, Oslo, 1937, p. 428.

[8] *Op. cit.,* vol. XIV, pp. 207, 323, cp. p. 23.

[9] T. Blanc, *Norges förste nationale Scene,* Kristiania, 1884, p. 206.

Shakespeare was not repeated.[10] Perhaps the very failure stimulated Ibsen to defend the venture and proclaim his Shakespeare program. At any rate, the work on this play lingered in his mind as a pleasant memory; several years later, in a letter of October 28, 1870, he referred to his recent stay in Rome as recalling the atmosphere of *As You Like It* by its "ideal peace" and its "carefree artistic community."

During his stay in Copenhagen and Dresden in 1852, he was led to Shakespeare in another way, too, than by seeing the plays on the stage. At that time he read the recently (1850) published book by Hermann Hettner, *Das moderne Drama,* and many biographers have pointed out the important effect on his mind from this reading. Hettner's book was a challenge to contemporary playwrights; it would not recognize any drama as fulfilling the highest literary demands except that which was firmly based on psychological dynamics. Hettner referred all future authors to Shakespeare as the great master and example, particularly in his historical tragedies. Shakespeare's greatness, he said, was that he broke away from the ancient idea of fate and always presented the dramatic catastrophe as the unavoidable consequence of the tragic guilt of the hero. The character of his persons was the essence and the real motive power of his dramas.

Ibsen felt the challenge as a release of his own deepest wants and endeavors. And what Hettner taught him by theory, Shakespeare demonstrated to him by practice. Perhaps it may be disputed which of the two affected him more forcefully. No doubt, both worked together to educate him for the task that was natural to him. More than anything else, however, the Shakespearean dramas must have fostered in him a will to emulate the highest examples. They inspired him with the passion of search for the psychological forces at the bottom of dramatic conflicts. Through them he learned to focus his efforts on the one decisive element of true drama, the study and depiction, merciless and merciful at the same time, of individual characters opposed in battle for life or death, living themselves out, so to speak, according to their innermost essence and for that very reason typically human in their individualities.

That was a response to the longings of his own soul. Throughout his whole life, Ibsen was struggling to find and to express the fundamentals of his personality. That was the incessant fight within himself, his own

[10] Contrary to some assertions, Ibsen never ventured to put any drama of Shakespeare's on the stage during all the years (1857-1862) he was the director of the "Norwegian Theater" in Oslo; see Audhild Lund, *Henrik Ibsen og det norske teater 1857-63* (Smaaskrifter fra det litteraturhistoriske seminar, xix), Oslo, 1925.

personal drama. He was extremely sensitive to impressions from all of life and all the forces surrounding him, consequently from literature too. That sensitivity was an element of his genius, but he felt it also as a weakness. In his youth he was inclined to imitate all kinds of literary patterns, and even when out of the first flush of youth he might bow to the claims of ruling currents of thought. Such impressions might stimulate him to opposition, to efforts at creating something different, as when *Svend Dyring's House* by the Dane Henrik Hertz impelled him to show what the Norwegian folk-ballad, as contrasted with the Danish, might lead to in drama (*The Feast at Solhaug*, 1855). Or as, at a later date, *A Gauntlet* by Björnstjerne Björnson made him scorn the pretentious preachers of truth in *The Wild Duck*. Always he searched and fought for his own self.

Shakespeare helped him find himself. Shakespeare entered his life as a force of liberation. What he, vaguely and immaturely, strove to achieve in *Catiline*, now grew to be a mighty conscious effort, conforming with his very nature.

The Renaissance had taken hold of the ancient, classic literature in order to arm itself for the fight for intellectual freedom. When the young generations of Europe, from the 1770s on, rebelled against a fossilized, tyrannical classicism, they found in Shakespeare a powerful ally and fellow-fighter whom they could place in the vanguard of a new host of liberty.[11] He remained the liberator even for later generations. We may compare his effect on Ibsen with that on Wergeland twenty-five years before. To Wergeland Shakespeare came at an earlier age and, from the start, overwhelmed him with such force as almost to drown his individuality. But soon he came to the surface again, refreshed and strengthened by the bath of passion and poetry; his poetic imagination had simply learned to find the rich expression corresponding to his innermost mind.

Ibsen was more mature when he met Shakespeare; he appropriated him more slowly, not with the violence of Wergeland, and he had no such period of complete Shakespearean imitation. Nevertheless, we can discern the first effects of Shakespeare in him by more material details than are visible in his later works. Such palpable traces of Shakespearean influence do not constitute the very essence of it. But they prove the fact, and they date its existence. That is what gives them their importance.

When Professor Francis Bull, of the University of Oslo, in the Norwegian literary magazine *Edda*, 1919, published the notice about Ibsen's lecture on Shakespeare at the "Society of December 22," he made at the

---

[11] See Hermann Hettner, *Literaturgeschichte des achtzehnten Jahrhunderts*, all volumes.

same time several suggestions regarding Shakespearean influence in some of Ibsen's dramas.[12] He found the first signs of it in the satirical comedy *Midsummer Eve,* written in 1852. This Ibsen play shows, in fact, very little originality. It is likely to have been conceived and begun in Copenhagen under the impression of some comedies by the Danish author J. L. Heiberg and to have been finished, or almost so, in Dresden where Ibsen saw the *Midsummer Night's Dream,* which was defined by Hettner as the foremost example of a comedy that would mix dreams and reality into a play of fancy. Obviously, the goblin of Ibsen's play is the twin of Shakespeare's Puck and performs the same part in the comedy.[13]

Here, however, the ideas borrowed from Shakespeare have produced no more than quite superficial imitations. The spirit of the great English dramatist had not yet penetrated to the real core of Ibsen's creative genius. Certainly only after his return to Bergen did he throw himself into a real study of Shakespeare and absorb deeper impulses from his works. Only then did Shakespeare become a truly decisive force in his development. What Shakespeare in this larger sense meant to him is first evident in his tragedy *Lady Inger of Östraat* (1854). The Shakespearean traits of this drama were emphasized in several particulars by Francis Bull; and a younger student, Olav Dalgard, made it the subject of a special study which partly confirmed, partly corrected, the suggestions of Bull.[14]

It was easy to detect in *Lady Inger* the formal technique taken over from Scribe, so much so that Edmund Gosse called the drama "a romantic exercise in the manner of Scribe." [15] It was useful to point out what Ibsen in this respect had learned from Scribe because it proved that he still was in the age of apprenticeship. On the other hand, there is in *Lady Inger* an outburst of liberated passion that testifies to a new epoch in the author's life. Dalgard asserts that Schiller represents the strongest literary influence in the drama,[16] and nobody can deny that much of it recalls the manner of Schiller. But Schiller was not a new element in Ibsen's dramaturgic growth; he had been dominant already in *Catiline.* The new force was Shakespeare.

Edmund Gosse remarked briefly: "There is some slight, but of course unconscious, resemblance to *Macbeth* in the external character of Lady

---

[12] *Edda,* vol. x, pp. 160-161.

[13] Francis Bull, in Henrik Ibsen, *Samlede verker,* vol. II, Oslo, 1928, pp. 12-13.

[14] *Edda,* vol. xxx, Oslo, 1930, pp. 1-47: *Studier over Fru Inger til Österaad,* see pp. 28-35 about the relations to Shakespeare.

[15] Edmund Gosse, *Henrik Ibsen,* London, 1908, p. 54.

[16] Francis Bull accepted this view in his *Norsk litteraturhistorie,* vol. IV, Oslo, 1937, p. 304.

Inger." [17] Clearly, it adds importance to the resemblance if we can state it—as I think we must—to be unconscious. In that case it demonstrates how completely Ibsen had appropriated the fundamentals of Shakespearean dramaturgy. Indeed, we cannot avoid recognizing *Macbeth* in the ghastly night scenes where Lady Inger wanders through the deserted halls half ecstatic, half sleepwalking, tormented by the black shadows of the past and by the conception of being both king's mother and king's murderer. Her monologues of the last act contain, besides, striking parallels to those of the last act of *Richard III*. Still more profound, however, appears her resemblance to *Hamlet*. Traits of his diseased will have been transferred to her. She is filled with the idea of her duty to accomplish a great task, that of restoring national independence, but she doubts and despairs of her strength to carry it through. One particular scene, the very first of the drama, directly recalls the churchyard scene that opens Act V of *Hamlet*. The influence of Shakespeare cannot be mistaken.

But the capital fact, surpassing all such details, is that the very method by which Ibsen makes his heroine unveil and unfold her character is fundamentally congruent with that of Shakespeare, such as is to be found in *Hamlet* as well as in *Macbeth*. The dramatic events by themselves lift to the light the deepest forces of her soul. Despite the manifest difference of external technique employed by Ibsen, his severe maintenance of the unity of time and place and his exploitation of all kinds of Scribean intrigue, the true motive power of the drama is the character of Lady Inger herself. The basic dramatic construction is truly Shakespearean, founded on the dynamics of psychology and passion. Justly, Dalgard refers to what Ibsen wrote in 1857 about the dramatic structure of *Hamlet*.

It is, however, well worth stressing the fact that the very problems of character which meet us in *Lady Inger* are essentially identical with those Ibsen had treated in *Catiline*. They were personal problems of his own inner self. But, from all points of view, artistic as well as psychological, it is a far cry from the drama of 1849 to that of 1854. In the latter we see him for the first time free and daring in the expression of his creative intentions. Here, finally, we face the powerful dramatic intensity which made for his greatness as an author. That quality is indeed Shakespearean. It was the essence of his own genius.

Ibsen still had to grow, and to do battle within himself, in order to be fully free from the pressure of external powers. In this fight he continued to have the help of Shakespeare. To a large extent he bowed to the demands of contemporary literary fashion in his later dramas from the

[17] *Op. cit.,* p. 56.

1850s, although the most successful of them, *The Feast at Solhaug* (1855) and *The Vikings at Helgeland* (1857), certainly excelled all other works of the same kind. Only indirectly—but even that is vital—is Shakespeare in them in so far as the author demonstrates his mastery of expressing human passions and depicting powerful characters.

Regarding *The Vikings* Roman Woerner has remarked [18] that the manner in which Ibsen exploited his sources is reminiscent of that of Shakespeare in the use of Holinshed and the Italian novelists; both of the dramatists knew how to mold their borrowings perfectly into the whole of the work so as not to appear like pieces of mosaic. I should think that, in this respect, Ibsen even improved on Shakespeare, in particular when we remember that he built this drama on two different sagas (the *Volsung saga* and the *Laxdoela*) and borrowed matters from a third (*Egils saga*). He always created dramas, never "histories."

Woerner also compares [19] the manner in which Ibsen in *The Vikings* keeps us waiting for the catastrophe by inserting the scene of Örnulf's complaint for the loss of his son, with the trick by which Shakespeare in *King Lear,* immediately before the catastrophe, makes us still more excited about the fatal issue of the drama—the dying Edmund is made to countermand the order for the murder of the king. I must admit that I do not see the congruency of the technique employed. Shakespeare really introduces a new element of tension, Ibsen simply leaves us waiting for some more moments.

More direct reminiscences of Shakespeare are to be found in *The Pretenders* (1863), the most brilliant of all of Ibsen's historical tragedies. From a certain point of view it may be called a drama of jealousy, and some outbursts of Earl Skule may remind one of *Othello.* In all of Ibsen's dramas, the villain Iago, the evil spirit of Othello, finds no closer counterpart than Bishop Nikolas in *The Pretenders,* the evil spirit of Skule. The fundamental contrast between Skule and King Haakon is partly sketched by Shakespeare in that between Macbeth and King Duncan's son Malcolm. Some particulars of *The Pretenders* lead back to *King Lear.* The dialogue between Skule and the poet Jatgeir has a close parallel in that between King Lear and the fool in Act 1, Scene 4. And the last wanderings of Skule through the forests seem almost a repetition of King Lear's strayings on the wild heaths, memories of which were steadily coming back to Ibsen's mind. A single phrase in his drama sounds like an echo of one from *King Lear,* appearing in the very first scene of that drama. There Cordelia defines her position in some words spoken aside: "What

[18] Roman Woerner, *Henrik Ibsen,* vol. I, 3rd ed., München, 1923, p. 92.
[19] *Op. cit.,* p. 96.

shall Cordelia do? Love, and be silent." Ibsen makes the betrayed Inge-
björg tell her fate in the same way: "To love, to sacrifice all and be
forgotten, that is the saga of woman" (in later editions corrected into:
that is my saga).

More striking still is perhaps the similarity pointed out by Roman
Woerner between *The Pretenders* and *Julius Caesar*.[20] This drama of
Shakespeare's is peculiar in having the title not of the real hero, who is
Brutus, but of the man who is the subject of the hero's acts and thoughts.
Caesar actually is killed at the beginning of the third act. But he remains the *perpetuum mobile* of the drama like the bishop in *The Pretenders,* and both of them reappear as ghosts after their death. Caesar
even reveals himself twice to Brutus, the first time in Act IV, proclaiming
himself, on the question of Brutus, as being "Thy evil spirit." The second
time Brutus exclaims:

> O Julius Caesar, thou art mighty yet!
> Thy spirit walks abroad, and turns our swords
> In our own proper entrails.

That is exactly the role of Bishop Nikolas, too, when his ghost appears
to Earl Skule.

Such are the distinct traces of Shakespeare in the dramas of Ibsen.
They offer irrefutable proof of the profound impression Shakespeare
exerted on the master dramatist of the nineteenth century. But I emphasize again that the important matter is not the details by themselves.
They simply help confirm the general observation of the effect of Shakespeare as assisting Ibsen in realizing the true essence of drama and liberat-
ing his genius.

After *The Pretenders* we observe no direct influence of Shakespeare in
Ibsen's works. A prominent American student of Ibsen, Professor A. E.
Zucker, has attempted to show reminiscences from Shakespeare's *Coriolanus* in Ibsen's *Brand* (written 1865).[21] He even asserts: "It would be
hard to find two other characters in the works of great dramatists who
are spiritually so closely akin as are Brand and Coriolanus." Certainly
there are parallels both in certain parts of the plots of the two dramas
and in some of the expressions used by their heroes. But the similarities
seem to me too trifling to prove any influence from the one drama upon
the other. Both of the heroes despise the "multitude," but from fundamentally different points of view, the one asserting the power of a class

---

[20] *Op. cit.,* p. 167.
[21] A. E. Zucker, "Ibsen-Hettner-Coriolanus-Brand," in *Modern Language Notes,* vol.
51, Baltimore, 1936, pp. 99-106.

of nobility by birth, the other championing the leadership of advanced
and clear-sighted individuals. Thus I see rather a contrast than an accordance between the two. I am more inclined to accept the suggestion
of Professor Zucker that the title of Ibsen's *An Enemy of the People*
(1882) may be traced back to Shakespeare's calling Coriolanus an "enemy
to the people" or "the people's enemy."

At the time Ibsen wrote *Brand* I think he had appropriated completely
what Shakespeare could give him, and he was a master of drama in his
own right. Edmund Gosse, who was no man of critical research but who
had a fine feeling of literary values, once remarked,[22] "There is something
of Shakespeare in *John Gabriel Borkman*." Undoubtedly he is right. But
in a way that holds true for the whole lifework of Ibsen that "something
of Shakespeare" is always present. It is the mighty breathing of high
dramatic passion that makes his works represent to us the eternal battle
of human hearts.

Ibsen developed and deepened the psychology he found in Shakespeare's dramas. He never placed before us a complete self-confessed villain such as we can meet with in Shakespeare—men who from the start
proclaim themselves as false and treacherous knaves by nature, like Richard III, or Edmund in *King Lear,* or Iago in *Othello*. Shakespeare attempted to explain his villains, at least partly. Ibsen never allowed his
persons to be mere villains; they are always thoroughly human, complex
by nature and in motive, studied and pictured down to their deepest
aspirations and qualities. In particular, he never introduced completely
villainous women; even evil-doers or criminals like Hjördis or Rebecca
West were excused and explained as acting out of love.

Much more than Shakespeare, Ibsen used the method of illustrating
different characters by opposing them to each other in rivalry or conflict.
Shakespeare, too, knew the art of dramatic and psychological effect won
by contrast of character. But he used it only in a few cases to bring out
more clearly the psychology of the protagonists of his dramas, such as
Antonio contra Shylock, Othello contra Iago, Macbeth contra Malcolm,
and then only very rarely are both characters treated and pictured with
the same care and completeness. As early as in *Catiline* Ibsen showed a
predilection for bringing together pairs of opposite characters who might
throw one another into strong relief and in that way make themselves
more markedly individualized. Remarkably often he contrasted two feminine characters in leading parts of his dramas, starting with Furia and
Aurelia and ending with Mrs. Rubek and Irene, repeatedly stressing the

---

[22] Gosse, *op. cit.,* p. 48.

H-117402

distinction and rivalry between them by making them sisters (thus in
*The Feast at Solhaug, The Vikings at Helgeland, The Pillars of Society,
John Gabriel Borkman*). Still more remarkable is his way of illuminating
the protagonist of his creation by a character of different type, most
brilliantly so in *The Pretenders,* but with clear intention and marked
success in many other works—from *The Vikings* and *Brand* to *An Enemy
of the People, The Wild Duck,* and *Rosmersholm.* In this respect, again,
we may say that Ibsen improved on Shakespeare. I think we may add that
in this method Ibsen took up a tradition from the old Norse sagas and
even directly learned from them.

In all such ways Ibsen endeavored to enlarge and to enrich the psychological drama which he received as the heritage from Shakespeare.
There lay the natural field of his own genius, and Shakespeare helped
him find it.

HEADQUARTERS
WEST GEORGIA REGIONAL LIBRARY

Ibsen's *Brand:*
Paradox and the Symbolic Hero

by Irving Deer

I

Among the many controversies that have been waged over Ibsen's plays, there is one which has received much less attention than it deserves. This is the controversy over Brand, the protagonist after whom Ibsen named the play which first earned his European fame. Simply stated, the controversy boils down to whether Ibsen intended him to be a hero or a villain. Thus baldly stated, this question may seem rather startling. Yet George Bernard Shaw, with his genius for creating startling controversies, had made it an issue deserving of close attention. Shaw defended and interpreted Ibsen's plays because he saw in them a profound attack on the unbending idealists he so firmly opposed. And nowhere did he believe Ibsen's attack on idealism to be more devastating than in *Brand*. From Shaw's point of view, Brand's intense idealism made him the personification of the highest type of villainy, the "idealist of heroic earnestness, strength, and courage" who destroys infinitely more out of good motives than the conscious villain ever destroys out of bad. Brand's popularity as an idealistic hero stung Shaw so sharply that he was forced to write of Ibsen's worshippers,

[They] have sometimes so far misconceived him as to suppose that his villains are examples rather than warnings, and that the mischief and ruin which attend their actions are but the tribulations from which the soul comes out purified as gold from the furnace.[1]

Since Shaw's remarks almost fifty years ago, the controversy over whether Ibsen is exposing Brand's villainy or extolling his heroism has

"Ibsen's *Brand*: Paradox and the Symbolic Hero" by Irving Deer. From *The Lock Haven Bulletin*, Series 1, No. 3 (1961), 7-18. Reprinted by permission of the author and *The Lock Haven Bulletin*.

[1] Bernard Shaw, *The Quintessence of Ibsenism* (London, 1929), p. 44.

been at times a lively one. What is most significant about the controversy, however, is something that goes beyond any final decision about Brand's goodness or evil. As abundant evidence will show, Shaw's interpretation is very questionable. Many critics have come to disagree with it. But they have failed to recognize adequately that the controversy over Brand may stem from ambiguities intrinsic to the ideas and techniques Ibsen used in the play.

II

The events to which Ibsen attributed his inspiration for Brand show clearly that he intended Brand to be a hero. Resentful over the harsh reception of his play *Love's Comedy*, notwithstanding the subsequent success of *The Pretenders*, Ibsen went into voluntary exile. He had interpreted the bitter attacks against him as marks of the essential cowardice and hypocrisy of his countrymen. Norway's and Sweden's unwillingness to help Denmark in the war against Germany over Schleswig-Holstein only deepened this conviction and increased his resentment. Passing through Berlin shortly after the fall of Dybböl, he witnessed an event which remained firmly in his mind. As he described it in a letter, he "saw the bellowing populace wallow amongst the trophies of Dybböl, saw them riding the gun carriages and spitting into the cannon—the same cannon to which we had given no help, but which had gone on shooting until they burst." [2] Recollecting his trip later, he wrote: "It was now that *Brand* began to grow inside me like a foetus." [3]

Deeply disturbed, he arrived in Italy at last, only to find there further evidence of the hypocrisy which disgusted him. Writing to his mother-in-law, Magdalene Thoresen, he bitterly described what he saw in Rome:

> Danish men and women sit on Sundays in the chapel of the Prussian embassy, amongst the Germans, at the very time of the war, and listen devoutly while the Prussian priest in the pulpit prays for the success of Prussian arms in the righteous war against the enemy. [4]

Moving to the country after two weeks in Rome, he turned his attention to his work. He began writing *Emperor and Galilean*, which he would not complete for nine years, and an epic poem which he would eventually rewrite as the poetic drama *Brand*. The warm serenity of his surroundings and the art masterpieces he enjoyed seemed for a time to

---

[2] Quoted in Halvdan Koht, *The Life of Ibsen* (New York, 1931), pp. 246-47.
[3] Quoted in Michael Meyer, *Brand* (New York, 1960), p. 13.
[4] Quoted in Koht, p. 257.

provide an escape from the hypocrisy he had tried to leave behind.[5] But
the folly of hoping to escape from the problems that had given him the
idea for *Brand* was soon apparent to him. Returning to Rome, he made
the acquaintance of a young Norwegian named Christopher Bruun, who,
like him, had been violently opposed to the German attack on Denmark.
Unlike Ibsen, however, Bruun had volunteered to fight with the Danes
at the battle of Dybböl. An uncompromising patriot of truth, a theo-
logian who hesitated to take holy orders because he saw a clash between
the doctrines of the Norwegian State Church and the demands of life,
Bruun provided Ibsen with new insights into the character and problems
he was attempting to convey in his epic poem. Within a year his ideas
for a dramatic version of the subject had crystallized and Ibsen wrote
ferociously, completing *Brand* in three months.

If the events preceding the writing of the play are not conclusive as to
Ibsen's intentions, his letters make it absolutely clear that he intended
Brand to stand as heroism incarnate. In a letter to the Danish critic,
Georg Brandes, he wrote: "I should have been quite able to apply the
same syllogism with equal propriety to a sculptor or a politician as to a
clergyman. I could have found as sure relief for the mood which drove
me to writing if, for instance, I had treated Galileo instead of Brand." [6]
What mattered to Ibsen was the kind of heroism for which Brand stood
—unflinching dedication to absolute truth—not the man himself. He
could have used Galileo—"except that then of course he would have had
to have held strongly to his beliefs, and not pretended that the earth
stood still." [7] In Brand, Ibsen saw what he described on another occasion
as "myself in my best moments." [8] While he was writing the play, his
enthusiasm over his hero made him feel what he described as "the exaltation of a Crusader." [9]

It may seem strange that with all the evidence for the heroic interpretation of Brand, there ever was any controversy over whether he was a
hero or a villain. The fact is, however, that long before Wimsatt and
Beardsley articulated their ideas about the "intentional fallacy," [10] some
critics were more interested in what a writer achieved than in what he
intended. Even those interpreters of Brand who relied most heavily on
biographical data turned for some justification of their position to the

[5] *Ibid.*, p. 247.

[6] *Letters of Henrik Ibsen,* translated by John Nilsen Laurvik and Mary Morison (New
York, 1905), p. 173.

[7] Quoted in Meyer, pp. 17-18.

[8] Laurvik and Morison, pp. 199-200.

[9] Quoted in Koht, p. 270.

[10] W. K. Wimsatt, Jr., *The Verbal Icon* (New York, 1958), pp. 3-18.

play itself.[11] And it was there, on the difficult reefs of paradox and symbolism, that some interpreters foundered.

Even the biographical data bearing on Ibsen's state of mind toward the play indicate the strong possibility that important ambiguities may have worked their way, both consciously and unconsciously, into the play. If he was exalted at the crusade he was waging through *Brand* against the hypocrisy and cowardice of his countrymen, by his own admission he also felt implicated in their guilt.[12] His discussions with Christopher Bruun had helped him to clarify the image of his hero, but they had also raised for him serious doubts as to his own qualifications to espouse the cause of heroism. Bruun had asked him point blank why, since he was so violently opposed to those who had not rushed to Denmark's aid, he had not himself volunteered to fight. He had answered, "We poets have other tasks." [13] But as his Prologue to the epic version of *Brand* shows, the question had hit home. Greatly dejected, he proclaimed that since he was a poet, he was "a hundredfold" more guilty than were ordinary citizens.[14] Art had attracted him as a way of escaping from his present responsibilities into a false dream world of the past, into a world of words instead of deeds.[15] He had long hoped that, on the contrary, he was using art as a way of squarely facing his responsibilities. He wanted nothing better than that it should do so. But from Bruun's question, he was forced to recognize that art was for him both an escape into a world of words and dreams and a way of assuming responsibility. The intense inner conflict he suffered from this ambivalent attitude toward art was not one easily to be resolved.[16]

III

Since Halvdan Koht's remarkable biography of Ibsen,[17] there are few reputable interpreters of the play who do not recognize in it some in-

---

[11] See for example, Koht, p. 282; A. E. Zucker, *Ibsen* (New York, 1929), p. 105; and Brian W. Downs, *Ibsen* (Cambridge, 1946), pp. 84-85.

[12] See Downs, pp. 100-102.

[13] Quoted in Downs, p. 100.

[14] *Ibid.,* p. 101.

[15] *Ibid.,* p. 102.

[16] In Ibsen's poems "In the Picture Gallery" and "On the Fells," both written in 1859, he had already expressed deep concern over the two opposing attractions which art had for him. During this dark period in Italy, he seemed to find renewed interest in "In the Picture Gallery" and rewrote part of it. *Love's Comedy,* written in 1862, also dealt centrally with the opposing attractions of art. And as his late plays *The Master Builder* and *When We Dead Awaken* show, this was a recurrent and vital issue for Ibsen to the end of his writing days.

[17] Koht, *The Life of Ibsen.*

direct reflections of the inner turmoil Ibsen suffered while conceiving and writing it.[18] However, Ibsen's claim that writing the play served him as a release for his pent-up hatred against hypocrisy[19] as well as the polemic zeal with which he wrote may have misled some interpreters into believing that he had resolved his distress in a single-minded approval of Brand. This interpretation—that Brand is fully approved—is as far from the truth as the opposite—that Brand is a hopeless villain. Ibsen's approval is great, but well qualified. If as a man totally dedicated to his calling Brand represented Ibsen in his best moments, Brand also represented him at moments when he held the virtue of total dedication in doubt. Failure to recognize either his approval or his qualifications can lead only to a distorted view of the play. For in both reside not only the complications of idea which have made the play difficult to interpret, but the clue to the complicated techniques which Ibsen invented to express his complex view.

There is an important clue to Ibsen's techniques in his remark that he "should have been quite as able to apply the same syllogism with equal propriety to a sculptor or a politician as to a clergyman." [20] From this remark and his subsequent one that he could have used Galileo if only Galileo "had held strongly to his beliefs," we can see that Ibsen was interested primarily in what Brand stood for, what he symbolized: the strong-willed man who sticks to his calling, whatever it is. What interpreters of the play fail to recognize is that Ibsen's approval of Brand remains primarily at the symbolic level, while his qualifications of Brand's behavior—his disapproval of them, if you prefer—remain substantially at a more literal or realistic level.

From Ibsen's remarks, one would expect the plot itself—the sequence of events—to symbolize the strong-willed man's (Brand's) struggle to fulfill his mission in life, no matter what sacrifices this entails. And it is precisely this which the events, taken as a whole, do approvingly symbolize.

All the characters are treated so as to illustrate and prove Brand's idealism. The only characters besides Brand who are not satirized are Agnes and the Doctor, and they are on his side. The Mayor and other

---

[18] See, for example, Brian W. Downs, *A Study of Six Plays by Ibsen* (Cambridge, 1950), pp. 47-49.

[19] On the desk where Ibsen sat writing *Brand*, he kept a scorpion in a glass. As he wrote to P. Hansen: "From time to time the little animal was ill. Then I used to give it a piece of soft fruit, upon which it fell furiously and emptied its poison into it—after which it was well again. Does not something of the same kind happen with us poets?" Quoted in Zucker, *op. cit.*, p. 103.

[20] Laurvik and Morison, p. 173.

officials are seen essentially as opportunists, liars, and hollow idealists. The community are essentially weak or irrational—all exactly as Brand defines them. Like the other characters, Brand himself illustrates an idea more often than he expresses a realistic character through conflict. From the first scene, he serves as a symbol of man in his most God-like aspect in search of the absolute. To the peasant who tries to stop him from descending the dangerous mountain snowfields, he explains that he must go on because he was charged by God to do so. His mission is to make men whole, no matter the cost. To do this, he must destroy the three enemies of wholeness: cowardice, as exemplified in the fear of the peasants who try to stop him; hedonism, as practiced by the pleasure-loving painter Einar and his sweetheart, the early Agnes who has not yet been swayed by Brand's zeal; and irrationality, as illustrated by Gerd, the insane gypsy girl who revels among the wildest and most dangerous peaks.

It is because Brand's mission at first draws him into conflict with those around him that most critics who agree with Shaw take him for a villain. His absolute demands alienate him from his mother and community and cost him the lives of his wife and child. He lets his mother die without absolution because, even on her deathbed, she will not give up the money she hoarded in life. Rather than move to a milder climate and give up his calling, he lets his sickly child die from the harsh weather. Demanding absolute fidelity to his mission, he forces his wife to accept the child's death as proof of her dedication and understanding of his cause. Though Brand is successful, his demands sap her waning strength, even as she sorrows for her dead child.

Critics who take these events as evidence of Brand's villainy fail to see that, to Ibsen, Brand's mission is much more than one of reforming others; it is ultimately one of realizing himself. Brand is tempted to give his mother absolution, to move away in an effort to save his child, and to allow his wife a sentimental memento of their dead child. His troubled rejection of all these temptations illustrates the horror and overwhelming odds against which he must fight in himself if he is to adhere to his cause. The reader should thus not think of Brand's child, wife, and mother as real people, only as symbols of the human ties which torment and frustrate him in his struggle with himself. As the play progresses Brand struggles less and less with those about him, more and more with the weaknesses within himself. When in the final moments of his life he is deserted and stoned by the community he has tried to lead to worship in the mountains, he is forced into complete self-confrontation. Standing completely alone at last, he must face himself. Having sacrificed everything else, he at last sacrifices his certainty about the rightness of his cause. He is overcome by doubt about the value of his absolutism. Facing death from an avalanche, he has just enough time to ask God whether he has earned salvation by his wholehearted dedication to his mission. Through the crashing thunder of the snow and ice which overwhelm him, a voice calls, "He is the God of Love." To those who feel Brand is a villain, the avalanche means that he is punished for never having displayed any love of his fellows, or at least that he gains salvation only because God has more mercy than he.

But punishment or mercy are not the only possible explanations of the ending. Since Ibsen has previously so fully illustrated the truth of Brand's claims, a more plausible if symbolic explanation is that Brand's uncertainty reveals his essential humanity and earns him salvation.[21] Even as he symbolizes the idea that man must struggle to achieve the absolute of wholeness, he also symbolizes the impossibility of man's ever achieving it. In the incident in the second act where Brand delivers absolution to a dying suicide victim, Ibsen vividly illustrates the heritage of debt which prevents man, and Brand as everyman, from achieving wholeness. The dying man had killed one of his children before the eyes of the other two. Brand recognizes[22] that it is the children who must suffer; they have inherited the sins of their father. Brand, too, has such a heritage. As a child he had seen his mother ransack the body and room of his dead father for money. He recognizes this debt when he says:

> Self completely to fulfill,—
> That's a valid right of Man.
> And no more than that I will!
> To fulfill oneself! And yet,
> With a heritage of debt? [23]

The question is answered for him by the invisible choir at the end:

> Never shalt thou win His spirit;
> Thou in mortal flesh was born?
> Spurn his bidding or revere it,
> Equally thou art forlorn.[24]

Man is doomed to defeat precisely because he is man and not God.[25] He must struggle for perfection, yet he must fail to achieve it. This is

---

[21] See Downs, *Six Plays*, pp. 43-44. Downs argues convincingly that Brand emerges as a new man after his doubt and his collapse on the mountain.

[22] Henrik Ibsen, *Brand*, translated by C. H. Hereford (New York, 1914), p. 52. Since the Hereford translation is still the most readily available, references are to it rather than to the less stilted Meyer or Garrett translations.

[23] *Ibid.*, p. 61.

[24] *Ibid.*, p. 248.

[25] See Downs, *Ibsen*, p. 86. Downs' Kierkegaardian interpretation supports this view.

man's tragedy as Brand illustrates it and as Ibsen sees it. In Brand's uncertainty before death, he reveals and recaptures his humanity.[26] He has given up everything to his cause including his certainty. And in following his calling to the letter, "Nought or All," he has learned the true meaning of the paradox he so often imposed on others: to be oneself is to lose oneself.

The limitations of Brand's total dedication are suggested (though not to Brand himself until the end) at those points in his struggle where he is forced to confront the realistic consequences of his absolute demands. To force his mother into conformity with his symbolic ideal, he must deny her literal absolution. To force his wife into conformity, he must deny her the real solace of a few mementos of her dead child; he must be willing to lose the human, real comfort of the father-husband ties which, in a totally human role, he would be unwilling to lose. To lead the folk to symbolic salvation he must deny them the realistic necessity of making a livelihood. And, finally, to achieve a symbolic victory in death, he must first recognize the excessive pride which led him to deny his human limitations and the ties of love.

If interpreters of the play have failed to recognize that Ibsen approves Brand at the symbolic level while qualifying his acts on the realistic level, they have, nevertheless, had a great deal to say about the play's symbolism.[27] From seeing the hawk as a symbol of love,[28] and the ice church to which Brand is leading his congregation as the symbol of the negation of love,[29] interpreters have gone to seeing the hawk as "the spirit of compromise" [30] in keeping with Brand's pronouncement on it, and the ice church as "whatever one rejects." [31] This lively traffic in symbol hunting indicates some of the difficulties which keep the play from being easily interpreted.

The ease with which the play's symbols lend themselves to various interpretations is, however, only one reason why interpreters have difficulty deciding what the play is about, and more specifically, whether Brand is a hero or a villain. Another perhaps more important reason is that Ibsen's ambiguities and paradoxes are difficult to analyze. At each point where symbolic approval and literal qualification impinge on each other, the situation is left ambiguous. The sequence of scenes near the end, just before Brand is overwhelmed by the avalanche, is a perfect

---

[26] See Downs, *Six Plays*, p. 44.

[27] See, for example, Downs, *Six Plays*, pp. 44-45 and Meyer, p. 18.

[28] Meyer, *op. cit.*, p. 18. Meyer attributes this view to Dr. Arne Duve in his book *Symbolikken I Henrik Ibsens Skuespill.*

[29] *Ibid.*, p. 18.

[30] Downs, *Six Plays*, p. 45.

[31] Meyer, p. 18.

case in point. Does Ibsen disapprove of Brand for not having shown love, or does he praise him for his absolute dedication to his cause? This is the question on which, as Brian W. Downs has remarked, "as many vary- ing opinions have been advanced as there have been critics concerned to give them." [32]

It is for the moment as if Ibsen himself is uncertain of the answer. As the artist confronted by an overwhelming sense of the limitations of complete dedication to his calling, is he perhaps reflecting in his hero for whom "life's an art" his own doubts? He may be. At any rate, he does not allow the ambiguity to remain. As with the other ambiguities he presents, he resolves this one through paradox. He would have us both approve and disapprove of Brand; approve Brand's symbolic significance, and disapprove of his human shortcomings. In the end, Brand goes be- yond indecision and doubt to a great symbolic victory through paradox; he loses himself in order to gain himself.

IV

The fluctuations between symbolic and realistic elements, as well as the use of ambiguity and paradox, are no mere mechanical devices for Ibsen. These techniques lie at the heart of his conception of Brand's struggle; they are necessary expressions of it. They penetrate every aspect of the play.

But they cause interpreters a great deal of difficulty. For not only does the occasional substitution of realistic elements in what is essentially a symbolic play seem inconsistent to those who do not understand its func- tion; it also results in an extremely confusing subjectivity for some readers. Ibsen seems at times to take away with one hand what he has given with the other. If Brand stands as an example for all men, he also stands as a case of extreme individuality. Ultimately, his struggle is with himself alone. One side of him cries out that he must meet the responsi- bilities of his actual condition as a son, father, and husband. The other drives him to give up everything for his ideal.[33] If he forsakes his mother on her deathbed and sacrifices his son and wife, he does so only after suffering the great anguish his choice entails. Even his wife Agnes can- not understand his decisions; they are so unique. She hangs back from total commitment to his cause, drawn by motherly love to her dying child. Only through sheer faith in him does she finally embrace his cause.

---

[32] Downs, *Ibsen*, p. 85.
[33] Hereford, Act III, *passim*.

With her death he is entirely alone, driven by values no one, least of all his community, can understand or share with him. And although we sense that Brand is intended to be heroic, we have almost as much difficulty as his community has in understanding his ideal. Since Ibsen occasionally allows Brand to engage in partially realistic conflicts, we cannot help judging him and his ideal by partially realistic standards. Judged by these, he seems dedicated to a destructive ideal. Thus the reader is often confused by the discrepancy between what Brand's ideal means to ordinary men and what it seems to mean to Brand—all-encompassing salvation. Hence, Brand appears at times a rather foolish and quixotic hero.

Even more confusing than the fluctuations between symbolism and realism is Ibsen's ambivalence toward Brand. Here again we see a parallel with Ibsen's own ambivalent attitudes toward his calling. Like Ibsen's ideal poet, Brand is a user of words. But Ibsen would have us believe that, unlike the ordinary Einar-type of poet, Brand is also a doer of deeds. And since Brand's success, when judged by realistic standards, is less than spectacular, Ibsen has a difficult time persuading us that Brand achieves anything. We can accept his success only on the symbolic level. The difficulty is that Ibsen conceives Brand's achievement like that of his ideal poet, as a paradox. Both the compulsion to act through words and the one to escape through them are in Ibsen's eyes real and strong. Neither can be avoided by the poet. Ibsen's only way out is to offer an enigmatic solution which encompasses both contradictories: to use words is to act. Here is the final answer to Bruun's question. The poet does not merely talk; he acts. And if he acts through words, so be it. Paradox and symbols are his weapons. Who is to say they are less effective than bullets?

This solution is as confusing to some readers as Brand's extreme subjectivity, and for similar reasons. In offering it, Ibsen, like Brand, seems to be acting through sheer faith in the ultimate value of his vocation.[34] The paradoxes which he uses to express his ideal and Brand's achievement are themselves only symbols of that achievement, not literal presentations of it. Like the play as a whole, which illustrates the grand paradox that Brand's defeat is his victory, each paradox in the play has a symbolic and a realistic aspect. Brand is symbolically victorious, but

---

[34] In their great faith Ibsen and Brand are like Kierkegaard's "Knight of Faith." This helps to explain why Kierkegaard is often attributed to have had a great influence on Ibsen. Like the experience of faith for Kierkegaard's hero, faith is a purely private affair for Brand. It is incommunicable. This, however, is not true for Ibsen. In writing the play for public reading, he is assuming that he can communicate his faith in his ideals. See Downs, *Ibsen*, pp. 79-93.

literally defeated. He gains himself symbolically while literally losing his life.

Only by accepting each paradox as a kind of higher all-embracing symbol in which the conflict between the symbolic and literal meanings is resolved can the reader see beyond that conflict. And see beyond it he must if he is to understand the play. For since paradox is at the heart of Ibsen's conception, it overwhelms the whole play. Brand must destroy to create. He must give up love to find love. In the end, he must lose everything to gain everything.

Considering the enthusiasm modern critics display toward the use of paradox in literature, it is surprising that many more of them have not pounced on Ibsen's plays. There they would find enough succulent paradoxes to gorge the most voracious of critical appetites. And, too, rightly understood, Ibsen's use of paradox would cause little confusion. For paradox is in a sense his whole point. If the artist must deal with beautiful illusion, he must also deal with life. And if man's ideals, like Godhead for Brand, are impossible for man to achieve, he must nevertheless continue struggling to achieve them. It is in the very complexity of Ibsen's conception that the play's significance lies. What could be one of Ibsen's private problems—his confusion about the value of art—becomes instead an expression of the human condition. Man is tragic precisely because he is man. If struggle is both necessary and futile for him, it is in the end its own reward. It is the best man can do. And despite the anguish of his struggle, he learns through one final paradox that doing one's best, though it falls short of the ideal, is in the end an ideal itself.

Peer Gynt

by Georg Groddeck

. . . Our search for psychoanalytic instruction in Wagner's Ring-cycle was not entirely fruitless, so we may look forward with some confidence to further progress through the study of Ibsen's *Peer Gynt*. It is unfortunate that the original cannot be widely read, for a translation cannot give all the many subtle indications of the unconscious, particularly those with which we are most concerned (e.g., in choice of words, diction, etc.). Imponderable qualities which the Norwegian reader appreciates without a thought, foreigners are unable to grasp, however much they study the language. To make matters worse Ibsen has an exciting way of burying all sorts of secrets in his dramas, so that with every fresh reading one discovers new treasure. This is intriguing for his readers, but it does not make for a good textbook. The fact that such secrets reveal a life which could hardly be dealt with in any other way, life which is not submissive to analytic reason, unconscious life, this fact ensures a rich harvest for psychoanalytic research, but it does not make the material easy to handle. A further hindrance, like the first an advantage from the literary point of view, is the god-like irony with which Ibsen endows his characters. And finally, just because Ibsen knew the unconscious better than almost anyone else, he writes as if for an audience already instructed in the subject, rather than for learners; it is less easy at first to understand the unconscious by reading the works of one who is familiar with its secrets than by studying one who innocently reveals them because he lives his life in unawareness. Wagner was innocent, Ibsen conscious of what he was doing. Certain points are common to both writers, but they are more sharply defined in *Peer Gynt* than they are in *The Ring*. It is those we shall start with.

In *The Ring* I tried to show that Siegfried sees his mother in the person of Brünnhilde, while Brünnhilde looks on him as a son, and from

"Peer Gynt" by Georg Groddeck. From *Exploring the Unconscious* by Georg Groddeck (London: Vision Press, 1950). Translated by V. M. E. Collins. Copyright 1950 by Vision Press, Ltd. Reprinted by permission of Vision Press, Ltd.

this I went on to say that everyone is compelled by the unconscious to hold fast to his mother, to love only that which has some sort of likeness to the mother. This is clearly represented in *Peer Gynt* also.

The play begins, you will remember, with a scene between Peer Gynt and his mother Aase, a very peculiar scene indeed, for both of them behave, not as though they were a grown-up son and a middle-aged woman, but as though a young mother and her little boy were having the usual sort of tussle together. She scolds him for tearing his clothes and for being lazy, while he has a boastful tale to tell of how he has ridden a reindeer over a knife-edge path with a dizzy precipice on either side and then, still astride his steed, has leapt into the lake far below. She takes it all in, as any young mother will do when her youngster tells her his lies; what he thinks and dreams about is for her reality, and when she knows he is lying, she cannot tell whether to laugh or to cry. The scene ends with Peer's swinging Aase up in his arms and rushing her across a brook just as the reindeer in his fairy tale galloped with him across the country. On the other side of the stream he sets her down on the roof of an old mill from which she cannot escape unaided, and runs away. Mere wantonness, the wantonness of a small boy. And that is how Aase herself sees him; she chases him with a stick to give him a beating. There can be no two opinions about it; for Aase, Peer is always the little boy whose behavior he shows us, and for Peer, Aase is the never-ageing mother, the beloved playmate. They live together in a play-world, and for neither of them is there any reality outside. In their world no one else has, nor ever will have, any share. Peer tells us this at Aase's death:

> So, mother, let's just talk of me and you, and trouble not ourselves with all the silliness and wrong outside.

When Aase tries to bring the talk round to Solveig, he uses much the same words again. He and his mother, that is his world, and as for her, after that first scene we may well conclude that she, too, was content to spend her life in this play-world. It is only after a long and roundabout journey that Peer Gynt can bring himself to the point of allowing another woman to have the honor of mothering him. This new mother, one need hardly say, is Solveig; she is the reincarnation of Aase. Peer Gynt feels that from the start. This and this alone it is that prevents him from remaining with her, for she is sacred to him, as a mother must be to her son. Never can she be for him mere woman. When he carries her into his hut, he carries her with arms outstretched before him, to keep her as far as possible from contact with himself:

> So I will carry thee, at arm's length, untouched.

He avoids any physical contact, completely misreading the situation and the girl's feelings because she is for him the mother-image. "Be off, give her up!" says the troll. "Give her up, be off! Were thine arm as long as the tallest pine on the hill-side, yet is she far too close to thee to escape with innocence and purity."

He wants an excuse for flight and he flees—to mother Aase. And when she dies he ranges over land and sea and never finds rest, until his own death approaches and he dreads being melted down in the spoon of the Button-molder. Then he lets out the secret which he himself has not known before, the secret which has dwelt in his unconscious mind and ordered all his doings: "Tell me if thou canst," he says to his new-found beloved, now grown old, "where have I been, with the spirit of a god in my breast, his signature on my brow?" Solveig answers: "In my faith, in my hope, in my love," but he cries: "Hush! those are dreadful words. For the boy whom thou bearest within thee, thou art the mother."

I have given the literal translation of Ibsen's words. They show how hard it is to give a real equivalent of unconscious material in a translation, for this last extract is commonly translated with an entirely different meaning: "Hush! Do not make my heart heavy. A mother fell in love with her son." One cannot make any sense of that, or see the real meaning, that this love of mother and son has shaped Peer's life, has forced him to wander hither and thither, to go round and round as the troll said, and never to find himself. One mother was taken from him, who could never allure him as woman. The other he loved as woman, not as mother, but he had to see her as his mother, and only at arm's length might he carry her.

To Solveig of course everything is quite different. Peer meets her at a wedding feast and invites her to dance. What does she do? At the bidding of the unconscious, she glances quickly—*skotte* is the Norwegian word and that conveys something of suddenness, untamed, unconscious—first down at her shoes, then to the kerchief at her bosom. Everyone who has seen anything of the workings of the unconscious will have noticed that a woman draws her skirt down when sitting opposite a man, and wears a posy at her breast if she desires to be embraced. And Solveig longs to be embraced; she follows after Peer wherever he goes, and atrociously as he behaves to her she continues to love him as only a woman does love, not all too morally, as men should recognize. She waits in patience year after year and is happy so to wait, happy at last to have an old and broken man for her child. Woman's morality is a wonderful thing; men can hardly even glimpse it in imagination. Solveig is radiant with morality, and never dreams of fearing what seems to her as natural as breath-

ing and living. She, a child from the depths of the country, still bound
to her prayer book and her mother's skirts, yet breaks with every convention and runs after a man she hardly knows, a man who the first
time she sees him is drunk, who takes a bride from her bridegroom before
her very eyes. She has the intuition of womanhood, for she guesses that
Peer Gynt is really a king among men, a king who can ride through the
air, and she never tires of hearing Aase's tales of Peer, because Aase, too,
has recognised his royalty.

It is always best to ask the great poets, if one wants to know what
women are like. Certainly they are very different from what we ordinary
men take them to be.

At one point in Ibsen's play the relations between Solveig and Peer
Gynt are clearly indicated. Solveig has sought him out in his hiding-
place in order, as her sister says, to take him a basket of food. That is
not the true purpose of her going, however, for without cause of offence
her first words are: "Come not near me, or I run away." And to Peer's
question: "Mean'st thou that I am dangerous to thee?" She only answers:
"Fie!"

What has he to be ashamed of? That he says outright what she was
hoping for? But at the end she runs away all the same—to return again.
And when she returns, Peer once again asks her: "Thou'rt not afraid to
come to me?"

Why must he ask this stupid question? He knows, he can see that she
wants to stay with him. He asks it because, and solely because, he is himself afraid. It is an old jest that those who are frightened only betray it
by their solicitude for others' fears. And why should not Peer be in terror, for she is young and beautiful, and yet he must not desire her because he sees her as his mother. He is terrified and he flees.

Here then once again we have the mother and child situation. Peer
ranges the whole world about, and at home there waits one who is at
the same time mother, wife and woman. That is the essence of life, except that man is not always fortunate in finding a Solveig to be both
wife and mother to him. As a rule he finds the second mother, the eternal
mother, only in that dark kingdom whither we all descend, our common
home. Peer Gynt speaks of this: "Now I go home, home underground,
into the land of darkness."

Homeward. Birth and the grave are one and the same. The Earth-spirit
tells Faust much the same as Peer Gynt says here in his own way:

> Forward or back, the length is the same.
> In and out are as broad as each other.

Out of the mysterious mother we come, back to the mysterious mother we go. And life? What is its end? That is always the same, we are children once again at the last. In growing old we become as children in everything; in everything. Truly it is better to grow childlike than to become childish. Best of all, to hear once again a woman singing a lullaby:

> I will rock thee, I will watch.
> Sleep and dream, my little babe.

It is no business of mine and has indeed nothing to do with the subject of this paper, but I cannot forbear saying a word or two about the staging of Peer Gynt. Unless the audience are at once struck by Solveig's likeness to Aase—which need not be exaggerated, though it must be sufficiently marked for others besides Peer Gynt to notice it—then the heart of the drama is lost. And this resemblance, slight at first, must deepen with every reappearance of Solveig so that at the end she seems to have taken on the very lineaments of Aase. Only in this way can the audience really understand what is happening; only then can they grasp the significance of the lullaby at the end. If this is not done the play lacks resonance, there are no overtones, no undertones; the deepest problem of the drama of Peer Gynt is not touched upon, Peer himself is nothing but an adventurous figment, a half-man who creeps back as a weakly, poverty-stricken graybeard to find refuge with his sweetheart of old, calling her his mother as though to assure her she has nothing to hope for from him. Absurd!

At the opening Aase is still comely enough, and there need not be more than twenty or so years' difference of age between her and Solveig. In the fourth act, when Solveig sings her song, she ought to look much the same as Aase in the first act, and at the end of the play she should have white hair and be clad like Aase. It is almost impossible to lay too much stress on the likeness of these two when producing the play.

It is equally wrong to make Peer Gynt die in the last scene. Solveig then has to sing her cradle-song "In the Splendor of Day" to a dead man. That is both stupid and tasteless.

> At the last crossing, Peer, we meet,
> And then we'll see—I say no more!

The voice of the Button-molder is heard at the end of the song, full of malice and enmity. Solveig replies with the surety of a mother protecting the child on her lap:

> I will rock thee, I will watch,
> Sleep and dream, my little babe.

How is it possible to stamp out the tender beauty of this scene by making Peer a dead man? He is not yet done with life, he will be ready for further experiences. To let him end as a frightened drunkard is not in accordance with the rest of the play nor with the dramatist's intention, for Ibsen describes him as a man of might.

"Sleep and dream," sings Solveig to her big baby. Be sure he will do that; all his life he has done nothing but dream, and for that he does not even need to sleep, since he daydreams, uninterruptedly, just like everybody else, you and I and everyman. Most of us do not know we are doing it, do not want to know. It conflicts with the so-called Reality-Principle, the "New Reality." Facts, realities! We have to reckon with what exists, and dreams, daydreams, too, are also facts; if anyone really wants to investigate realities, he cannot do better than start with such as these. If he neglects them, he will learn little or nothing of the world or of life.

What would become of the world, if we were not ceaselessly dreaming? Psychoanalysts have been at considerable pains to prove the importance of dreams: their failure, or at least their relative lack of success, is due to their writing special textbooks instead of revealing to people what is in books they already know, books that would never have been written had not their authors been daydreamers. It is quite unnecessary, when analyzing anyone, to wait for him to dream in sleep. Ibsen knew that, just as Freud does, and everyone else who keeps his eyes open for the unconscious. Illness itself, though certainly not a dream in the ordinary sense, may be described in a sense as a daydream, a dream of that unconscious self which directs organic as well as psychic processes, and shapes the whole pattern of life. You will see at once what I mean if you study the *Peer Gynt* textbook. There you will find set out clearly things which were only hinted at in Wagner, set out in every scene and every incident.

Already in the first scene Peer Gynt's greatest dream is made manifest. Aase scolds him. He is sorry that she grieves on his account, so he gives her the best thing he has:

> Mother, little cross mother,
> Only trust me, be patient a while.
> In a little time you will be honored,
> The village will make you their queen.
> In a little time I shall do something
> So great, if you only can trust.

Aase still scolds:

> If you knew just the one thing,
> How to mend that tear in your trews!

And he bursts out, unheeding her gibe:

> A king, an emperor I will be!
> Give me but time, and I shall do it.

An emperor he will be, and no common emperor either, but one who rides through the air on a wonderful horse with hooves of gold:

> They all shall see
> Peer Gynt the Emperor ride through the air.
> Nickel and silver he throws down like pebbles.
> The village and everything in it shall prosper.
> The prince of the land stands and waits on the shore,
> And with him the fairest of all the fair maidens
> Emperor and barons bow down before him
> And stand at his court on the steps of his throne.

It is not ambition which vaunts itself thus. Peer has not an ounce of ambition in him and cares not a jot what other people think about him, recks as little of their scorn as of their jests. In this sense he is himself, and so he remains to the end of his life. He never troubles about Solveig's opinion of him, not even when the Button-molder wants to melt him down. What makes him free is neither her faith, her belief, nor her love, but the suddenly emerging conviction that she is able "to cradle him in her soul," that she is at one and the same time mother, wife and comrade, that she does not judge him.

Peer Gynt is just as all other men are—that is true even though not every man can see the truth—only unfortunately many of us try to seem different. He is really himself, he does not need to grow to himself. He is a dreamer, but he knows quite well that he dreams and fantasies. Other people call him a liar—the first words in the play are those of his mother: "You are lying"—the prince of liars, but that is sheer stupidity on their part, for he is essentially sincere. By nature man is forced to daydream, to build his fantasies, but his fancy must be self-sufficient; the man who wants to turn fantasy into reality, or who thinks for a moment that this is possible, that man is the liar, for he does not remain true to himself. Peer never cherishes this vain intention, but keeps fantasy and reality clearly apart; his fantasies represent no aim in life for him, he merely lives in them and has no other use for them. He remains himself when he is daydreaming just as he does when he eats or drinks or peels his onion. Never does he lose hold of himself in his dreams, never does he make the usual feeble compromise of transferring some small part of dream life into the world of every day. He is always Emperor Peer Gynt. Certainly he does little for the state or the well-being of his fellow-countrymen; the words spoken by the pastor at a burial apply equally to him:

> A breaker of the law? Perhaps—
> Yet something shines above all laws,
>   Even as the crown of mist
> Above the mountain-top.
> A worthless citizen, who served
> No king or country?
> Yet was he great because he was himself,
> Because he never stilled the voice within,
> That voice which sighed like muted violin.

Peer himself adopts this verdict as his own epitaph:

> A time will come when yonder worthy man
> Shall say the same of me.

And now that time has come, for Ibsen's readers are inspired by Peer's vitality, some of them without understanding why, and some even completely mistaking what it is in him that makes him so sympathetic a character. Many of those who read or see the play imagine that Solveig is the salvation of a ruined and depraved Peer, but Solveig is not very different. She, too, is herself, only she knows nothing about it, can know nothing, being woman. For the Philistine—and it is very hard to come out of Philistia—Peer Gynt wastes his life in trifles, dabbles in wickedness without ever committing an honest crime, and is not even worth sending to hell but must be melted down in the Button-molder's spoon. Is Solveig, though, any whit better? Does she not also waste her life by sitting in the mountains and waiting for a man with whom she has only spoken three times, whom everybody calls a liar—and judged by their standards he deserves the name—who is the son of a drunken father and a crazy mother, who holds nothing sacred, but rushes about the world, is slave-owner and false prophet, who falls into the power of trolls, and snaps his fingers at the devil? Has Solveig nothing better to do than mind a few goats? Is she to be forgiven for deserting her worthy parents, and throwing herself at the head of a stranger, a notorious swindler? Does she not dabble in wickedness also, or is she supposed to be better because the word "fidelity" governs her life? To whom, then, is she faithful? Only to herself. Not to Peer Gynt, for she does not know him. To herself. Just as he remains himself, so also does she, only she is a woman and he a man. Both of them are honorable dreamers, amazingly sincere people whom the devil can do nothing with.

In spite of all I have said there are probably some of you who still doubt whether Solveig and Aase have the same significance so I will cite yet other evidence. When Peer is first in direst need, he calls for help to Aase (in the Rondane Keep), and not long afterwards, when nearly overcome by the Boyg, he calls for Solveig. When he deserts Solveig it is to go to Aase. When he returns to his home he first seeks Aase's house, then goes to Solveig. Solveig's love flares up at first sight, but she nourishes it upon Aase's love. When Aase tells her in the fullness of her heart about Peer, she fills her own heart with the story and takes over Aase's very thoughts. The third act has special significance in this respect. The second ends with Solveig, the third begins with Peer's thoughts of his mother:

> Restless thou art because no little mother
> With careful hands is here to keep thy house.

The next scene is in Aase's cottage: she is looking through all her rubbish to find clothes for her boy. In the following scene Solveig comes again to Peer, and again in the next scene he goes to Aase. Nothing is left undone that could be done to make it clear that Aase is both mother and sweetheart, Solveig both sweetheart and mother.

At the end there comes still another proof of that, the strongest, poetically the strongest, because it is rooted in the depths of the unconscious. When Peer was still a child in years, Aase took him into fairyland and there they rode together through ice and snow on the great mare Grane to the castle of Soria-Moria. When Aase in old age returns to childhood, Peer wraps her in coverings and takes her over the fjord to Heaven's Gate. He takes his thanks from the lips of his dead mother, as once that mother was thanked by him. For all of us there comes a time when our children see we need their help, and we old children bless the hands of these younger mothers and fathers. So it was with Peer and Aase. And with Solveig and Peer the situation is reversed. At first Solveig is the child for whose salvation Peer goes through every hardship; in the endless years of waiting she is transformed into the mother, in the endless years of trouble Peer becomes the child. There is so much to learn from this play, it is quite impossible to refer to everything.

Between Aase and Solveig stands the green-clad troll, the negative of the mother-image. Three times does Peer seek to break loose from the ties of the mother-beloved: with Ingrid—the stolen bride, with the three milkmaids, and with the Troll-woman. It is a terrible progression in

which the struggle against his fate is expressed, first one, then three, and
finally one again, a ghost. He tries to flee from sin and falls into sin.
And the worst comes at the end, the lusting in thought. Is it not a
marvellous bit of psychoanalytic teaching that the desire for the mother,
the incest-wish, drives men into the swamp—or rather the repression of
the incest-wish, the denial of its existence?

"Djavlen star i alt som minder," says Peer, . . . "Remembrance is the
devil himself."

With the Troll-woman Peer begets a child, the child of a fantasy
brought into the world of reality. And this son, when grown to inordi-
nate size—thoughts are dangerous, Peer, thoughts, desires, wishes—feels
nothing but contempt for his father and tries to slay him with an axe.
Have you not also, Peer, repressed the wish to kill your father when in
his drunkenness he would lay hands upon your mother? Thus it is in
life. And what a deep knowledge of the unconscious the Troll-woman
shows us. When Peer's jaw drops in overweening terror she says to her
son: "Give your father drink, his mouth is open." There you have in a
sentence the motive for drunkenness, escape from fear. Aase says much
the same:

> From time to time we have to drown our thoughts,
> Some men choose wine, and others, lies.

There are other revelations of the unconscious to be found, the
mother's death-wish, for instance, against her own son. When Peer is
climbing up into the mountains after the rape of the bride, Aase calls
out in her rage: "If only you would fall!" and then, frightened of the
omnipotence of thought, she at once follows this up with: "Be careful
as you mount." Thoughts, thoughts, they have to be repressed. "Give
her up, be off," cries the Boyg. "I must go round and round in my mind.
That is the way to shake it all off and forget," says Peer as he deserts
Solveig, and he manages to shake it off very completely, for not a single
thought does he devote to her. He represses and forgets. "One keeps true,
and one forgets." And how do we repress? One does it with wine, another
with lies or dreams. "Dream then, my little one."

Peer's dreams are countless, but two things are always to be found in
them, women and riding. Have these any connection with each other?
Surely people knew that ages ago or we should never have had the pro-
verb: "Rule a horse and a woman with sugar and whip." Riding is a
symbol of loving, that one cannot doubt; indeed, one might even surmise

that the idea of riding was derived from the experience of sexual congress, that riding was due to the mighty power of Eros.

> By the bridle you can tell if a man is well-bred.

No woman was ever thought, ever dreamt of, by one better bred than Peer in his fantasies of Solveig; he says the mere sight of her makes him a saint; he dare not touch her. The rider adores Solveig:

> O maiden without fault or blame,
> I would be cradled in thy soul.

Man's first horse is his mother; in her body he rides, a true Emperor of Heaven.

Peer tried to repress his love for his mother, but only half succeeded. She still stands between him and other women, between him and Solveig, and in her role as the bearer of a child even between him and children. Like Siegfried he remains childless, unless you take the homunculus of the Troll-dream to be a child. But recollect how he rages when he thinks of marriage and of children on board the ship. He wants to bear children himself and be a mother, just as Siegfried did, and Faust, and every man who is a full human being. We have the homunculus theme again here, you see. Hate and yearning desire. "Mothers, Mothers. It sounds so marvellous."

To be emperor, that is Peer's main theme, emperor of the air, of the desert, of the new realm Gyntiana, emperor of all past time. And when by the irony of fate he is at length made emperor by the mad asylum-doctor, he is broken for a moment, but quickly recovers himself, and as he sits peeling the onion he is just as indifferent to the outer world as ever he was. He is in himself an emperor, so need not trouble to become one. Only one thing remains to trouble him, and this he curses as the devil.

"*Djavlen star i alt som minder*," he says. The ordinary translation fails to give the essential meaning of this phrase. "May the plague take all this" gives no inkling of the fact that here we have the key to the whole play. "All this" is in no sense the equivalent of "*som minder*," i.e., "all that reminds me"—"Remembering is the devil."

In this sentence Peer repeats what is told us in another saying of deep import: "He that loseth his life shall find it," and again, "Except a man be born again, he shall in no wise enter into the Kingdom of Heaven." It is, alas, the fate of Peer Gynt as of every man, to be confronted always in the world and in his own life by things that force him to remember.

What else does psychoanalysis teach us, if not that the repressed material of the immensely powerful unconscious, the kingdom of darkness, of the *djavlen,* is bound to reappear in one shape or another, in sickness, crime, madness—or in art and deeds of might. For it is not true that a repression, *"som minder,"* always or even very often produces evil. The devil—as we know from Faust—wants to do evil but his evil turns to good. And so it is with *"som minder."*

And so it is, too, with what Peer in the same breath sends to the devil: *"Djavlen star i alle kvinder!"* (The devil take all women!) Women, too, are connected with *"som minder,"* or at least the one most important woman, the mother.

We know, and the whole play turns round this fact, that Peer Gynt is fast bound to his mother Aase, and to his memories of her, that he never ceases to be the child of his mother. That is his destiny, but since every evil carries good along with it, it is also his good fortune. Because he always remains a child he does not need to grow childish, he can take up with trolls, with strange passers-by, with the devil and the Button-molder, with the Boyg, and also with Solveig. All the same, he is not wrong in wishing women to the devil. Who was it taught him to live in what men call a world of lies? Who encouraged his dreaming? Or rather, who gave him the stuff of his dreams? For no man can live without his fantasies, the stupidest has his daydreams. Who then gave him the stuff of his dreams? They came from his childhood. And who directed his childhood, who was it instilled into him the strange good and evil which are to be found in him? None but Aase, his mother, while his father roamed over the countryside soaking and gluttonizing. She tells this to Solveig:

> There we two sat at home together
> And strove to put away all thoughts of grief
> For as I never could contend with him
> It brought no joy to look fate in the face.
> From time to time we have to drown our thoughts,
> And some men will choose wine and others, lies.
> Ah well! And so it came about that we
> Made sport with trolls, and princes, and every sort of beast.
> Even rape came in for who could think
> That tales like these would stay in the boy's mind?

Many people now know that they do, and so we have the very wise ones trying to shut children out of fairyland, thinking this best for them. There are plenty of such careful and conscientious parents today—it is the enviable privilege of parents to consider themselves conscientious!—

who will not let their boys revel in Red Indian stories, or their girls delight in love-stories (save the mark!) and who think even fairy tales may
work harm; Struwwelpeter himself is now under suspicion lest he should
put naughty ideas into the heads of good children. But children are not
good. Heaven preserve us from such, they are far the worst of all! I am
not joking when I hold up Struwwelpeter as a good book for children,
and a still better book for grown-ups, since it is perhaps the most important textbook ever written on the workings of the unconscious.

It is from Aase, then, that Peer gets material for his dreams. Here we
have the same lesson as in the dictum "Man is the child of his childhood." And so he should be. That is an ancient doctrine which, thank
heaven, gives no support to the view that the human race can be improved by half-baked attempts to bring up children on psychoanalytic
lines. In spite of his dreams about empire and trolls, in spite of his building castles in the air and riding the winds, Peer Gynt is shown to us
winning his way from the misty mountains to the land of sunshine.
Indeed it is precisely because of the fantasies he learned from his mother
that he is able to succeed at last, for fantasy is the opposite of repression,
which has its origin in the poor compromise that seeks to transfer fantasy
into the world of every day and by so doing deals it its death-blow.

There is, however, another order of reality. Peer lives in his dreams,
impossible, unreal dreams, yet so real for him that they become actual.
He comes in fact to the Ronde Castle, he joins the trolls, he really speaks
to the strange passenger, the lonely moralist, he actually meets the Boyg,
he has dealings with the Button-molder, he plays tricks on the devil,
he journeys with his mother to heaven. To get all this experience the
rest of us would have to use alcohol or morphia, or we wait till sleep
gives it us in dreams, and even then our "reality" would be a poor thing
by the side of Peer's. Reality? Certainly. Whoever can, like Ibsen, make
his fantasy so real that it begets an actual child, so real that it can figure
on the boards of the stage, that man is a dreamer who shows us up as
miserable weaklings. Peer Gynt is, beyond us all, an Emperor.

Peer Gynt's dreaming teaches us with shattering sincerity that we are
all dependent upon the experiences of our childhood, though it is not
always the mother who directs the forces which determine the rest of
life. Aase asks Peer:

> Remember'st thou that priest,
> —From Copenhagen came he,—
> Who asked thy name?
> And swore thou answer'st him
> Like a prince?

There is the "trauma," the psychical wound. To a small boy it must
have been a great experience that a priest, a foreigner to boot, should
call him a prince. What a priest says, for a little boy, is true, so the
whole responsibility for Peer's dreaming does not lie with Aase. Let us
be just to her even where she was responsible. If she had not taught the
little Peer to dream so wonderfully, he could never have driven her over
the frozen wild to the castle of Soria-Moria, nor would she in old age
have been held in honor or heard the Master's voice: "Old Aase here
may freely pass." Could anyone wish that scene struck out of men's
memories? Yet it could only come about in the way it did because Peer
Gynt was himself, was the son of his mother.

Himself? Yet it is made clear over and over again in the play that he
was anything but himself, that he lived according to the wisdom of the
trolls: "Man, be self-sufficient," and not as wise men counsel: "Man, be
thyself." Let us go back to the scene where the distinction is first made
clear between "Be thyself" and "Be sufficient unto thyself." The old
troll is speaking of the difference between men and trolls: "Out there in
the sunlit world it is deemed the highest wisdom to say 'Man, be thyself,' but here amongst us trolls the counsel given is 'Troll, be sufficient
unto thyself.' Let that henceforth, my son, be thy life's motto."

The troll-wisdom "Be sufficient to thyself" is easy enough to understand, but the human wisdom is obscured by translation. The original
"vær dig selv" implies that the "thou" is an objective thou, and not a
subjective one. If a small child tells you something about itself it does
not say "I did so and so," but "Hans—or whatever its name is—did so
and so." The child stands—or can stand—in an objective relation to
itself. It sees its own being as a self and not as an "I." Peer Gynt, too,
can regard his "self" as an object, he can *"være dig selv,"* he can give up
his ego and take the child's attitude to the self, making himself a part
of the great whole, the universal. If the oft-repeated words *"dig selv"* be
taken in this sense, all the difficulties of interpretation disappear. It is, of
course, not possible to make this clear in a stage representation, but if
the audience are prepared they will not be led astray by the performers.

It should be obvious to everyone that the self is not identical with
the ego, for the ego is something entirely personal and in essence illusory,
something existing only in our own imagination. It comprehends but a
very small part of a man. The self, on the other hand, is the whole
man. We all know it, yet none of us lives in accordance with our knowledge, for we are all under the spell of the ego-idea. It is as though we
were trolls, as though we took troll-nature in place of human nature.
"With the Ronde-folk everything has two sides," says the green-clad

troll. "Be sufficient to thyself" is the wisdom hidden within us, troll-wisdom. It is part of man, for man is ambivalent.

> Black seems white and big seems small,
> Coarse seems fine, and dirt seems clean.

Peer, like ourselves, is not a half-man, but a double. We all live and think as though we had individual personalities, yet we know we have not. Everyone tries to flatter himself into the belief that he is a personality, an "I," and only at rare moments does he achieve a knowledge of the self. Self-knowledge is literally knowledge of the self, not of the ego, and only he can win to it who is willing to think again as he thought in childhood, "Hans did it."

Ibsen has emphasised time and time again that Peer Gynt was such a man and uses this very means to make it clear, for Peer Gynt mostly refers to himself by his name and seldom makes use of the pronoun "I." Only once, if I remember the original correctly, does he say *"jeget"* in place of *"selvet,"* and that, characteristically enough, is at his second encounter with the old troll when he says: "I have brought my royal I to the pawnshop. Let others redeem it."

Still clearer, once one has grasped the antithesis of the ego and the self, is the scene in the mad-house, a scene which is immensely effective on the stage but only theatrically effective if one has not the clue. Dr. Begriffenfeldt acknowledges Peer as emperor of the self and crowns him as such, afterwards presenting to him one patient after another, as people who are also themselves. Here, of course, he utterly confuses ego and self, for in the insane the self is lost and only the exaggerated ego-feeling survives. Perhaps it was Ibsen's conscious intention to represent the mad asylum-doctor as a German who could not keep straight about the ego and the self, for the German puts "Ich" and "selbst" next each other as though they meant the same thing, when others say me-self or myself.

The last words Peer Gynt speaks before he is crowned are in abdication of the ego: "What am I? I am anything you like, a Turk, a criminal, a troll of the mountains."

He gives up his ego, though of course he can do this only for a few moments, realizing himself as nameless, a self, independent, impersonal. He gives up the ego and then reveals what has always filled his mind, though hidden in the unconscious, and governed his life, driving him up and down the world, always in haste, for his ego is mightier than that of other men. He is told by the Button-molder to find the will of the Master, and when he asks what a man may do who has never discovered the Master's will, he is told to hazard a guess. And Peer must guess, for he knows it not, and his hunt all over the world has not merely been a flight from anxiety—that is only its negative side—but also a search after the Master's will.

Peer Gynt gives us a definition of the self: "The Gyntian self is a host of wishes, pleasures and desires, a dance of dreams and challenges." He tells us more in the finest scene of the whole play, while he sits peeling an onion: "Thou are no emperor, thou art an onion! And now, Peer, I am going to peel that onion." And he peels and peels away until he comes to the end:

> It does not stop, there's only layer on layer.
> Is there no core, not even in the innermost?
> I find just peel, getting smaller and smaller.
> Dame Nature is a wit!

True, she is a wit. We all of us fancy we must have a core at the center, something that is not merely shell; we would like to hold within us some specially dainty kernel, to be a nut protecting the future, the everlasting. And we do not realize, cannot realize, that we have in fact no kernel, but are made up of one leaf on top of another from outermost to innermost, that, in fact, we are onions. But in the onion every leaf shares its essential nature. The onion is honest right through, and only becomes dishonest, rotten, if it tries to grow a kernal different from the rest of it, and to destroy the peel as though it were something false, something no honorable onion should acknowledge. Peer understands this at first only intellectually. His heart will not accept it, and that is the same with us all. Just before, he was talking of himself as emperor of Beastland, and just afterwards he wants his epitaph to be written: "Here lies No-man." But even No-man has a kernel, he is complete and not just a peeling. No man wants to be that, and yet we are all just that. Everything in us is a peeling, but in every peeling is the essential nature of the whole. The self is an onion-self; only in others do we become a whole. "Cradle me then within thy soul."

In the play there is one character who knows himself and has no ego; that is the one of whom Peer asks: "Who art thou?" and three times receives the answer: "Myself." When at last Peer changes his question to: "*What* art thou?" he is told *"Den store Bojgen."* That it sometimes translated "the big Hunchback," but the actual meaning is "the bender"; he bends himself and he bends others. He is the self, the objective self, the opposite to the ego; he cannot be destroyed. Or can he? Who knows? He is the sphinx, at once lion and woman. And he cannot hurt Peer because "there are women at his back," Aase and Solveig.

Peer Gynt is in terror of the Bender, and it is when the two are in conflict that he utters those strange words:

> Forward and back the length is the same,
> Inward and outward are just as narrow.

One can interpret that in different ways, perhaps as the way between ego and self. But, perhaps, we may find another reference there to the road Peer has journeyed himself. Out of the mother we come at birth, back to the mother we must go at death—in and out and roundabout. Narrow is the path at birth, narrow the way to the grave. Birth, the grave, and always the mother. Women stand at the back of us, mother, bride and wife.

In the Sun-splendor, we hear:

> Sleep then, my babe,
> I will rock thee and keep watch.
> The treasure on my lap
> Who brought this joy to me,
> He sleeps now at my breast.
> God keep thee, blessing and hope.
> Sleep on, my dearest babe
> While I rock thee and keep watch.

And once again in the Glory-of-Day:

> I will rock thee and keep watch,
> Sleep and dream, my little babe.

Emperor and Galilean

by Paulus Svendsen

Ibsen's world-historical drama is, literally, his central work. No other play lies nearer the chronological center of his authorship. In a curious way it stands alone, surrounded by a kind of dramatic void. When it appeared in 1873, four years had passed since *The League of Youth,* and four more years would pass before *Pillars of Society.*

Ibsen's work with *Emperor and Galilean* fell in that time of life which the Greeks called *akmé,* when the poet was felt to stand at the peak of his creative power.

No other of Ibsen's plays took so long to write. Including interruptions, he worked on it over a period of nine years. He could justifiably say that he had sacrificed many years of his life to this book. It is understandable, then, that we have more notes, preliminary studies, and drafts than for any other of his plays, and this material shows that Ibsen carried out painstaking studies, and was a man of learning. He could legitimately accept the doctor's degree he received at Uppsala in 1877.

Emperor and Galilean is the play that Ibsen, on several occasions, designated as his masterpiece. And, as far as I know, it is the only play about which he said: "The positive view of the world which the critics have so long demanded of me will be found here" (July 12, 1871). It would seem that he admitted the justice of this demand; his mission should also be to answer.

Not only the critics, but people generally had begun to grow impatient. They expected something more than new riddles and new revelations of life's corruption. It was one of Ibsen's admirers, Arne Garborg, who wrote in 1873: "For all his richness of thought, Ibsen has really nothing to give. He is, himself, only a seeker. He dissipates himself in a night of doubt."

Of course, it was not only to comply with the impatient desires of

"Emperor and Galilean" by Paulus Svendsen. Translated by Allen Simpson. From *Edda,* LVI (Hefte 4, 1956), 338-50. Copyright © 1956 by *Edda.* Reprinted by permission of the author and *Edda.*

his critics and public that Ibsen now believed he could give them his positive view of the world, but it was, certainly, of significance that he addressed himself to a perplexed age. He was himself suffering under all the confusion, in "this meaning-darkened time" [*denne menings-mörke tid*] as he called it (1872). Sometimes he felt mortally threatened by chaos. "There are actually times when the whole history of the world seems to me to be one great shipwreck. The only thing to do is save oneself." He wrote this two months after he had begun work in earnest on *Emperor and Galilean* and had finished the first act (September 24, 1871). He added: "The whole human race is on the wrong track, that's the trouble." His colleague Björnson wrote, in the summer of 1872: "Never in the memory of man have we had such a glorious year in Norway. Joy is everywhere in the land." Ibsen was not blind to "the profusely blooming life around us," but this could not shake his conviction that "the whole of mankind has gone astray."

He worked out his play about Julian the Apostate from a deep personal need to find a meaning and a design in human history. It seems that Ibsen felt that a phase in his life was at an end. He had travelled much, between Egypt and Stockholm, and had followed intently the violent events of the time and tried to form an opinion about them. While preparing his poems for publication he had reviewed his shifting points of view over the past years. Now he felt the need to work out his own, positive relationship to the past and the present and then let "the final verdict upon the struggle and the victory" shine out from his massive world-historical drama.

As he thus lifted the historical material into the currents of his age, and so made it contemporary, he engaged himself so personally that he could say: "What I am putting into this book is a part of my own inner life; what I describe I have myself experienced in different forms," and there is "much self-anatomy in this book" (October 14, 1872 and February 20, 1873).

As a result, we find several layers in the play: the historical, the contemporary, and the subjective; and the investigator is thus confronted by special problems of interpretation.

Ibsen restricted himself here as in no other of his historical dramas; he wanted to keep strictly to his sources, and many speeches of the characters are taken directly from this source material. It is advantageous to know as much as possible about these sources, so that we avoid misinterpreting the text wherever we have available the means for checking it. Ibsen was once brought to tears by a misinterpretation due solely to ignorance.

During his preliminary studies, Ibsen avoided strongly colored accounts of Julian. He wanted to see him with his own eyes, make himself Julian's contemporary. He had developed this faculty for contemporaneousness in his earlier historical plays, but never had he devoted so much effort to "synchronization" as here. Moreover, he had to bring into relief those features of the historical material that could create contact with his own age—Ibsen deliberately placed himself under this requirement. Any interpretation must keep this in mind as well.

His intentions went even further. He did not want to depict only a struggle related to special situations separated in time by 1,500 years. By calling the play "a world drama" and later "a world-historical drama," he wanted to point to something valid for us all, shaped as we are by our civilization—indeed, the powers active there are universal. The play "deals with both heaven and earth" (February 6, 1873).

Through painstaking concentration on his sources, an intense preoccupation with contemporary conditions, and the frankness of confession, Ibsen wanted to elevate history, his fellow man, and himself to a confrontation with eternal powers. So much did he expect of his *Hauptwerk*.

There was, in the situation of his time, more than ample cause for attempting this. Political, social, philosophical, and religious attitudes were in great conflict. To mention just a few: the Franco-Prussian War was followed by great crises in both the warring countries; the rebellion of the Paris commune coincided more or less with the cultural struggle going on in Germany. The Catholic Church was involved in both external and internal conflict. The Vatican Council declared the pope infallible in doctrinal and moral-theological questions, leading to the establishment of a new religious sect, the Old Catholic Church. Italian troops brought to an end the more than thousand-year-old Papal State. In 1870, the hundredth anniversary of Hegel's birth was celebrated with a flood of books and articles. Hegel's ideas of government were, in a way, confirmed when history's first Protestant empire was founded the following year. The leading thinkers of the day were Schopenhauer and Eduard von Hartmann, both of whom gave support to pessimism as a way of life and a world-view. Sometime in the 1870s Bismarck asked the members of the Reichstag if those gentlemen had ever seen a satisfied German. In 1878 the French Academy recognized the concept "pessimism."

Of course, "optimism"—a word recognized about a century earlier—also had its spokesmen. Darwin's *Descent of Man* appeared in February

1871; and his most prominent champion in Germany, Ernst Haeckel, wrote that future generations would celebrate this date as the beginning of a new, beneficent era in the evolution of man.

In orthodox Protestant circles the signs of the times were interpreted somewhat differently. The same year that Haeckel published *Natürliche Schöpfungsgeschichte* (1868), in which he called the theory of evolution the greatest victory of the human spirit, Gisle Johnson and C. P. Caspari published their Norwegian translation of the Lutheran confessions, where these words appear: "Human nature becomes more frail as the world ages . . . Nature ages and becomes by degrees weaker, and iniquities multiply." In orthodox circles the view of man was not very different from that which Petter Dass had expressed so tersely two hundred years earlier: "We are worse than our fathers."

The intellectuals of the period were bound to be preoccupied with the hectic activity going on about them. They reacted, of course, in different ways. To shed light on Ibsen's mood and thought at this time, it may perhaps help to place some of his observations alongside the statements of a man he almost certainly never met, but whom he resembles in many ways, Henri Frédéric Amiel. Both of them despised the masses, and both of them applied a moral criterion to civilization. Especially striking is how similarly they expressed themselves at the beginning of the 1870s. On February 4, 1871, Amiel assessed the situation in these words: "Our struggles are the unceasing pursuit of an unattainable goal, that is, a noble madness." Ibsen wrote, on September 24 of the same year: "Is there really anything tenable in the present situation, with its unattainable ideals, etc.?"

During the war, Amiel wrote (February 15, 1871) that there was something in both the warring countries which had to disappear. France, for example, must rid herself of rhetoric and pomp; she had to lose her illusions. Two months before, on December 20, 1870, Ibsen had written something similar: "The old illusory France has been crushed," and he added that when "the new, *de facto* Prussia is crushed too, we will enter the age of the future in one leap." Amiel had the same expectation: "I sincerely hope that from this war a new equilibrium will emerge, a new Europe."

Amiel hoped that, in this new Europe, the cardinal principle of society would be the government of the individual by himself, so that the individual would not be regarded as a means to an end, as an instrument for Church or State. He anticipated that a free and voluntary society for common ideals would emerge, with everyone contributing joyously to the common goal. Two days later, on February 17, 1871, Ibsen wrote:

> The state is the curse of the individual. . . . Away with the State! . . .
> Undermine the concept of state; make voluntary participation and spiritual
> kinship the only essentials for a union. . . . That's the beginning of a
> freedom worth something.

In 1871, while Ibsen was writing the first part of *Emperor and Galilean,* where questions about freedom and necessity, history's goal, and the clash between Greek joy of life and Christian guilt are so central, Amiel wrote (January 20) that two concepts of the world oppose one another, the moral, which takes into account man's freedom, and the fatalistic. In one form or another the question always returns: Has the universe a goal, or hasn't it? Both the law of nature and the law of freedom govern man; therefore, the most popular churches are Epicureanism and orthodoxy—perhaps, Amiel suggests, they will end by merging. Out of such thoughts and moods in a time of crisis, the expectation grew in Amiel of an earthly, harmonious empire of the future which, in any case, it is our pious duty to believe in. Similar thoughts and moods at precisely the same time gave birth to Ibsen's belief in "the third empire."

Ibsen was in accord with many when he judged conditions in Europe harshly. He was also in accord with many when he expressed his longing for a new epoch.

Ibsen felt as though he were witnessing a "struggle to the death between two epochs" (1872). This battle was going on all around him when he lived in Germany, and therefore he could later say that *Emperor and Galilean* was written under the influence of German intellectual life. But he also kept up with the intellectual struggle as it was developing in the North. He read not only Georg Brandes' lectures on the "Main Currents of Nineteenth Century Literature," but also, undoubtedly, the analysis which Brandes' teacher, the Danish philosopher Hans Bröchner, made of the time. Bröchner maintained that the Christian and the humanistic stood as fundamental antitheses in the consciousness of the age. What was taking place was nothing less than the breaking up of the traditional union of Christianity and humanism. The intellectual struggle was concerned with the question of Christianity as the basis of European culture. There is much contemporary evidence to show that Bröchner's analysis was felt to be accurate. And, viewed from our time, it is clear that *Emperor and Galilean* came into being in a crucial epoch and addressed itself to people who were witnessing an abrupt change in the cultural life of Europe.

Ibsen took from this change what was perhaps its most essential characteristic: apostasy.

C. S. Lewis, in his inaugural address at Cambridge in 1954, maintained that while Europe's history could earlier be divided into a pre-Christian and a Christian era (the cultural shift began about the time of Julian), we must now speak of a post-Christian era as well. We must place this new boundary somewhere between Walter Scott and ourselves—in Norway we would say between Wergeland and ourselves. Europe's de-Christianization is obviously not absolute and complete, but Europe's Christianization had not been either. In any case, the transition which began in the last century was, Lewis maintained, greater than the cultural transition Europe had experienced in its conversion to Christianity.

If we consider Ibsen's Julian in this perspective, then it is clear that Ibsen must have experienced the beginning of that de-Christianization which for many—both Christians and non-Christians—stood as a fact in the 1870s. And, in this situation, Ibsen then portrayed a figure that history itself had selected as the prototype of the defector, the apostate. The readers of the time, too, saw clearly that Julian was "modern."

In his portrayal of apostasy, Ibsen combined the historical material, the realities of his own time, and his personally shifting attitudes in a way which scarcely has a parallel in the literature of the period.

He has described Julian's apostasy, and especially its consequences, in such a way that this particular instance—determined by the age in which it took place and by Julian's psychology—becomes typical of apostasy as such. It has become a symbol in Goethe's sense: the fate of an individual—a historic fact—has become representative of something universal. Apostasy has acquired *Bedeutung*.

We must seek the background for Julian's apostasy in the kind of Christianity he abandoned. It is a Christianity stamped by God's categorical demands. God is the god of wrath and retribution. Such a religion engenders in Julian a boundless anxiety, and with it a need for self-assertion and power. His fondest dream soon becomes to conquer.

From childhood on, this frail, awkward boy has had instilled in him the belief that he is a new Achilles. He relates this belief to the expectations that both the Christians and heathens have of him. He comes to believe he has a mission, and this reinforces the great thoughts he has about his own significance: it is he who shall defend Christianity against the more educated among its antagonists. Therefore he goes to Athens: "The Lord God has called to me with a mighty voice. Like Daniel, I will go boldly and joyously into the lion's den."

The first sign of apostasy is the weakening of his sense of mission. He tries to conceal this by seeking out "this Christianity which is to be saved"—and he can find it neither in the Emperor nor in the bakers in Constantinople. Not for a moment does he suspect that Christianity might be sought within himself. His sense of mission is thereby without engagement: "If Christ wants anything of me, then he must speak clearly."

There is no battle of intellects between Julian and Libanios in Athens. It annoys him, too, when Libanios ceases to flatter him. When he is drawn to Maximos, this happens not least because the mystic is a man who understands Julian's dimensions and holds out to him the prospect of performing the greatest tasks and winning the greatest victories. The emptier Julian becomes, the more easily he falls victim to those who say they believe in him. Maximos then becomes the one who helps him put the unengaged mission into the service of self-assertion. From Maximos he acquires his historic perspective: Moses, Alexander, and Jesus were only forerunners of Julian. His thoughts of greatness soon know no bounds. If he is to be history's greatest man, then he must first of all eradicate the Galilean and his teachings—in fact, everything written about him must be destroyed. He is strengthened in his hatred of the Galilean by the concealed and open hypocrisy and lies of the Christians.

The portrayal of Julian's apostasy is made credible by the fact that both his inner development and outer circumstances work together to this end. Many aspects of this apostasy have universal validity.

In the second part, the apostasy acquires an even more pronounced symbolic meaning. Various critics have maintained that the second part does not measure up to the first. Brandes, understandably, was irritated over Ibsen's having robbed Julian of his real greatness. But, if we wish to see the necessary coherence and consistency between the two parts, we should perhaps direct our attention first of all to the consistency within the nature of apostasy itself.

The first phase in the apostate emperor's life is sympathetic. Julian appears as a modern, enlightened representative of tolerance. He proclaims "complete freedom for all citizens" in religious matters. No indignity shall befall the god of the Galileans. Personally, Julian wants to restore to the Greek gods of his forefathers "their ancient rights," but "everyone has his freedom" to worship the god or gods he wishes. The apostasy, therefore, is first that Julian personally "turns back" to the "immortal" Greek gods. In that way he will resurrect Greek beauty, which Christian "truth" had sought to kill.

Apostasy leads him to restoration, or—to put it in Julian's language

—from *apostatis* he goes to *apokatastasis*. The question then becomes whether such a restoration is possible.

The Dionysus-procession he leads through the streets of Constantinople is his first bitter disappointment. He has to ask himself: "Was there beauty in this? . . . What has become of beauty? Will it not return at the bidding of the emperor?" It is more than a disappointment; it is a defeat.

To fall *from* Christianity is one thing. The question is: what can Julian fall *to?* Greek beauty, in any case, shows itself incapable of being an alternative to Christianity. What, then, of faith in the old gods?

Julian knows, of course, what is professed about the gods, but this "we dare not believe unreservedly," he tells Oribases. "The gods, whose nature has by no means been adequately explored, seem at times—if I may say so—either to be asleep, or to intervene only very little in the affairs of men." Julian, who in his youth had envied the Greeks because their gods were so far away, must not admit that he seeks vainly to make contact with them, for he needs them as compensation for his lost faith. He sacrifices to many gods: "one of them must surely hear me. I want to call upon something outside me and above me."

Julian has lost his Christian faith without gaining any new, valid faith in return. The Greek religion is dead and powerless, irrevocably gone. Thus both pagan beauty and pagan truth are without content or sustaining power. No alternative exists to Christianity after all. Julian's apostasy from Christianity is an apostasy to nothing. And that is the apostate's curse, his tragedy. These scenes, which many readers find long and dull, seem to have the function of exposing apostasy as a fall, a falling away into emptiness.

This recognition is brought out in many ways. Inwardly Julian has lost all reference points. Absolute skepticism becomes the inevitable consequence of apostasy, and he admits it: "Does anything exist in and for itself?" he asks Maximos. "From this day on I can think of nothing," he adds—and kicks at an Apollo head! His inner self resembles the ruins he sees around him: "Isn't this whole world a rubbish heap?"

His relationships with other people deteriorate too. He is absorbed at night in study, but the wisdom he subsequently offers is rejected and he reaps scorn, hate, and mockery. The result of this is misanthropy. "I have no use for you," he says to his pagan "friends." Although he sees apostasy everywhere, no true fellowship arises among the apostates.

Apostasy leads not only to isolation from his fellowmen; the religious longing he feels for the pagan gods remains unfulfilled. The gods are silent, they give him no sign. "Alone! No longer a bridge between the spirits and myself."

Julian has to admit that the Galileans, in spite of their errors, have

something which he and his kind lack. Through his speeches runs
wonder over the "riddle" which is "fundamentally beyond our comprehension," that the carpenter's son, with no external power, could found
a kingdom "with twelve humble men, fishermen, ignorant folk," and
that this kingdom is held together by "women and unlearned people
for the most part." This must be because the Galilean's kingdom is
founded on a principle totally different from the power principle underlying the state. Julian perceives this too: "He who shall rule must be
able to rule over the will, over the mind, of man. It is here that Jesus
of Nazareth opposes me and contends with me for power."

Only such a power over the mind can unite humanity in true fellowship and inspire the individual to a self-sacrifice that could lead even
to martyrdom. Therefore Julian also says to those closest to him:

> These Galileans, I tell you, have something in their hearts which I wish
> very much you would strive for. You call yourselves followers of Socrates,
> of Plato, of Diogenes. Is there any of you who would gladly go to his death
> for Plato's sake? Would our Priskos sacrifice his left hand for Socrates?
> Would Kytron let them cut off his ear for Diogenes? Of course, you
> wouldn't! I know you, you whited sepulchres! Get out of my sight.

The second part of the drama also brings a confrontation between
Julian and the Christian friends of his youth. After their happy life
together in Athens their ways had parted. Gregor and Basilios had, like
Julian, Christian faith from the beginning, but it was no force in their
lives. The splendor of Greek art and learning took such a powerful
hold on these two that the Christian demand of renunciation failed to
reach them. To be sure, they suffered because of all the inner strife and
contention in the Church, but they kept away from this and cultivated
their personal interests. Only when the persecutions began did they find
their way to courageous, self-sacrificial faith in the service of the Church.
Then they understood something Julian never learned, that commitment inevitably involves renunciation. Before accepting the Church's
call, Gregory, like Jacob, wrestled with God: "What went on inside me
during the night . . . I do not know. But I do know that before the
cock crew, I spoke face to face with our Crucified Lord. Then I was his."

Julian's road had been entirely different. From guilt-ridden, routine
Christianity he had gone through apostasy to an emptiness which he
tried to fill with a raging struggle against Christianity.

Even as a young man in Athens Julian had discovered that the old
Greek beauty was no longer beautiful, and as emperor he confirmed

this discovery by experience. In Athens he believed he had also learned that the new Christian truth was no longer valid. But as emperor he was forced to experience that there can be, in any case, a tremendous strength in the Christian "delusion."

> He is alive on earth, Maximos, the Galilean is alive, I say, however thoroughly both the Jews and the Romans imagined they had killed him . . . he is alive in men's rebellious minds; he is alive in their defiance and scorn of all visible power.

He is alive in another way too: "The Galilean, the carpenter's son, reigns as the king of love in the warm, believing hearts of men." Julian knows that he, like Alexander and Caesar, will only "be remembered with respectful acknowledgement by certain clear and cold minds." Ibsen, in a speech he gave in 1874 to a procession of students who had come to honor him, referred to these lines as "derived from something I have lived through."

When apostasy back to the old and dead paganism turns out to be no alternative to Christianity, Julian ostensibly clings to Maximos' compromise: the third empire, which builds on both the free, beautiful Greek world and on Christian renunciation, an empire which hates and loves both the tree of knowledge and the tree of the cross.

To succeed in paving the way for this empire, however, he would have had to make good his words that "we must strive to become a new generation." But he never lets this demand apply to himself; he directs it constantly to others—he himself continues only to hate. This, his hatred, which is apostasy's last consequence, becomes so gigantic that he says:

> Oh, if I could lay waste the world! Maximos, is there no poison, no consuming fire, that can lay waste creation as it was on that day when the Solitary Spirit moved upon the face of the waters?

Had he lived in the atomic age, he would not have needed to ask.

This absolute apostasy from Christianity, and its necessary consequences, which Ibsen saw signs of in his own contemporaries and here calls to account, is graphically illustrated in the fate of this brief life. Julian and the Galilean died at exactly the same age, and the spear with which Agathon kills the emperor is the same one with which Longinos, according to legend, pierced the side of the Galilean. By Julian's deathbed Basilios alludes to the words of the Epistle to the Romans when he asks: "Is it not written: one vessel is made unto dishonor and another unto honor?" Thus Julian's tragedy is also that, against his will, he served only to strengthen the Galilean's empire by his struggle against it. Just as Cain and Judas, by their infamous deeds, served to strengthen God's kingdom, so Julian's persecution of the Christians led "not to death, but to resurrection." And the necessity of apostasy, which, by willing what he had to will, Julian fulfilled, will surely be reckoned in his favor "on that great day when the Mighty One shall come in a cloud to pass judgment on the living dead and the dead who live!" These are the final words of Makrina, the pure woman.

In letters and speeches Ibsen returned again and again to what he meant, in *Emperor and Galilean,* by the term "the third empire." He does this in such a way that we must see it as something of a personal confession of faith. None of the conflicting parties of his time were able, however, to use this doctrine to further their own cause. He remained standing alone with his "positive view of the world." Georg Brandes could by no means use this "banner," nor could anyone else. This was because Ibsen's third empire could not apply to any single cause; it was something new which was yet to arise.

The concept of the three empires not only helped Ibsen to greater clarity about the relationship between freedom and necessity in history and between the individual and the world-will. It also strengthened his almost apocalyptic belief that catastrophe and collapse are always omens that something new and better is near. Behind many of Ibsen's intense revelations of squalor, lies, and deceit—revelations never accompanied by outbursts of sorrow or despair—seems to lie an optimistic faith that if only all this is brought into the open, it will contribute to a change —"so much the sooner will vengeance come and hold judgment on the deceits of the age." He was convinced that a will keeps watch in history, "a demon with eternal power," a moral will which, amidst all the corruption, lies, and deceit, will suddenly appear and sweep the board clean. Therefore he can use the words he does: "We will enter the age of the future in one leap," "the moment's wind is changing," and the new age will dawn "very soon."

Perhaps he also saw his own work in this light. He was a pessimist when it concerned his age, which could appear to him as a shipwreck, an iron age destitute of beauty, or an age carrying the corpse of the past on its back. But with respect to the future he was an optimist. A great many things would and must topple, and he himself would be there to help pull down whatever was rotten and crumbling. Then, he believed, a new life-force would emerge. His plays are about this life-force too, this force for transformation.

Ibsen's Search for the Hero

by John Northam

I am very grateful to have this occasion[1] for paying homage in his own country to one of the greatest dramatists, not merely of Norway, or even of modern times, but in the history of drama. This I say not by way of sycophancy, but as an introduction to my theme.

I cannot hope to support this estimate by discussing the verbal poetry of Ibsen—that is a task properly left to your own countrymen; nor do I intend to delve into his relationship with the culture of his time, for that too is virtually the preserve of Norwegian scholarship. I intend, in fact, to approach Ibsen by a devious route which will yet, I hope, lead eventually to the heart of the matter—hence "Ibsen's Search for the Hero."

It may be a personal eccentricity, or a bias encouraged by the syllabus at Cambridge, that a question emerges from much of my reading in whatever literary form: "What is the modern tragic conflict; or, where is the tragic hero to be found in modern life?" This seems to me a pertinent question to ask about the literature of the last hundred odd years and particularly of the last decade. It is pertinent not merely because ordinary people nowadays are not very heroic in their daily lives —I doubt if they have ever been that—but because our own generation is so peculiarly deficient even in the *idea* of a hero. Unlike the Greeks and the Elizabethans, we have no definite and exalted place reserved in our scheme of things for the hero. The most prevalent fashion in our literature is to explore, sometimes with a wry humor, the suffering and the defeat, the pathos of human existence, or to express anger; but rarely does it offer any more invigorating example.

It is because tragedy is so invigorating, besides being dreadful and terrifying, that it is vital to the spiritual health of an age. It suggests to

"Ibsen's Search for the Hero" by John Northam. From *Edda*, LX (Hefte 1-2, 1960), 101-120. Copyright © 1960 by *Edda*. Reprinted by permission of the author and *Edda*.
[1] This paper reproduces the substance of two lectures delivered in Oslo in September 1959.

us standards by which, even in the commonplace society which we in-
habit, life can become an expression of nobility. That is why Ibsen is
so vitally important to us, for he seems to me to be the only dramatist
to have created great tragedy out of a society that can still be called
fundamentally modern.

Tragedy has resisted definition long enough for it to be in no danger
from me; but it will help the argument if I indicate crudely and briefly
what I understand by the term. Tragedy explores the extent to which
man is responsible for his own fate. Exploration is needed, because although man acts on the assumption that he is free to choose, he comes
into conflict with powers in the universe over which he has no ultimate
control. There is no fixed or clear demarcation between freedom and
necessity.

Whether, in any particular play, man will be portrayed primarily as
an individual or as a figure representative of mankind as a whole seems
to depend on the attitudes current in the community out of which the
play is created. It is not surprising that in the prime of the Athenian
city state, a tightly organized society, the tragic heroes of Aeschylus were
presented not as individuals but as great symbols of mankind. It is the
cross-fertilization of medieval and Renaissance ideas that enables Shakespeare to present figures that are simultaneously great typical figures and
also individuals observed with miraculous attention to detail.

For Ibsen, coming when he did in time, there could be no question
but that the hero must be represented primarily as an individual. So that
one of the problems facing Ibsen, if we can credit him with a constant
ambition to write a modern tragedy,[2] was this: how to present on the
stage a convincing portrait of a modern individual—a man of sophisticated and subtle thoughts and feelings, of modern manners and of everyday speech—and at the same time show him as possessing the full stature
and grandeur of a hero.

And here we must turn to the other element in the conflict, the powers
over which man has no ultimate control. For we judge a man's heroism
by reference to his opponent, David in relation to Goliath. It is essential
to the tragic vision that the tragic hero should be seen to be in conflict
with forces that are powerfully represented.

Like the hero, the forces are differently represented in different ages.

[2] Implicit in the way he constantly relates his plays, however "antique" in subject
and technique, to his own concerns and to the society around him; also in the spas-
modic but repeated attempts, amongst these "antique" plays, to try a modern one—
of *Midsummer Eve, Love's Comedy, League of Youth, Brand.*

The Greeks called them Gods, operating through (and sometimes operated upon by) Fate. It is possible to formulate the most sophisticated Elizabethan or Jacobean view of the tragic conflict as being a conflict between a hero and a chaos of forces of good and evil in a universe ordained by God to observe Order and Degree, the order having been shattered by some human sin or folly, and the apparent chaos being an obscurely purposeful return toward stability. In both Greek and Elizabethan tragedy, man is in some way in conflict with forces that are divine and which therefore work in ways not fully comprehensible, and certainly not controllable, by him.

For a man of Ibsen's generation the great opponent of man was seen to be society—not just society in its "problem play" aspect, the source of definable, limitable, and often remediable misery, but society as a force working through a myriad of obscure agencies and trivial occasions, but working with a power and a mystery comparable to that displayed by the Greek gods or the Elizabethan universe. Or perhaps I should say that Ibsen had the wit to see society in this light; but having seen it, there remained for him the problem of presenting this vision in the theater.

Ibsen's problem as a dramatist was therefore a double one: to present a convincing portrait of a modern individual and still make a hero out of him; and to present a portrait of modern society that is accurate and lifelike but which shows it as operating as an inexorably powerful force upon the tragic hero. And by present, I emphasize that Ibsen had to do all this in terms of the theater. So that although my theme is a general one, it is also a severely limited one. By Ibsen's search for the hero I do not mean merely his search for the *idea* of a hero but his search for the technical means of expressing that vision in the theater. I wish now to glance briefly at Ibsen's early plays to see in them the growth of the technique.

To simplify the references (and this can be done, thanks to the devoted work already carried out on the sources of the early plays by so many scholars) I shall use "Shakespeare" to mean not only the direct influence of Shakespeare but also his influence transmitted through other writers—at second-hand and often combined with other elements, but still unmistakably Shakespearean. With that preamble, it can be said that Ibsen relied at first upon two principal models, Shakespeare and Scribe. From Shakespeare he certainly obtained a sense of man's inherent greatness, together with an incentive to express this in events and actions chosen for their grandeur, and in language that was manifestly and unashamedly colorful, rhetorical, figurative, and artificial. But Shakespeare could give Ibsen no model of modernity; nor could Ibsen derive from him any help toward the neat construction of a modern play.

Construction he learnt from Scribe. But Scribe, though he could provide a model of modernity, was too prosaic of imagination to entertain any vision of heroic greatness. Consequently Ibsen had two inadequate models: one a model of human greatness romantically and poetically expressed but remote both from everyday life and from the conditions of the modern theater; the other close to modern life in appearances, suited to the conditions of the modern theater, but lacking in heroism. What was Ibsen to do?

Using "Shakespeare" in this general sense, the first three plays, *Catiline, The Warrior's Barrow, Midsummer Eve* seem to me simply Shakespearean and, as plays, poor. One recognizes, of course, that the issues involved are those of deep and personal concern to Ibsen himself, that many of the themes and some of the personalities and situations are dear enough to be used elsewhere in poems and later plays; but as plays, these works are juvenile.

It is not until the appearance of *Lady Inger of Östraat* that Ibsen moves on a step by accepting wholeheartedly the assistance of Scribe's example in plot construction. In the event, the construction is over-enthusiastically elaborated, but at least Ibsen is acknowledging the need for construction. *Lady Inger* may be a crude mixture of Shakespeare and Scribe, but it served its purpose.

However, for a man with a rooted ambition to write a modern tragedy, all four of these early works remain remote from the times he lived in. There are heroes and heroines galore, but they are from an earlier time. Ibsen is having to clothe his own deepest and most personal feelings in fancy dress.

Two more plays in more or less the same vein, *The Feast at Solhaug* and *Olaf Liljekrans,* completed Ibsen's dissatisfaction with their artificiality and turned him in a different direction. The turning point, familiar to you all, is *The Vikings at Helgeland,* where he draws upon the sagas for material. What is more important, Ibsen derives the general tone and atmosphere from the same sources; and what that was Ibsen himself has described in describing the saga: "a great, cold, rounded and self-contained epos, essentiallly objective, and exclusive of all lyricism." I am told that the language of the play is more simple than the language of the earlier plays. It is clear that the play depends more upon implication than upon direct expression; there are no monologues in the play.

If the language as a whole is more restrained, so too is the construction. Scribe is still the model, but Ibsen has digested his lesson better so that the tricks are far less obviously used. Because of this avoidance of artificiality both in language and in construction, the play moves nearer to real life.

But Ibsen was in danger of losing something of value while he made his gain. For it was through exploitation of elevated language that he was able in his earlier plays to reveal the inner complexities of his characters; now he is denying himself this method of character-creation through words. He was all the more likely to feel the restriction because, for all its characteristic understatement, the saga material demonstrates a keen observation of human personality. How could Ibsen retain this suggestion of deeply understood individual personality when he was abandoning the poetical method he had used so far for its expression?

It is surely not a coincidence that in this play for the first time Ibsen begins to take a serious interest in the appearance of his characters. The hero Sigurd and his wife appear in splendid, brightly colored clothes; the old warrior Örnulf wears darker clothes suggestive of his age; the sordid traitor, Kaare, wears the color gray; while Hjördis, the evil, vicious, murderous Hjördis, wears black. Quite clearly, the costumes are meant to give us a visual impression of the sort of people the various characters are. But what is more interesting is that Ibsen tries to do more with this suggestive detail. He tries to suggest *development* of personality by *changes* of costume. Hjördis is a murderous woman because she is disappointed in her love for Sigurd. But during the play she discovers that Sigurd loves her after all, and this discovery sets free all the latent warmth and passion in her soul. Ibsen underlines this change at the relevant point in the play by having her take off her black clothes and put on a splendid Viking dress. You see, what I am suggesting is that having lost, or rather, having sacrificed the use of long, poetical speeches, Ibsen tries to suggest some of the poetry of personality and feeling through his use of costume.

This is of course a small point, and not likely to make Ibsen feel that he had solved his technical problem. After all, although one could say that the restraint of the language in *The Vikings* is a move toward the reticence of modern speech, the play remains far removed from modern life. And at this point Ibsen seems to have become impatient, to have decided to turn away from the past and make a direct attempt to represent his own times on the stage in *Love's Comedy*. It is a play that contains many of Ibsen's most serious thoughts about life in society, and it is full of local material. But although he was at home with the material, Ibsen found the technical problem a difficult one. At least, that is my interpretation of the long gap that exists in time between this play and the one before—four years or more. It was not Ibsen's first modern play but it was the first *serious* modern play that he attempted, the first play in which he tried to show the possibility of heroic behavior in modern times. It was clearly meant to be an heroic play; he uses some of the material he had discovered in the sagas, and it has been called the most Kierkegaardian of his plays with the possible exception of *Brand.*

For all that, I think the play fails to achieve its objects. There is a lot of talk about heroism, but the play does not contain any convincing embodiment of heroism on the stage, there is no heroic figure. Compared with Sigurd and Hjördis, Falk and Svanhild are thin creations that lack the stature and the glamour of the earlier heroes and heroines. Ibsen has been able to deal with a modern situation only by simplifying. His characters for the most part are stock social types created merely for the purpose of social satire. The style, I understand, is uneven. And the final verse form that he adopted after his unhappy attempt to write the play in prose gives the whole an air of artificiality that distances the play from the reality it claims to comment upon. It does not occur to Ibsen at this stage that he could use costume in a modern play to retain some of the poetical implications of character.

In view of all that he had had to sacrifice to write this play in modern form, it is not surprising that for his next he should make quite certain that he regained all the old glamour and the obvious, unmistakable greatness of his earlier work. After the experiment, he returns to the safety of his earlier models, Shakespeare and Scribe in *The Pretenders.*

He uses them with much greater tact than he did earlier, but *The Pretenders* does not strike me so much as an advance as a summing up. It is a splendid play in many respects; the play seems to me to do better what he had already done. But it does not break in new ground. As such it could not satisfy Ibsen. Once again, the play is about his own deeply felt concerns, but, once again, these are disguised in fancy dress. He cannot yet write a modern play about modern conflicts and modern heroes. But he had gone as far as he could go in that particular set of conventions.

It took him fourteen years to find his way forward as a dramatist. He was faced with a technical problem that he could not solve within the conventions that he knew, and to solve it he was forced virtually to abandon the theater for this long period of time.

Of course, he did not stop writing, and as you well know wrote some of his masterpieces during this time; but they were not dramatic masterpieces, and that is all that I am interested in at this point. He wrote

Brand, Peer Gynt, League of Youth, and *Emperor and Galilean.* I want to consider them not as great works in their own right, which some of them are, but as an experimental stage in the creation of modern tragedy and the modern hero.

By the time that he wrote *Brand,* Ibsen had at last discovered the idea of the modern tragic conflict and of the modern tragic hero. But he could not compress all that he needed to say to create this tragedy within the limits of any play that he was capable of writing at that time. *Brand* is an epic or, at most, a dramatic poem. It can be made into a play by careful editing, but it is not a play as its stands. But what I want to draw your attention to is the fact that in this apparently undramatic work, Ibsen was quietly developing the technique that he had begun to use in the *Vikings.* In the earlier play he had used costumes to suggest character—here he extends this: he uses more subtly than before the landscape and the weather to act as symbols of Brand's character and of the feelings that sweep through him—for example, when Brand's icy spiritual rigor begins to melt at the end of the play, so does the ice-church, and there is the avalanche. That is just one example.

But much more important than that is Ibsen's new use of more trivial, everyday things for the same purpose of telling us something about a character. Let me illustrate this important development by talking for a moment about the candlelight in *Brand.*

You remember the situation; Brand returns from a long journey during which his wife has been left alone, after the death of their son. One of the problems about Brand is to decide what we are supposed to feel about him; is he admirable, is he too harsh, does he lack the necessary warmth and feeling? Brand's words at his entry are kindly enough:

> I am with thee, child, once more.

But Ibsen expands the words into a vital comment on the inner personality of Brand by means of a stage direction: as Brand says: "I am with thee, child, once more," *he lights a single candle, which throws a pale radiance over the room* . . . a single candle, a pale, chill, inadequate light . . . that is what Brand is to other people.

Compare this with the other use of the candles later: Brand himself is now in doubt and perplexity. He calls for his wife:

> Light, Agnes, light, if light thou hast.

Agnes opens the door and enters with the lighted Christmas candles; a bright glow falls over the room . . . You see, Ibsen is giving us a visual equivalent of Agnes' warmth of character to contrast with the cold harshness of her husband, and he is doing it with a candle, that is to say with a trivial, everyday, material object that is made into a theatrical metaphor because it is used consistently. There is nothing in the candle that could not be translated into stage lighting in a prosaic modern play.

And we have to note not only real objects used in this fashion, but people too. Gerd is an attempt to make a living creature symbolize at the same time, not just a social type, but a mysterious spiritual force at work in the universe. The figure of Gerd is not successfully defined, but we can see what Ibsen was trying to do.

I have no time to say anything about *Peer Gynt* except that there too, in his exploration of many situations that are potentially tragic, Ibsen needs the spaciousness of epic to present his material. He cannot present *Peer Gynt* in play form.

Ibsen, I repeat, had an ambition above all to be a playwright and to write the modern tragedy. For all the success of *Brand* and his own confidence in *Peer Gynt,* he could not rest where he had reached in those works. Dissatisfied with his inability to form this rich material into play form, he next wrote one of the most theatrical of his plays, as if to show that he could still write for the theater. The play is *League of Youth*. He has fallen back on his old model, Scribe. It is a serious play, it is a modern play, it is an actable play—and it is a play in which Ibsen develops his command of modern colloquial speech. But what a price he had to pay for this. It is a play devoid of greatness. Nor did it occur to Ibsen even at this stage that he could carry over into a modern prose play some of the suggestive devices that he had been developing. *League of Youth* showed that Ibsen could still write a neat play for the modern theater, but it also showed that he could not yet write the modern tragedy.

And so, just as after *Love's Comedy,* Ibsen felt the need to recapture his sense of the heroic and the tragic even if it meant going back into the past again for fancy dress to clothe his modern conflicts. *Emperor and Galilean* is a work on an obviously heroic scale, in every sense of the word. It is not a direct comment on modern life but an oblique one. Nor is it fully dramatic—it is more akin to a long novel than to a play. And yet here again, in this apparently undramatic work, Ibsen continues to exploit the technique that we have seen so slowly emerge over the years. He uses costume more subtly than in the *Vikings*—the fact that Julian's court dress sits uneasily upon him is a visual indication that Julian is a rebel; that his fingers are inky is a trivial indication of his tendency to be a scholar. The lighting is used to emphasize and evaluate the great conflict that underlies the play, between Christianity and paganism. The Christian church in the play is brilliantly lit; Julian's paganism is associated with gloom and darkness. Ibsen is suggesting a comment on the relative values of these two ways of life through a theatrical effect. Furthermore, Ibsen uses the set to indicate the position occupied by Julian in this conflict. In Act I we see Constantinople; the Royal Chapel is illuminated, while around it lie the overthrown statues of pagan deities; Christianity is triumphant in Constantinople.

But in Act II we are in Athens, and there paganism is still alive: the set shows a square in which the pagan statues are still standing.

In Act III we see Julian's position visually represented: in the background of his house, we see a small court containing statues. Julian's link with paganism is made clear through the set.

Of course, this work is so enormously long and so painfully explicit that these details are not strictly required. But still Ibsen bothered to put them in, they were important for him. And you can see that basically he is attempting nothing that could not go straight into a modern play and be translated into costume, scenery, lighting, and makeup.

After *Emperor and Galilean* Ibsen worked hard for another four years before he could produce another play. In all he worked for some seven years on *Pillars of Society*. During the time that he was considering *Pillars of Society*, he could reflect as follows: "I have discovered my modern hero in Brand, and I can see where the tragic conflict is in modern society. But I can't go in the style and technique of *Brand*, because it is too far remote from ordinary life still, and it lacks the concentration necessary for a play. What can I do instead? I have now explored the resources of modern prose speech in *League of Youth* and I can construct a modern play without relying too obviously upon Scribe. But I have yet to solve the problem of retaining some sort of poetry and grandeur in my dramatic portrayal of modern life—not the poetry of words but of feeling and situation. But I have found out something that may help: I can do quite a lot by manipulating the prosaic details of my plays so that they become theatrical metaphors and come to mean more than what they are; I have used costume in this way, lighting, scenery, landscape, and weather; I have used trivial, everyday things like inky fingers and candles; and I have used living figures as symbols of spiritual forces that act upon the hero. Perhaps these things could be brought into the context of a modern realistic play to help me to portray the modern hero and the tragic conflict which I now understand so well."

I chose *A Doll's House* to show how Ibsen succeeded because it is not generally thought by the public to be a tragedy, and yet Ibsen refers to it in a draft as "The Modern Tragedy." My method will be that of close

analysis of the development of the play, that is to say of the growth of
the play's meaning from first curtain to last, in an endeavor to show how
Ibsen suggests, through devices similar to those that we have observed in
the earlier plays, a tragic struggle that lies behind the trivial anxieties
of a housewife, a struggle involving an heroic figure in conflict with the
secret, powerful, and ineluctable forces of society. If in this brief analysis
the usual regard is not paid to the words, it is not, of course, because I
consider that the words can be ignored, set aside, or in any way demoted
from their rightful role of being the prime agent of communication. But
I am suggesting that Ibsen emphasizes certain parts of the dialogue, and
of the plot, to bring out his tragic pattern. The emphasis is gained partly
by manipulation of prosaic detail, and since this is not a commonly noted
element in Ibsen's plays, I may seem to exaggerate its importance. I do
so only for purposes of demonstration.

The curtain rises, Nora comes in, humming gaily—a happy woman—
a happy mother, for with her comes a Christmas tree carried by a porter
—and a Christmas means parties, and presents, and children. Nora is
not mean with her money: the porter charges 6d, she gives him 1/.
She is childish—she still loves macaroons—she is not above concealing
the fact from her husband: all this we learn about Nora in the first few
seconds of the play, with hardly one important word spoken. Ibsen obviously means to make use of our imagination to construct his characters
from small points in the stage picture and stage action.

It is a charming room. And it is a charming family; we enjoy seeing
this happy mother and her loving husband arguing about money. Perhaps the husband gets a little angry when he reminds Nora that she takes
after her father in her extravagance—"that sort of thing is hereditary"—
but Nora is happy to retort "I wish I had inherited many of Papa's qualities" and that blows over—but we shall remember the reference. They
are both so happy that the visitors who interrupt them stand in cold
contrast. The first is a Mrs. Linde and Ibsen makes a sharp contrast here.
Nora is happy, Mrs. Linde is "downcast and hesitant"; she is pale, thin,
and old, much older than Nora, though they are of the same age. Nora
chatters happily about her family—Mrs. Linde has none—and nothing
to live for besides. Mrs. Linde has had to fight her way in the outside
world by keeping a shop, and school—anything, in fact, to support her
mother and her two young brothers. Now the mother is dead, the boys
grown up, and she is free—but very unhappy to be free. It is true that
we learn that Nora has had some troubles in the past—she has had to
borrow secretly large sums of money to save her husband's health and
even life, and it has been difficult to find the money to repay—but the

contrast still remains between a woman happy because she has her family, and a woman desolate because she is alone.

The first blow to Nora's happiness falls when the maid lets in Krogstad. Clearly his visit worries her, although her words tell us little: when Krogstad goes into Helmer's study, Nora goes at once to the stove and stokes the fire—his presence has chilled her.

It is important to grasp this first hint of unpleasant elements in a Doll's House existence because it is closely followed by the first hint of another kind of unpleasantness in the person of Dr. Rank. Within a few seconds of his entrance he has a very important speech.

> *Nora.* Come, Dr. Rank—you want to live yourself.
> *Rank.* To be sure I do. However wretched I may be, I want to drag on as long as possible. All my patients, too, have the same mania. And *it's the same with people whose complaint* is moral. At this very moment Helmer is talking to just such a moral incurable— . . . a fellow named Krogstad, a man you know nothing about—corrupt to the very core of his character. But even he began by announcing, as a matter of vast importance, that he must live!

Now this speech is very important for two reasons: first, because it shows that Rank, like Nora, has a hidden source of disquiet, a physical one—he is wretched in a way that threatens his life; and second, because his speech equates physical illness with moral illness; so that from this point onwards, Ibsen can use physical illness as a symbol of moral illness.

At this early point in the play, such gloomy notes are muted; we are still to feel that, taking everything into consideration, Nora has been very fortunate in her sheltered existence. But the theme of illness is renewed as the scene closes—Nora invites Rank back for the evening—he accepts, provided that he feels well enough—Ibsen does not intend us to forget the somber theme of disease. Exit Rank, leaving Nora to romp with her children and create an image of family bliss. Krogstad, the moral incurable, enters; the children leave the room and that is the end of Nora's happiness in the play. For Krogstad is not so easily defeated as Nora expected—threat of dismissal makes him merely more dangerous, since his position at the bank means everything to him. He threatens Nora that if she allows Torvald to dismiss him, he will tell her husband that Nora borrowed from him the money needed to send Torvald away for his health—a terrifying threat in itself because Torvald detests borrowing, but horrifying when Krogstad accuses Nora of forging her dying father's signature to get the money, and threatens her with the legal consequences of forgery.

Nora tries to pretend that the *legal* aspect of the affair leaves her unmoved—if the law does not allow a wife to forge when she wants to spare her father anxiety and to save her husband's life, then the law must be stupid. No, she says, it is impossible—she did it for love.

This is not a very sensible attitude to take, but it represents a desperate attempt to protect her threatened Doll's House existence merely by *asserting* that her home, her family, *must* come first, before legal obligations and suchlike—but Ibsen reinforces this impression of her trying to thrust other considerations aside by using the Christmas tree again. Nora asks the maid to bring in the tree, and place it in the middle of the floor.

We, the audience, can see the tree, suggestive of family security and happiness, set defiantly in the center of the stage to dominate it, as if its mere presence could banish Nora's troubles. It is a visual equivalent of Nora's obstinate, but uncertain, persistence that everything will be all right, merely because she says so.

But of course mere assertion that her Doll's House values are right, and the values of the outside world are wrong, is useless. Nora soon gets a worse shock; she learns something which terrifies her far more than the threat of mere legal action: her husband, in all innocence, points out that Krogstad's real crime was not forgery, but concealment of forgery. That made him deceitful, and since then he has contaminated his own children with his own moral sickness.

This revelation causes a number of our earlier impressions to fuse together into a theme. At once we perceive that Nora too, who is also deceitful in her own way, could perhaps transmit moral corruption to her own children; and we have seen, in the figure of Dr. Rank, how terribly a parent can ruin a child. Nora now believes that she is corrupt because of her deceitfulness; she is terrified to think that she may corrupt and poison her own children with a moral corruption as foul as Rank's physical sickness. Rank gives us the size of the horror she faces.

At the curtain of Act I, Nora is still trying to convince herself that this new danger of contaminating her children morally is no more real than the earlier legal threat from Krogstad. "Corrupt *my* children!—Poison *my* home! It's not true! It can never, never be true!"—but her face is "pale with terror"—and she now believes that the poison of moral corruption runs in her veins. She is fighting against Death.

So Nora faces two terrors—the threat of legal action and disgrace, leading to the destruction of her Doll's House; and the certainty of moral disaster for her children if she continues as their mother. The joy has gone out of family life, and Ibsen provides a fitting stage picture for her anguish. She has tried to push away the threats by mere assertion of her own standards—and Ibsen brought the Christmas tree into the center of the stage picture; but now, as the curtain goes up on Act II a day later, we can see from the set that she no longer hopes to succeed—she is terrified now, the family unity and gaiety are spoiled, she will not, dare not, play with the children—and the Christmas tree has been pushed into a corner of the room, it is stripped of ornament, and the candles are burnt out. What a fine symbol of dejection.

Now that Nora is firmly established as in some sense a spiritual incurable, the link between her and Rank, the physical incurable, is immeasurably strengthened. Early in Act II, we hear all about the spinal disease he inherited from his father—and from then on we can see both Rank and Nora as carriers of an obscure and secret poison slowly killing them.

This is not Rank's play, it is Nora's. Rank is a minor character—but he plays a vital dramatic role. His function is to act as the physical embodiment, visible on the stage,[3] of Nora's moral situation as she sees it. Nora is almost hysterical with terror at the thought of her situation—almost, but it is part of her character that with great heroism she keeps her fears secret to herself; and it is because of her reticence that Rank is dramatically necessary, to symbolize the horror she will not talk about. Nora feels, and we feel, the full awfulness of Rank's illness, and she transfers to herself the same feeling about the moral corruption which she imagines herself to carry. Nora sees herself, and we see her seeing herself (with our judgment reserved), as suffering from a moral disease as mortal, as irremediable as Rank's disease, a disease that creeps on to a fatal climax. This is the foe that Nora is fighting so courageously.

Nora tries to relieve the superficial part of her anxiety by persuading Torvald to let Krogstad have his job back—that might save her from public disgrace—but she only makes her deeper anxiety worse, because Torvald loses patience and reminds her that her own father was not above suspicion—this increases her sense of being corrupt, because, we recall, she inherited some qualities from her father. And her sense of being infectious, of being a danger to her family as Rank's father proved to him, is increased when Torvald expansively tries to soothe her by saying that of course he would take upon his own shoulders whatever evil threatened her. So her deceit will ruin not only herself by public disgrace, and her children, but her beloved husband. This is the last straw. She now feels a moral leper. Torvald's self-sacrifice would be wonderful,

---

[3] Comparison with Lear and Gloucester, mental blinding and physical blinding as a violent comment upon it, is not out of place here. Also perhaps the relationship between Teiresias and Oedipus in Sophocles' *Oedipus Tyrannus*.

but at the same time, terrible. At all costs it must be prevented—and so begins her somber interview with Dr. Rank, her one last chance of getting enough money to buy off Krogstad's revenge and escape death.

This interview, as you all know, is the somewhat puzzling one in which Nora appears to joke about Rank's terrible sickness, to tease him with her silk, flesh-colored stockings, and then, when she seems to have worked him into a state where he would promise her anything, she rejects his offer of devoted service.

I have called the scene somber, without hesitation. First of all, there is the lighting (*during what follows it begins to grow dark*). And then there are the contents of the scene. This, you recall, is Nora's last effort to find a way out of the legal part of her fatal situation, to avoid disgrace and so prevent Torvald's self-sacrifice. We learn at once that Rank too has only one last investigation to make of his diseased body to know with certainty when he will begin to break up—his physical illness creeps on to its climax side by side with Nora's moral and nervous illness. We know very well that Nora is fully informed about the seriousness of Rank's disease—why then should she pretend that it does not exist, or why flippantly attribute it to his father's over-fondness for champagne and truffles? The answer is quite obvious when we read, or hear, this snatch of conversation:

> *Nora.* Why, you're perfectly unreasonable today. I did so want you to be in a really good humor.
> *Rank.* With death staring me in the face?—And to suffer thus for another's sin! Where's the justice of it? And in one way or another you can trace in every family some such inexorable retribution—
> *Nora (stopping her ears).* Nonsense! Nonsense! Now cheer up.

She shuts her ears because she recognizes the situation as her own— Rank suffers for his father's sin, Krogstad's children have been corrupted by their father's moral incurability, Nora fears that she will ruin her own children and poison her home. The interruption proves that she feels the application of what Rank says to herself—and after that, her determined effort to remain bright and cheerful, and to joke Rank into compliance can be seen not as frivolousness, heartless levity, but as a heroic triumph of reticence in the face of the equivalent of death.

But this interview, although it shows Nora at her best, heroically fighting disaster without whimpering, also shows her at her worst. All this sexual teasing of Rank, for example, with her stockings and her tasteless jokes about his disease—as I read it, Ibsen is showing us here the bad results of her upbringing, first by her father and then by her husband.

She can get her own way with men by cajoling, by teasing—and she has learnt no other way more self-respecting. That is why she flirts so cruelly with Rank—not because she gets fun out of it, but because it is the only way she knows of dealing with men. It is the spoilt Nora who does the flirting—it is the heroic woman underneath, the woman of fundamentally sound principles who puts a stop to the nonsense when it begins to offend her sense of rightness. She puts an end to the interview even though it means throwing away her last chance of salvation from a fate that she sees as dreadful.

That is why the scene is important—another instance of heroism.

Nora's doom moves a step nearer: Krogstad calls again, to tell her that instead of informing the police, he intends to blackmail Helmer. This is the end for Nora—when Krogstad leaves, but drops the blackmailing letter into the letter-box, she cries, in genuine anguish, "Torvald, Torvald—now we are lost." Mrs. Linde offers to help by influencing Krogstad and leaves Nora to keep Torvald away from the letter-box until she returns—but so far as Nora is concerned, the end is upon her; as she sees it, the moment has come when the poison must work to its crisis. Like the tarantula's victim, she can only dance a mad dance in a last, vain effort to expel the poison—she expresses her intolerable anxiety in the tarantella.

Now had Ibsen wanted simply to express feverish anxiety, any dance would have served—in fact, in one draft version of the scene, Nora is made to dance Anitra's dance from *Peer Gynt*. But Ibsen chooses the poison-spider dance (and he makes sure that we know it *is* a tarantella, by naming it enough times), because it is so appropriate to the theme of disease and death, this picture he has created of Nora suffering from the slow, malignant working within her of a secret moral disease, and it helps again to link her with Rank.

Nora has shot her bolt—she has kept Torvald from reaching the letters, but she no longer hopes to avoid the inevitable—only to postpone the wonderful but terrible moment when she must kill herself to prevent Torvald from assuming the burden of sin.

The last act opens—it is nighttime. Mrs. Linde is waiting for Krogstad to call while the Helmers are upstairs at the fancy-dress party where Nora is to perform her tarantella. Mrs. Linde once loved Krogstad, and proposes marriage to him now. He accepts. A piece of machinery out of a well-made play—the secondary characters are being tidied up, the villain is being reformed in the most economical way. But why bother to reform the villain? For Mrs. Linde after all refuses to let him demand

back his black-mailing letter. No, the real point of the scene is to demonstrate the one fundamental truth about women.

> I need someone to be a mother to, and your children need a mother.
> You need me, and I—I need you.

This is Mrs. Linde speaking, the woman who at the beginning of the
play had nothing to live for, who had earned her own living, mixed with
the outer world, and found life profoundly depressing and aimless without the anchor of a husband and children. This scene describes for us
in advance the painful void into which Nora consigns herself at the end
of the play. "What a change!" says Mrs. Linde, "what a change! To have
someone to work for, to live for, a home to make happy!"—immediately
before the entrance of Nora, who is to lose all this.

Nora's costume, as she enters from the ball upstairs, makes a strong impression on us. She wears the Italian costume appropriate to her character as a girl from Capri, with a large black shawl over it. Festival and
funeral combined. Or, to be more precise, make-belief and death, although in the nature of things, precision here is impossible. The fancy
dress suggests to us that she still inhabits that world of make-belief, the
Doll's House, with its fictitious values; the black suggests to us her
thoughts of suicide to end her sickness. And the costume suggests this
without Nora's having to say one unrealistic word of self-revelation.

Ibsen also emphasizes the climax of the disease and death theme by
bringing on Rank. Nora has danced her tarantella at the party upstairs—
her last fling. At the same party, Rank had enjoyed his last fling—at the
champagne—before retiring to his death-bed. The last link which Ibsen
forges between the two victims of poison and corruption is that their
deathwarrants share the same letter-box: Rank leaves behind him a visit-
ing-card marked with a black cross, a sign that he has crawled away to
die; the card lies beside Krogstad's letter to Torvald, and when Torvald
reads that, Nora must die so as not to inflict her moral disease on others;
physical and moral corruption are to burn themselves out together.

She waits for the right moment, when Torvald promises again to
shoulder his wife's burdens. He, of course, is merely romanticizing; she
takes him seriously, and sends him off to read the fatal letter. She will go
out and drown herself to prevent this heroic sacrifice.

This is women's magazine stuff—but we must remember that Nora
has no means of finding out that her Doll's House standards and values
are all of that order. And she believes in them still with desperate
earnestness. That is why we see her in fancy dress, the dress of illusion,
while the intensity of her resolve to die, which in poetic drama would

have merited a soliloquy, is compressed into a detail of costume. Reticence is preserved, but so is emotional color: as she prepares to leave the house, she covers herself in black; she puts on her black shawl again, and Helmer's black evening cloak. We thereby *see* her attitude of mind —and this is Ibsen's comment, not Nora's self-dramatization.

You all remember what happens. Helmer does not perform a miracle when he reads Krogstad's black-mailing letter. He explodes into vulgar rage—he calls his wife a hypocrite, a liar, a criminal; he throws her father into her face: "I ought to have foreseen it. All your father's want of principle—all your father's want of principle you have inherited— no religion, no morality, no sense of duty!" This is an aspect of the problem which had not occurred to Nora before—but she remains quiet —perhaps she is a victim like Rank, as well as a carrier of corruption.

The miracle has not happened. Nora realizes that she has been living an illusion; and one does not die for illusions if one recognizes them for such. It is irrelevant to her that a note should arrive from Krogstad returning her I. O. U.'s, that Helmer should say, with sickening egotism, "I am saved! Nora, I am saved." That part of her problem, the legal or public side now assumes its rightful place as trivial compared with the moral problem, which remains. Nora realizes numbly that her life has been an elaborate make-belief. She does not say so just yet—she is cold, almost silent. But her costume speaks for her. As she discards her illusions, so she discards her fancy-dress and her black cloak and shawl, and appears in her everyday dress—to symbolize her entry into a world of cold fact and commonsense.

From her new, sad viewpoint, her notion of heredity becomes as wide as ours, the audience's, has long become. She agrees that she is not fit, in her present state of moral health, to have charge of the education of her children. But Helmer's words have made her bitterly aware that the poison did not originate with her:

> I have had great injustice done me, Torvald, first by father, and then by you.

They have both treated her as a doll-child. It is the men who run society who have condemned Nora to a stultifying life. That is the real crime, the real corruption, as she clearly sees, not her forgery or her little lies, but the male conspiracy to debase the female; and she now recognizes that she had begun to bring up her own children as if they too were dolls. It is the Doll's House attitude that is the corruption which must not be transmitted. She must go into a hostile world and educate herself.

She does not say much about how she expects to enjoy this new life, but Ibsen has already prepared us—from the point for point contrast with Mrs. Linde, we realize that Nora leaves the play as Mrs. Linde entered it—lonely, unhappy, with no one to love or live for, and much, much older; and from the parallel with Rank we get the impression that her going out into the alien world beyond the Doll's House is like Rank's departure out of life altogether: the culmination of a long, painful, and fatal illness. Her life in the outer world will be a life-in-death. At her final exit, she puts on a black shawl again, to suggest visually the melancholy exile she enters upon with only the hope of a miracle to end it.

What has Ibsen done in this play that he did not do before? He has, above all, exercised the art of concentration. He has written a modern play about a modern woman in a modern situation, but he adds new stature and a new dimension to it by concentrating different kinds of imagery to suggest that society works upon Nora like some dreadful, hidden, and inexorable disease. The final draft version of the play lacks this concentration, and this power. He guides our attention to this theme through his verbal imagery (e.g., Rank's first speech), but he maintains it by a concentration of suggestive detail—Nora's black shawl, the sympathetic night light of Act III, the figure of Rank, the tarantella-dance— all of these help to create the sense of fatality; and Nora's consistent fight against that, a fight in which she will sacrifice no basic principles however desperate her situation, makes her into a heroine. Ibsen has discovered his modern hero.

I suggest that it was some such vision that Ibsen had in mind when he called the play "The Modern Tragedy." I suggest that you will find themes of similar or greater majesty created in later plays, which must be seen not as realistic plays, or, in contradiction, as plays full of verbal symbolism, but as plays filled with metaphors and images drawn from the whole range of theatrical material; plays filled thereby with a sense of the poetry of life, even of modern life. My point may be summarized if I say that Ibsen's prose plays present the poetry of life in the imagery of the theater. In that sense, I, a foreigner, can salute Ibsen as a great poet.

Ghosts: The Tragic Rhythm in a Small Figure

by Francis Fergusson

The Plot of Ghosts: Thesis, Thriller, and Tragedy

Ghosts is not Ibsen's best play, but it serves my purpose, which is to study the foundations of modern realism, just because of its imperfections. Its power, and the poetry of some of its effects, are evident; yet a contemporary audience may be bored with its old-fashioned iconoclasm and offended by the clatter of its too-obviously well-made plot. On the surface it is a *drame à thèse*, of the kind Brieux was to develop to its logical conclusion twenty years later: it proves the hollowness of the conventional bourgeois marriage. At the same time it is a thriller with all the tricks of the Boulevard entertainment: Ibsen was a student of Scribe in his middle period. But underneath this superficial form of thesis-thriller—the play which Ibsen started to write, the angry diatribe as he first conceived it—there is another form, the shape of the underlying action, which Ibsen gradually made out in the course of his two-years' labor upon the play, in obedience to his scruple of truthfulness, his profound attention to the reality of his fictive characters' lives. The form of the play is understood according to two conceptions of plot, which Ibsen himself did not at this point clearly distinguish: the rationalized concatenation of events with a univocal moral, and the plot as the "soul" or first actualization of the directly perceived action.

Halvdan Koht, in his excellent study *Henrik Ibsen,* has explained the circumstances under which *Ghosts* was written. It was first planned as an attack upon marriage, in answer to the critics of *A Doll's House.* The story of the play is perfectly coherent as the demonstration and illustration of this thesis. When the play opens, Captain Alving has just died,

"*Ghosts:* The Tragic Rhythm in a Small Figure" by Francis Fergusson. (Original title: "*Ghosts:* The Theater of Modern Realism".) From *The Idea of a Theater* by Francis Fergusson (Princeton: Princeton University Press, 1949). Copyright 1949 by Princeton University Press. Reprinted by permission of the author and Princeton University Press.

his son Oswald is back from Paris where he had been studying painting, and his wife is straightening out the estate. The Captain had been accepted locally as a pillar of society but was in secret a drunkard and debauchee. He had seduced his wife's maid, and had a child by her; and this child, Regina, is now in her turn Mrs. Alving's maid. Mrs. Alving had concealed all this for something like twenty years. She was following the advice of the conventional Pastor Manders and endeavoring to save Oswald from the horrors of the household: it was for this reason she had sent him away to school. But now, with her husband's death, she proposes to get rid of the Alving heritage in all its forms, in order to free herself and Oswald for the innocent, unconventional "joy of life." She wants to endow an orphanage with the Captain's money, both to quiet any rumors there may be of his sinful life and to get rid of the remains of his power over her. She encounters this power, however, in many forms, through the Pastor's timidity and through the attempt by Engstrand (a local carpenter who was bribed to pretend to be Regina's father) to blackmail her. Oswald wants to marry Regina and has to be told the whole story. At last he reveals that he has inherited syphilis from his father—the dead hand of the past in its most sensationally ugly form —and when his brain softens at the end, Mrs. Alving's whole plan collapses in unrelieved horror. It is "proved" that she should have left home twenty years before, like Nora in *A Doll's House;* and that conventional marriage is therefore an evil tyranny.

In accordance with the principles of the thesis play, *Ghosts* is plotted as a series of debates on conventional morality, between Mrs. Alving and the Pastor, the Pastor and Oswald, and Oswald and his mother. It may also be read as a perfect well-made thriller. The story is presented with immediate clarity, with mounting and controlled suspense; each act ends with an exciting curtain which reaffirms the issues and promises important new developments. In this play, as in so many others, one may observe that the conception of dramatic form underlying the thesis play and the machine-made Boulevard entertainment is the same: the logically concatenated series of events (intriguing thesis or logical intrigue) which the characters and their relationships merely illustrate. And it was this view of *Ghosts* which made it an immediate scandal and success.

But Ibsen himself protested that he was not a reformer but a poet. He was often led to write by anger and he compared the process of composition to his pet scorpion's emptying of poison; Ibsen kept a piece of soft fruit in his cage for the scorpion to sting when the spirit moved him. But Ibsen's own **spirit** was not satisfied by the mere discharge of venom; and one may see, in *Ghosts*, behind the surfaces of the savage story, a partially realized tragic form of really poetic scope, the result of Ibsen's more serious and disinterested brooding upon the human condition in general, where it underlies the myopic rebellions and empty clichés of the time.

In order to see the tragedy behind the thesis, it is necessary to return to the distinction between plot and action, and to the distinction between the plot as the rationalized series of events, and the plot as "the soul of the tragedy." The action of the play is "to control the Alving heritage for my own life." Most of the characters want some material or social advantage from it—Engstrand money, for instance, and the Pastor the security of conventional respectability. But Mrs. Alving is seeking a true and free human life itself—for her son, and through him, for herself. Mrs. Alving sometimes puts this quest in terms of the iconoclasms of the time, but her spiritual life, as Ibsen gradually discovered it, is at a deeper level; she tests everything—Oswald, the Pastor, Regina, her own moves—in the light of her extremely strict if unsophisticated moral sensibility: by direct perception and not by ideas at all. She is tragically seeking; she suffers a series of pathoses and new insights in the course of the play; and this rhythm of will, feeling, and insight underneath the machinery of the plot is the form of the life of the play, the soul of the tragedy.

The similarity between *Ghosts* and Greek tragedy, with its single fated action moving to an unmistakable catastrophe, has been felt by many critics of Ibsen. Mrs. Alving, like Oedipus, is engaged in a quest for her true human condition; and Ibsen, like Sophocles, shows on-stage only the end of this quest, when the past is being brought up again in the light of the present action and its fated outcome. From this point of view Ibsen is a plot-maker in the first sense: by means of his selection and arrangement of incidents he defines an action underlying many particular events and realized in various modes of intelligible purpose, of suffering, and of new insight. What Mrs. Alving sees changes in the course of the play, just as what Oedipus sees changes as one veil after another is removed from the past and the present. The underlying form of *Ghosts* is that of the tragic rhythm as one finds it in *Oedipus Rex*.

But this judgment needs to be qualified in several respects: because of the theater for which Ibsen wrote, the tragic form which Sophocles could develop to the full, and with every theatrical resource, is hidden beneath the clichés of plot and the surfaces "evident to the most commonplace mind." At the end of the play the tragic rhythm of Mrs. Alving's quest is not so much completed as brutally truncated, in obedience to the requirements of the thesis and the thriller. Oswald's collapse, before our eyes, with his mother's screaming, makes the intrigue end with a bang, and hammers home the thesis. But from the point of view of Mrs. Alving's tragic quest as we have seen it develop through the rest of the play, this conclusion concludes nothing: it is merely sensational.

The exciting intrigue and the brilliantly, the violently clear surfaces of *Ghosts* are likely to obscure completely its real life and underlying form. The tragic rhythm, which Ibsen rediscovered by his long and loving attention to the reality of his fictive lives, is evident only to the histrionic sensibility. As Henry James put it, Ibsen's characters "have the extraordinary, the brilliant property of becoming when represented at once more abstract and more living": i.e., both their lives and the life of the play, the spiritual content and the form of the whole, are revealed in this medium. A Nazimova, a Duse, could show it to us on the stage. Lacking such a performance, the reader must endeavor to respond imaginatively and directly himself if he is to see the hidden poetry of *Ghosts*.

Mrs. Alving and Oswald: The Tragic Rhythm in a Small Figure

As Ibsen was fighting to present his poetic vision within the narrow theater admitted by modern realism, so his protagonist Mrs. Alving is fighting to realize her sense of human life in the blank photograph of her own stuffy parlor. She discovers there no means, no terms, and no nourishment; that is the truncated tragedy which underlies the savage thesis of the play. But she does find her son Oswald, and she makes of him the symbol of all she is seeking: freedom, innocence, joy, and truth. At the level of the life of the play, where Ibsen warms his characters into extraordinary human reality, they all have moral and emotional meanings for each other; and the pattern of their related actions, their partially blind struggle for the Alving heritage, is consistent and very complex. In this structure, Mrs. Alving's changing relation to Oswald is only one strand, though an important one. I wish to consider it as a sample of Ibsen's rediscovery, through modern realism, of the tragic rhythm.

Oswald is of course not only a symbol for his mother, but a person in his own right, with his own quest for freedom and release, and his own anomalous stake in the Alving heritage. He is also a symbol for Pastor Manders of what he wants from Captain Alving's estate: the stability and continuity of the bourgeois conventions. In the economy of the play as a whole, Oswald is the hidden reality of the whole situation, like Oedipus' actual status as son-husband: the hidden fatality which, revealed in a series of tragic and ironic steps, brings the final peripety of the action. To see how this works, the reader is asked to consider Oswald's role in Act I and the beginning of Act II.

The main part of Act I (after a prologue between Regina and Engstrand) is a debate, or rather agon, between Mrs. Alving and the Pastor. The Pastor has come to settle the details of Mrs. Alving's bequest of her husband's money to the orphanage. They at once disagree about the purpose and handling of the bequest; and this disagreement soon broadens into the whole issue of Mrs. Alving's emancipation versus the Pastor's conventionality. The question of Oswald is at the center. The Pastor wants to think of him, and to make of him, a pillar of society such as the Captain was supposed to have been, while Mrs. Alving wants him to be her masterpiece of liberation. At this point Oswald himself wanders in, the actual but still mysterious truth underlying the dispute between his mother and the Pastor. His appearance produces what the Greeks would have called a complex recognition scene, with an implied peripety for both Mrs. Alving and the Pastor, which will not be realized by them until the end of the act. But this tragic development is written to be acted; it is to be found, not so much in the actual words of the characters, as in their moral-emotional responses and changing relationships to one another.

The Pastor has not seen Oswald since he grew up; and seeing him now he is startled as though by a real ghost; he recognizes him as the very reincarnation of his father: the same physique, the same mannerisms, even the same kind of pipe. Mrs. Alving with equal confidence recognizes him as her own son, and she notes that his mouth-mannerism is like the Pastor's. (She had been in love with the Pastor during the early years of her marriage, when she wanted to leave the Captain.) As for Oswald himself, the mention of the pipe gives him a Proustian intermittence of the heart: he suddenly recalls a childhood scene when his father had given him his own pipe to smoke. He feels again the nausea and the cold sweat, and hears the Captain's hearty laughter. Thus in effect he recognizes himself as his father's, in the sense of his father's *victim;* a premonition of the ugly scene at the end of the play. But at this point no one is prepared to accept the full import of these insights. The whole scene is, on the surface, light and conventional, an accurate report of a passage of provincial politeness. Oswald wanders off for a walk before dinner, and the Pastor and his mother are left to bring their struggle more into the open.

Oswald's brief scene marks the end of the first round of the fight, and serves as prologue for the second round, much as the intervention of the chorus in the agon between Oedipus and Tiresias punctuates their struggle, and hints at an unexpected outcome on a new level of awareness. As soon as Oswald has gone, the Pastor launches an attack in form upon Mrs. Alving's entire emancipated way of life, with the question of Oswald, his role in the community, his upbringing and his future, always at the center of the attack. Mrs. Alving replies with her whole rebellious philosophy, illustrated by a detailed account of her tormented life with the Captain, none of which the Pastor had known (or been willing to recognize) before. Mrs. Alving proves on the basis of this evidence that her new freedom is right; that her long secret rebellion was justified; and that she is now about to complete Oswald's emancipation, and thereby her own, from the swarming ghosts of the past. If the issue were merely on this rationalistic level, and between her and the Pastor, she would triumph at this point. But the real truth of her situation (as Oswald's appearance led us to suppose) does not fit either her rationalization or the Pastor's.

Oswald passes through the parlor again on his way to the dining room to get a drink before dinner, and his mother watches him in pride and pleasure. But from behind the door we hear the affected squealing of Regina. It is now Mrs. Alving's turn for an intermittence of the heart: it is as though she heard again her husband with Regina's mother. The insight which she had rejected before now reaches her in full strength, bringing the promised pathos and peripety; she sees Oswald, not as her masterpiece of liberation, but as the sinister, tyrannical, and continuing life of the past itself. The basis of her rationalization is gone; she suffers the breakdown of the moral being which she had built upon her now exploded view of Oswald.

At this point Ibsen brings down the curtain in obedience to the principles of the well-made play. The effect is to raise the suspense by stimulating our curiosity about the facts of the rest of the story. What will Mrs. Alving do now? What will the Pastor do—for Oswald and Regina are half-brother and sister; can we prevent the scandal from coming out? So the suspense is raised, but the attention of the audience is diverted from Mrs. Alving's tragic quest to the most literal, newspaper version of the facts.

The second act (which occurs immediately after dinner) is ostensibly concerned only with these gossipy facts. The Pastor and Mrs. Alving debate ways of handling the threatened scandal. But this is only the literal surface: Ibsen has his eye upon Mrs. Alving's shaken psyche, and the actual dramatic form of this scene, under the discussion which Mrs. Alving keeps up, is her pathos which the Act I curtain broke off. Mrs. Alving is suffering the blow in courage and faith; and she is rewarded with her deepest insight:

> I am half inclined to think we are all ghosts, Mr. Manders. It is not only what we have inherited from our fathers and mothers that exists again in us, but all sorts of dead ideas and all kinds of old dead beliefs and things of that kind. They are not actually alive in us; but they are dormant all the same, and we can never be rid of them. Whenever I take up a newspaper and read it, I fancy I see ghosts creeping between the lines. There must be ghosts all over the world. They must be as countless as the grains of sand, it seems to me. And we are so miserably afraid of the light, all of of us.[1]

This passage, in the fumbling phrases of Ibsen's provincial lady, and in William Archer's translation, is not by itself the poetry of the great dramatic poets. It does not have the verbal music of Racine, nor the freedom and sophistication of Hamlet, nor the scope of the Sophoclean chorus, with its use of the full complement of poetic and musical and theatrical resources. But in the total situation in the Alving parlor which Ibsen has so carefully established, and in terms of Mrs. Alving's uninstructed but profoundly developing awareness, it has its own hidden poetry: a poetry not of words but of the theater, a poetry of the histrionic sensibility. From the point of view of the underlying form of the play—the form as "the soul" of the tragedy—this scene completes the sequence which began with the debate in Act I: it is the pathos-and-epiphany following that agon.

It is evident, I think, that insofar as Ibsen was able to obey his realistic scruple, his need for the disinterested perception of human life beneath the clichés of custom and rationalization, he rediscovered the perennial basis of tragedy. The poetry of *Ghosts* is under the words, in the detail of action, where Ibsen accurately sensed the tragic rhythm of human life in a thousand small figures. And these little "movements of the psyche" are composed in a complex rhythm like music, a formal development sustained (beneath the sensational story and the angry thesis) until the very end. But the action is not completed: Mrs. Alving is left screaming with the raw impact of the calamity. The music is broken off, the dissonance unresolved—or, in more properly dramatic terms, the acceptance of the catastrophe, leading to the final vision or epiphany which should correspond to the insight Mrs. Alving gains in Act II, is lacking. The action of the play is neither completed nor placed

---

[1] *Ghosts,* by Henrik Ibsen. Translated by William Archer.

in the wider context of meanings which the disinterested or contemplative purposes of poetry demand.

The unsatisfactory end of *Ghosts* may be understood in several ways. Thinking of the relation between Mrs. Alving and Oswald, one might say that she had romantically loaded more symbolic values upon her son than a human being can carry; hence his collapse proves too much —more than Mrs. Alving or the audience can digest. One may say that, at the end, Ibsen himself could not quite dissociate himself from his rebellious protagonist and see her action in the round, and so broke off in anger, losing his tragic vision in the satisfaction of reducing the bourgeois parlor to a nightmare, and proving the hollowness of a society which sees human life in such myopic and dishonest terms. As a thesis play, *Ghosts* is an ancestor of many related genres: Brieux's arguments for social reform, propaganda plays like those of the Marxists, or parables *à la* Andreev, or even Shaw's more generalized plays of the play-of-thought about social questions. But this use of the theater of modern realism for promoting or discussing political and social ideas never appealed to Ibsen. It did not solve his real problem, which was to use the publicly accepted theater of his time for poetic purposes. The most general way to understand the unsatisfactory end of *Ghosts* is to say that Ibsen could not find a way to represent the action of his protagonist, with all its moral and intellectual depth, within the terms of modern realism. In the attempt he truncated this action, and revealed as in a brilliant light the limitations of the bourgeois parlor as the scene of human life.

The End of Ghosts: *The Tasteless Parlor and the Stage of Europe*

Oswald is the chief symbol of what Mrs. Alving is seeking, and his collapse ends her quest in a horrifying catastrophe. But in the complex life of the play, all of the persons and things acquire emotional and moral significance for Mrs. Alving; and at the end, to throw as much light as possible upon the catastrophe, Ibsen brings all of the elements of his composition together in their highest symbolic valency. The orphanage has burned to the ground; the Pastor has promised Engstrand money for his "Sailor's Home" which he plans as a brothel; Regina departs, to follow her mother in the search for pleasure and money. In these eventualities the conventional morality of the Alving heritage is revealed as lewdness and dishonesty, quickly consumed in the fires of lust and greed, as Oswald himself (the central symbol) was consumed

even before his birth. But what does this wreckage mean? Where are we
to place it in human experience? Ibsen can only place it in the literal
parlor, with lamplight giving place to daylight, and sunrise on the
empty, stimulating, virginal snow-peaks out the window. The emotional
force of this complicated effect is very great; it has the searching intimacy
of nightmare. But it is also as disquieting as a nightmare from which we
are suddenly awakened; it is incomplete, and the contradiction between
the inner power of dream and the literal appearances of the daylight
world is unresolved. The spirit that moved Ibsen to write the play, and
which moved his protagonist through her tragic progress, is lost to sight,
disembodied, imperceptible in any form unless the dreary exaltation of
the inhuman mountain scene conveys it in feeling.

Henry James felt very acutely the contradiction between the deep and
strict spirit of Ibsen and his superb craftsmanship on one side, and the
little scene he tried to use—the parlor in its surrounding void—on the
other.

> If the spirit is a lamp within us, glowing through what the world and the
> flesh make of us as through a ground-glass shade, then such pictures as
> Little Eyolf and John Gabriel are each a chassez-croisez of lamps burning,
> as in tasteless parlors, with the flame practically exposed. There is a positive
> odor of spiritual paraffin. The author nevertheless arrives at the drama-
> tist's great goal—he arrives for all his meagerness at intensity. The meager-
> ness, which is after all but an unconscious, an admirable economy, never
> interferes with that: it plays straight into the hands of his rare mastery of
> form. The contrast between this form—so difficult to have reached, so
> "evolved," so civilized—and the bareness and bleakness of his little northern
> democracy is the source of half the hard frugal charm he puts forth.[2]

James had rejected very early in his career his own little northern
democracy, that of General Grant's America, with its ugly parlor, its
dead conventions, its enthusiastic materialism, and its "non-conducting
atmosphere." At the same time he shared Ibsen's ethical preoccupation,
and his strict sense of form. His comments on Ibsen are at once the
most sympathetic and the most objective that have been written. But
James's own solution was to try to find a better parlor for the theater
of human life; to present the quest of his American pilgrim of culture
on the wider "stage of Europe" as this might still be felt and suggested
in the manners of the leisured classes in England and France. James
would have nothing to do with the prophetic and revolutionary spirit
which was driving the great continental authors, Ibsen among them.
In his artistry and his moral exactitude Ibsen is akin to James; but this

[2] *London Notes,* Jan.-Aug., 1897.

is not his whole story, and if one is to understand the spirit he tried to realize in Mrs. Alving, one must think of Kierkegaard, who had a great influence on Ibsen in the beginning of his career.

Kierkegaard (in *For Self-Examination*) has this to say of the disembodied and insatiable spirit of the times:

> . . . thou wilt scarcely find anyone who does not believe in—let us say, for example, the spirit of the age, the *Zeitgeist*. Even he who has taken leave of higher things and is rendered blissful by mediocrity, yea, even he who toils slavishly for paltry ends or in the contemptible servitude of ill-gotten gains, even he believes, firmly and fully too, in the spirit of the age. Well, that is natural enough, it is by no means anything very lofty he believes in, for the spirit of the age is after all no higher than the age, it keeps close to the ground, so that it is the sort of spirit which is most like will-o'-the-wisp; but yet he believes in spirit. Or he believes in the world-spirit (*Weltgeist*) that strong spirit (for allurements, yes), the ingenious spirit (for deceits, yes); that spirit which Christianity calls an evil spirit— so that, in consideration of this, it is by no means anything very lofty he believes in when he believes in the world-spirit; but yet he believes in spirit. Or he believes in "the spirit of humanity," not spirit in the individual, but in the race, that spirit which, when it is god-forsaken for having forsaken God, is again, according to Christianity's teaching, an evil spirit—so that in view of this it is by no means anything very lofty he believes in when he believes in this spirit; but yet he believes in spirit. On the other hand, as soon as the talk is about a holy spirit—how many, dost thou think, believe in it? Or when the talk is about an evil spirit which is to be renounced—how many, dost thou think, believe in such a thing?[3]

This description seems to me to throw some light upon Mrs. Alving's quest, upon Ibsen's modern-realistic scene, and upon the theater which his audience would accept. The other face of nineteenth century positivism is romantic aspiration. And Ibsen's realistic scene presents both of these aspects of the human condition: the photographically accurate parlor, in the foreground, satisfies the requirements of positivism, while the empty but stimulating scene out the window—Europe as a moral void, an uninhabited wilderness—offers as it were a blank check to the insatiate spirit. Ibsen always felt this exhilarating wilderness behind his cramped interiors. In *A Doll's House* we glimpse it as winter weather and black water. In *The Lady from the Sea* it is the cold ocean, with its whales and its gulls. In *The Wild Duck* it is the northern marshes, with wildfowl but no people. In the last scene of *Ghosts* it is, of course, the bright snow-peaks, which may mean Mrs. Alving's quest in its most

[3] Kierkegaard, *For Self-Examination and Judge for Yourselves* (Princeton University Press, 1944), p. 94.

disembodied and ambivalent form; very much the same sensuous moral void in which Wagner, having totally rejected the little human foreground where Ibsen fights his battles, unrolls the solitary action of passion. It is the "stage of Europe" before human exploration, as it might have appeared to the first hunters.

There is a kinship between the fearless and demanding spirit of Kierkegaard, and the spirit which Ibsen tried to realize in Mrs. Alving. But Mrs. Alving, like her contemporaries whom Kierkegaard describes, will not or cannot accept any interpretation of the spirit that drives her. It may look like the *Weltgeist* when she demands the joy of living, it may look like the Holy Ghost itself when one considers her appetite for truth. And it may look like the spirit of evil, a "goblin damned," when we see the desolation it produces. If one thinks of the symbols which Ibsen brings together in the last scene: the blank parlor, the wide unexplored world outside, the flames that consumed the Alving heritage and the sunrise flaming on the peaks, one may be reminded of the condition of Dante's great rebel Ulysses. He too is wrapped in the flame of his own consciousness, yet still dwells in the pride of the mind and the exhilaration of the world free of people, *il mondo senza gente*. But this analogy also may not be pressed too far. Ulysses is in hell; and when we explore the Mountain on which he was wrecked, we can place his condition with finality, and in relation to many other human modes of action and awareness. But Mrs. Alving's mountains do not place her anywhere: the realism of modern realism ends with the literal. Beyond that is not the ordered world of the tradition, but *Unendlichkeit,* and the anomalous "freedom" of undefined and uninformed aspiration.

Perhaps Mrs. Alving and Ibsen himself are closer to the role of Dante than to the role of Ulysses, seeing a hellish mode of being, but free to move on. Certainly Ibsen's development continued beyond *Ghosts,* and toward the end of his career he came much closer to achieving a consistent theatrical poetry within the confines of the theater of modern realism. He himself remarked that his poetry was to be found only in the series of his plays, no one of which was complete by itself.

Illusion and the Self in *The Wild Duck*, *Rosmersholm*, and *The Lady from the Sea*

by Robert Raphael

A conscious and, it often seems, purposeful development of ideas appears to form in Ibsen a philosophical, if not dramatic, totality beyond the limits of any single drama, so that a convenient way to approach the whole is not so much by parts as by the revelation of some salient philosophical trend which can be seen clearly to evolve throughout at least a large grouping of the plays, but preferably in the entire body of mature works. I shall confine myself to the problem of illusion and the self, a problem which commences in a major key with what are commonly considered to be the first three plays of Ibsen's late period: *The Wild Duck* (1884), *Rosmersholm* (1886), and *The Lady from the Sea* (1888).

Illusion first assumes the proportions of a major philosophical theme in Ibsen's *Weltanschauung* with *The Wild Duck*. Actually *The Wild Duck* is a play about two kinds of illusion: traditional and transcendental. Illusion is self-deception and, quite obviously, a very common mode of human behavior. Its function is to provide the personality with fixed patterns of value, which are nothing but orientative patterns in the mind that guarantee a certain amount of meaningful continuity to it beyond the randomness and disturbance of external data and experience. These valuable orientations tend to sustain the personality in its constant struggle with reality, so that it is not surprising to find that against such strongly fixed patterns of illusion the reality often is as nothing. Reality, after all, exists to suit and confirm the orientative patterns in the mind and, except in strictly scientific method, not the reverse.

In the Ekdal household, and especially for old Ekdal and little Hedvig, value is provided by the attic which contains a wild duck, along with

"Illusion and the Self in *The Wild Duck, Rosmersholm,* and *The Lady from the Sea*" by Robert Raphael. From *Scandinavian Studies,* 35:1 (February 1963), 37-50. Copyright © 1963 by *Scandinavian Studies.* Reprinted by permission of the author and *Scandinavian Studies.*

many other treasures of illusion such as unusual pigeons and rabbits which thrive in a game forest invented by old Ekdal with five withered Christmas trees. Old Ekdal hunts there, carrying a gun that is very old. For Hedvig there is an old giant clock that no longer runs, and cupboards full of interesting books like a *History of London* with its numerous illustrations of castles and churches and great sailing ships. Hedvig and her grandfather approach their world with a devotion and ritual akin to religious reverence, for the attic with the duck and other treasures may be considered a metaphor for the Christian paradise: it performs in their lives exactly the same function as does a traditional church for many people. Existing on the top floor of the Ekdal microcosm, the attic is the *summum bonum* in their lives; it provides them, just like heaven, with a world of pure value, a realm of nearly perfect orientation. The Ekdals keep returning to this private religion for sustenance just as people do with any traditional illusion that is sacred to them. Significantly enough, this whole realm of self-deception, in fact everything in the Ekdal existence, has come at one time or another from wise old Werle, the merchant and manufacturer. Actually, Werle has given them not only the wild duck, but also—like some god—he has fashioned into their lives all the major values of existence ever since the time, about fifteen years before, when he bestowed single-handedly on Hjalmar Ekdal, the young head of the household, not only his home and his training in photography but even his wife and child. The other objects in the attic come from an old sea captain who once lived there long ago. Hedvig implies that he may be the Flying Dutchman who brought all his treasures from "the bottom of the sea," the sea which invariably serves as a symbol for the unconscious self. In other words, all value has come into their lives from outside. Nothing is their own.

What the attic is for old Ekdal and little Hedvig, Hjalmar Ekdal's great "invention" is for him. Hjalmar cannot indeed give any specific details of this invention; he says only that

> when I resolved to dedicate myself to photography, it wasn't just with the idea of taking portraits of all kinds of everyday people. . . . I swore that were I to consecrate my powers to this craft, I should also exalt it to such a height that it would become both an art and a science. And that is why I decided to make the great invention.[1]

Not surprisingly, this valuable illusion has been purposely brought into his existence from outside, too; this time by Dr. Relling, who cultivated

---

[1] All references to the texts of the dramas are to the *Hundreaarsutgave* of Henrik Ibsen's *Samlede Verker*, 22 volumes (Oslo, 1928-1957). English translations are my own.

Hjalmar's self-deception that he would make some remarkable discovery in photography some day. Whatever originality Hjalmar had, Dr. Relling points out, "was torn out of him completely already in his boyhood." The real Hjalmar, Dr. Relling continues, only "had talent for prettily declaiming the verses and thoughts of others." Hjalmar, Ibsen is saying, is, like most people, merely an imitator; no artist, but only a photographer who is sustained by an illusion of some great invention that never comes off. Value has been introduced for him, as for the rest of the Ekdals, by old Werle and Dr. Relling.

The Ekdal microcosm subsists more or less happily on these traditional illusions for almost fifteen years, until one day young Gregers Werle arrives. Rebelling against his father's wisdom, and admittedly seeking to cure his "sick conscience," Gregers comes knocking at the Ekdals' door with his "claims of the ideal." What Gregers means are the demands of his transcendental illusion. A remark of Sigmund Freud in a letter of August 13, 1937, reads like a commentary on Ibsen's train of thought at this time. Freud writes that "the moment a man questions the meaning and value of life, he is sick, since objectively neither has any existence." [2] We do not have to conjecture whether Gregers is sick; he tells us this himself when he reveals the neurotic motivation behind his life mission by telling his father that "It's thanks to you that I go around hunted and gnawed by a guilt-laden conscience." Gregers now decides to "save" Hjalmar from what he judges to be the falsehood and deception that are ruining him. Ibsen, however, now unmasks the real purpose behind Gregers' missionary zeal with a single stunning stroke when he has him state: "Besides, if I am to go on living I must try to find some cure for my sick conscience." He admits that his motives are entirely selfish; there is no question of any empathy involved. In this way, Ibsen analyzes, or begins to analyze in this play, the whole reason for being of the transcendental hero.

Hjalmar's world of second-hand illusions places him in a rather vulnerable spot when Gregers comes along—he actually moves in with the Ekdals so he can perform at close range—in order to consecrate him and his wife, Gina, to an entirely new way of life, "a communion in truth and without any deception." Hjalmar, we find, is soon declaiming Gregers' thoughts. He interprets the "new life" to his wife and daughter on the authority of "claims of the ideal," which he defines as "certain demands that a person cannot set aside without injuring his soul." Ironically, of course, the claims of the transcendental hero violate the very "soul" which they intend to protect and elevate, for the transcen-

[2] *Letters of Sigmund Freud* (New York, 1960), 436.

dentalist with his sick conscience questions the meaning and value of existence, in fact the very conditions of experience. In itself this is harmless, but Ibsen shows repeatedly from now on that such questioning inevitably gives rise to the religious impulse, which is the impulse to "save" people from their traditional, low-bred orientations, in short, from themselves, by imposing on them a loftier illusion. In this attempt at a noble synthesis of reality with a transcendental ideal, as Ibsen saw it, the missionary not only fails by destroying himself, but also inevitably ends up by wounding and finally destroying the personalities of those who are subjected to his vision. Again and again in Ibsen, beginning with this play, the noble synthesis turns out to be a heroic self-deception, and one that always proves to be a fatal error, whether one is speaking of Gregers Werle or Rosmer, of Solness or Allmers, John Gabriel Borkman or Rubek.

Gregers seeks to redeem the very conditions of experience of the Ekdals by the imposition of his transcendental authority. Fortunately, his aims are thwarted by Dr. Relling, who comes into the sick world as the author's *raisonneur;* a diagnostician and a potential healer in a microcosm that seems to him like one big hospital. In fact, he diagnoses the sickness of the transcendental hero to perfection when he tells Gregers that he suffers from a bad case of "self-righteous fever," and adds that he "always goes around wallowing in a delirium of religious impulse; always must have something to look up to beyond your own limits." Transcendental illusion, the doctor knows, just like traditional illusion, provides a needed screen against the rigor and disturbance of reality; but Relling is keenly aware also that traditional illusion is more preferable by far, since it will not justify the violation of other personalities. The whole world is sick, unfortunately, Dr. Relling says, but the remedy is the purposeful cultivation of stimulating and life-sustaining illusion by anyone who is strong enough to stand alone, and above illusions. Such a man is then in a position to help other people to live their lives by manipulating and sustaining their self-deceptions, both large and small.[3] Gregers' sickness proves to be so insidious that in the end it claims little Hedvig as a victim, for Hjalmar, under Gregers' coaching, has ruthlessly exposed his daughter's illusion of the wild duck. "Life could be quite pleasant after all," the doctor concludes, "if we might only be left in peace by these blasted fools who pester us poor folk with ideal demands." But even though Hedvig is dead, Gregers has learned

---

[3] Ibsen is very explicit about this in his "Second Sketch" for the play, where Relling describes himself as a doctor who must "inject a little illusion" now and then into those about him.

nothing. He states that he shall go on with his mission of being the thirteenth man at table. His allusion to the New Testament Christ here is obvious.

Dr. Relling's whole point is that the attic permits people to *live*, whereas the transcendental ideal of Gregers is an illusion that is neither stimulating nor life-sustaining; it is, in fact, destructive, for it claims the life of Hedvig and almost destroys the Ekdal marriage. At this stage in Ibsen's development, the only redemption seems to lie in being able to engage with reality by an escape into some traditional kind of illusion, as old Ekdal, Hedvig, and Hjalmar willingly do. The only persons who preserve real and complete identity are old Werle and Dr. Relling. They are the only ones who can bear reality more than most people; and Ibsen knows that most people can stand very little reality, indeed. Only old Werle and Dr. Relling are able to cope with reality by looking at all the hell of the world and the personality without casting up strong defenses.

In *The Wild Duck*, Ibsen analyzes and satirizes transcendentalism with its missionary hero. *Rosmersholm,* however, is no satire. Ibsen is now writing in dead earnest, so that this play turns out to be a truly frightening magnification of what had been, in the final result, really only potentially frightening, and often even quite farcical, in *The Wild Duck.* In *Rosmersholm,* Ibsen obviously wants to find out in much greater detail just how the transcendentalist sets himself up as god, and in what manner and why he goes about violating another personality. Unlike the Ekdal microcosm with its attic, which may be viewed as a metaphor for the general human condition, Rosmersholm is no microcosm but rather an abstraction in Ibsen's mind, a supposition. It is a place where men never laugh and children never cry: a realm of pure transcendental value.

By rejecting his one-time role as a respected clergyman, a conservative pillar of the community, and turning himself into a freethinker and atheist who yearns to play god, Rosmer has merely substituted a traditional illusion for a transcendental one in order to help him survive in self-imposed isolation. He also yearns to cure his sick conscience: he is sick with guilt over what he believes to have been his share in the suicide of his wife, he is haunted by the "white horses" in his mind. Thus he becomes Gregers Werle all over again, but with an important difference. Johannes Rosmer is no caricature and no buffoon. He is the transcendental hero *par excellence,* and being a more serious and more consistent transcendentalist than Gregers he is far more dangerous.

In order to cure his sickly conscience Rosmer wants to dedicate all his powers to setting up a true democracy in the country. But *his* "democracy," of course, is not any political one. The true mission of Rosmer's democracy is "to make all men in the country into noblemen by emancipating their minds and purifying their impulses." Fortunately, he has an opportunity to try out his form of ennoblement on only one person, Rebekka West. She perishes; but not without having first illustrated by the example of her downward course the whole terrifying dilemma of the transcendental hero. She proves that no matter how noble one's ideal, how lofty one's principles, or how deserving of fulfillment one's "higher" morality might be, that to impose them on another human being not only violates his personality, but also obliterates his sense of identity and selfhood. In short, it kills happiness, which is the joyful gratification that derives from the full realization of selfhood, and the right of the self to form its own moral judgments. Let us see how this happens.

Frustrated in love by Rosmer's god-like morality beyond any possibility of relief, a love which is the complete expression of her selfhood, his wife Beate easily falls prey to Rebekka's wiles. When Rebekka first came to Rosmersholm, she makes clear, her sense of self was secure, free, and fearless. She was filled by a wild and uncontrolled passion for Rosmer in those days. "It was like one of those storms we can get up north in the winter," she tells him. This is what made her finally drive her competitor, Beate, out to her death over the falls of the millstream. But Rosmer cheats Rebekka of her hard-earned victory, for instead of then finding in Rosmer a passionate lover or husband, Rebekka eventually becomes infected by the Rosmer view-of-life. Instead of being able to tackle whatever turned up, she has now, at the end, lost the power to act. Rosmersholm, she explains, has at last overpowered and crushed her:

> It is the view-of-life of the Rosmer race—or *your* life-view in any case— which has infected my will . . . and made it sick. A slave to laws that had no meaning for me before. . . . The Rosmer view-of-life does ennoble, but it kills happiness.

When Rebekka tells Rosmer that she must henceforth go about the world dragging behind her a crippled life—even though her impulses have been chastened and ennobled—she means to inform him that her once robust and free conscience has been replaced by a sickly, guilt-ridden one. Now that her awareness of selfhood has been completely crushed, she becomes a victim of what George Bernard Shaw calls "the superstition of expiation by sacrifice." [4]

As irony would have it, just as Rebekka says she has been won over to Rosmer's vision, Rosmer himself confesses that he now faces only the frightful emptiness brought on by the bankruptcy of his missionary ideal. The discomforting data of reality is encroaching on his transcendental paradise, so that he finds his back to the wall at last and admits: "I no longer believe in my power to transform people. I do not trust myself in anything anymore. I believe neither in myself nor in you." Like Brendel, his old friend, Rosmer also finds himself "a deposed monarch amid the ash-heap of his burnt-down castle." But Peder Mortensgaard, Brendel insists, "is master of the future. Peder Mortensgaard has in him the strength of omnipotence. He can do anything he wants. For Peder Mortensgaard never wants to do anything more than he is able. He can live his life without ideals. And that, you see, is precisely the great secret of action and victory. It is the sum of all our world's wisdom." Like old Werle and Dr. Relling, Ibsen seems to be saying, Mortensgaard can always survive comfortably because he is not dependent on illusion of any kind. Rosmer, however, escaped not into reality, but away from it into a world of transcendental illusion with himself as hero. Such an escape might in fact have functioned for him were he not haunted by "white horses," by what Rebekka calls "this business of guilt." Rebekka says she, too, now catches a glimpse of white horses, for she has become subject to the Rosmer view-of-life. That is why she tries to persuade him, at the last moment, to take up his work again by attempting to ennoble hundreds, thousands.

But Rosmer's transcendental armor is already cracked and crumbling, and only Rebekka can help him put the pieces back together again. That is why Rosmer now commits one more preposterous act: the total effacement of Rebekka for the confirmation and glorification of his illusion. Rebekka must play the sacrificial lamb. Rebekka states: "I am subject to the vision of Rosmersholm now. Where I have sinned I must expiate," by which she wishes to inform Rosmer that from now on she will get out of his life completely. But Rosmer cannot be contented with just that. He will be convinced that his ideal is *real* only if Rebekka is willing to sacrifice herself for him by going the same way that Beate went: to her death in the millstream. Only this, he emphasizes, can remove all doubt.

In this way, Rosmer forces his transcendental authority directly on

[4] George Bernard Shaw, *The Quintessence of Ibsenism*, New York (Hill & Wang, 1958), 105.

Rebekka, and by this very act he robs her completely of the right to create her own moral responsibility and to form her own moral judgment. When he tells Rebekka: "There is no judge over us. And therefore we must see to it that we pass judgment ourselves," he is saying actually: I am judging you. As she approaches her end, however, Rebekka unmasks Rosmer's transcendentalism for what it really is with the question: "Suppose you were deceiving yourself? Suppose it was only an illusion? One of these white horses of Rosmersholm?" Having suggested that his noble synthesis is in fact a self-deception, Rebekka raises another disturbing question which Rosmer cannot possibly answer: "Tell me this first. Is it you who follow me? Or is it I who follow you?" Rosmer can only say that they both follow each other, "for now we two are *one*." The irony of this answer is shattering: in order to enter the world of pure value we must die; this is our only possible union. Ibsen is telling us to be wary of the transcendentalist who for his illusion's cause is willing to sacrifice himself. He will just as willingly sacrifice others, too.

Rosmersholm evolves the problem of transcendental illusion to a point where, at the last, its subjective ideal triumphs over the objective reality of life itself. The Rosmer illusion, Rebekka says, "does ennoble, but it kills happiness." The only possible redemption that Rosmer could have brought Rebekka would have been to permit her to carry out her own moral judgment, through the exercise not of his moral authority but through an assertion of empathy; that is, in perceiving and confirming, not violating and subjugating, her identity. In the end he makes her moral, but scarcely morally responsible, when he imposes his authority on her by force and thus destroys her right to choose. This outcome helps to explain why Ibsen in his next play turned to the question of self and its exercise of moral responsibility, as well as the task of empathy in confirming the value of another personality.

What now follows is a play about a carp pond and the sea.

Years before the play begins, Ellida Wangel, the Lady from the Sea, was reconciled and united to her real self by her symbolic marriage to the Stranger, the sea-man. At that time he took a ring he always wore and, placing it on a key-ring with a ring of Ellida's, the sea-man cast them both into the waters' abyss. With that the Stranger departed, and Ellida was left to enter a traditional marriage with Dr. Wangel, with whom she also shares the company of two daughters from his former wife. But the sea, which is, we recall, a metaphor for the depths of selfhood, constantly haunts Ellida so that she feels compelled to maintain contact with it. That is to say, she must bathe in the fjord every single day without exception. She must, she insists, maintain contact

with the self which "repels and attracts," for she cannot resist the
terror, she tells her husband, the terror which she admits is the attraction
in her own mind.

During the first few years of marriage with Dr. Wangel she almost
learns to forget her own self-realization, until she has a child who has
exactly the same eyes as the sea-man, whom she last saw years before.
"The child's eyes," Ellida explains to her husband, "changed color like
the sea. If the fjord lay still in sunshine, so were his eyes. And so in
storm." As one would expect, the child from the sea does not survive
for long on land, in the "carp pond" which Ellida's stepdaughter, Bolette,
describes:

> I don't think we live so very differently from the carp down there in the
> pond. They have the fjord so near them, where the schools of large, wild
> fish pass in and out. But about that the poor, tame house-fish know noth-
> ing. And they can take no part in that. . . . No, we must go on living
> out our lives here in the carp pond.

A short while later, Ellida makes very clear just what Bolette is talking
about. She says that "If only people had from the first accustomed themselves to live on the sea—or in the sea perhaps—we should now have
been perfected in quite a different way than we are, both better and
happier." We see from this that "ennoblement" for Ellida, if any, would
have to come from a place that is directly opposed to Rosmer's and
Gregers' transcendental realms. It would have to be evolved from the very
abyss, from the self. Ibsen's rather complex metaphorical structure in
this play functions properly only if one considers Ellida's child to be
an offspring of her selfhood, and hardly of her union with Dr. Wangel.
Then, the symbolism—admittedly cryptic on the surface—of the child's
strange resemblance to the sea-man, its uncanny death, and the estrange-
ment of wife and husband which immediately ensues all becomes clear.
It simply means that Ellida's true sense of identity, her real self with all
its hell and disturbance, is threatened with extinction in the carp pond,
in her being forced to play a social role in her legal union with Wangel,
a role which endangers and violates her personality.

Then the Stranger from the sea—he bears a certain resemblance to
the accursed Flying Dutchman—comes to the carp pond, since Ellida
will not return to the sea. In Act III, when Ellida is first confronted by
him again and suddenly has a glimpse of all the terror and attraction
of selfhood once more, she can only react with fright and horror. The
Stranger emphasizes that if Ellida wishes to be with him she must come
freely, never by force. She must have the freedom to choose. At the
moment, however, Ellida cannot even bear for him to look at her; that

is, it is now too disturbing for her to contemplate the self within. And this is precisely what she tells her husband, who has given the Stranger a stern warning to keep away from his wife and never come back. First, we see Ellida clinging passionately to Wangel and imploring him to save her from the strange man. But interestingly enough, the very next thing she says is: "Save me from myself. There is the attraction in him. The man is like the sea." Ibsen could not make his point any clearer.

The Stranger has given Ellida a choice. She must await him on the following night, when she must be prepared either to return with him to the sea for all time, or else to expect his departure from her forever, after which he will be a dead man for her. In the beginning, Wangel seeks to coerce her judgment by saying that he dare not set her free. He claims that he has no right to do so for her sake, but instead he must exercise *his* right and duty as a husband in protecting her from herself. If we think this is a violation of her personality, *à la* Nora and Torvald Helmer, we are perfectly right. Ellida, in fact, tells him that he did exactly this when he came to her home to "buy" a wife to fill the emptiness of his home and to find a new mother for his two girls. Ellida admits that she should have never sold herself, that the meanest work would have been better after one's own choice. In metaphorical terms, only her first sea-marriage to the Stranger was real and complete. Now, she implores Wangel to give back her freedom. She insists that she must be able to choose for either side. She feels that she must plunge into the terrible abyss. It is a terror which repels and attracts, for that terror, she confesses, "is no outward force which threatens me. The terror lies deeper, Wangel! The terror is the attraction in my own mind." There is actually nothing for Wangel to protect her from; instead, she must herself be able to regard the whole terror of the personality, and choose. Ellida distresses her husband even more by admitting that from the very first she had felt completely rootless in his house, and she now sees no ties whatever that might bind her to him, since no empathy exists between them. That is the reason why she demands her freedom, the freedom to live her real life. But the keeper of the carp pond replies that he must, as her husband and her doctor, take away her freedom to act on her own behalf. He will act and he will judge for her.

When the Stranger returns, Dr. Wangel still insists on this right; he soon notices, however, that Ellida is fast slipping away from him, that she is being lured into the unknown, lured by the terrible, fascinating power of the sea. Wangel realizes at once that he must give her the freedom she demands. He tells her that she can choose her path now in perfect freedom, and as soon as she hears these words she wants to know the reason for his unexpected decision. In his reply: "because I love you so dearly. . . . The years and the living together have done that," Ellida experiences from him the first expression of genuine empathy. And suddenly she begins to draw back from her rush into the unknown, for now she sees that choosing in freedom and on her own responsibility changes everything. Ellida can now make an irrevocable choice: she will never go off with the sea-man. As for the unknown? "It neither lures nor frightens," she announces to Wangel, "I have been able to see into it, go out into it, if only I myself had desired. I have been able to choose it now. That is why I could also renounce it."

Finally given the responsibility of exercising her own judgment with complete freedom, Ellida not only turns from the sea to Wangel, she also firmly renounces it. She could have "seen into it," but instead she elects not to do so, for she no longer feels constrained to regard the whole hell of the personality, to face the abyss of selfhood which both repels and attracts. Instead of facing it she now finds herself free to disregard it, while understanding that it always exists. Ellida's comprehension of the self gives her the strength to accept her role in the carp pond, but what enables her to accept it willingly is without a doubt Wangel's first expression of real empathy for her; an empathy he demonstrated *after* he gave Ellida complete freedom of choice, so that for her his motive is beyond question.

In rejecting freedom in favor of what had been previously an unhappy existence as mother to children who are not her own, and wife to a man whom she does not love, Ibsen is saying that if one is not strong enough to stand alone, is not sturdy enough to bear reality without the comforting illusions provided by society and its social roles, then existence in the unfree carp pond might be made at least supportable— and perhaps even gratifying—through the operation of empathy; an empathy which asserts, not destroys, the value of another personality. In this fashion, Ibsen seems to be showing that empathy can function in much the same way as the attic does in *The Wild Duck:* it permits people to live.[5]

[5] In the past, there has been a tendency in Ibsen criticism to seek out psychoanalytic interpretations for *The Lady from the Sea.* Typical of this approach is the comment of the Ibsen scholar, Roman Woerner, who insists that Ibsen intended Ellida to be a study in neurosis (Roman Woerner, *Henrik Ibsen* [Munich, 1923], II, 210). This simply does not make sense. Ibsen is not Strindberg, nor is he a Tennessee Williams. Obviously, *The Lady from the Sea* is no more a play about abnormal psychology than *Rosmersholm* is a play about emancipated politics and free-thinkers, or *The Wild Duck* a play about a duck.

Thematic Symbols in *Hedda Gabler*

by Caroline W. Mayerson

Criticism of the "naturalistic" plays of Ibsen has been so largely directed toward establishing his stature as psychologist and social iconoclast that his characteristic use of functional imagery in *Hedda Gabler* has been for the most part neglected. Of course such statements as Gosse's that there is "no species of symbol" in the play[1] have not stood uncorrected. But Jeannette Lee's interpretation of Hedda (committed, by her own admission, to the Gyntian policy of going "roundabout") as "a pistol, deadly, simple, passionless, and straight," [2] is confusing, and Miss Lee's allegorical exegesis, in which the soul of the poet (the manuscript) is destroyed through the combined efforts of animality (Madame Diana) and cold intellect (Hedda), despite the efforts of love (Thea),[3] may be regarded as an oversimplification of the ironic worldview to which Ibsen's total achievement bears witness. Auguste Ehrhard more convincingly interpreted Lövborg's book as the future, which Hedda, the demon of destruction, attempts to impede and destroy,[4] but Ehrhard's discussion omits consideration of other important symbols. In short, while these studies have indicated another perspective from which Ibsen's artistry may be profitably examined, their effect is to provoke reinvestigation of, rather than to explain satisfactorily, the meaning and function of the symbols.

During the course of the play, Ibsen places considerable emphasis upon Thea's hair, upon the manuscript as her "child," and upon General Gabler's pistols, and his treatment of these items suggests that he intended them to have symbolic significance. We shall be concerned

---

"Thematic Symbols in *Hedda Gabler*" by Caroline W. Mayerson. From *Scandinavian Studies*, 22:4 (November, 1950), 151-160. Copyright 1950 by *Scandinavian Studies*. Reprinted by permission of the author and *Scandinavian Studies*.

[1] Edmund Gosse, *Ibsen* (London, 1907), p. 190.

[2] *The Ibsen Secret: A Key to the Prose Dramas of Henrik Ibsen* (New York, 1910), p. 26.

[3] *Ibid.*, pp. 73-74, 154-156.

[4] *Henrik Ibsen et le Théâtre Contemporain* (Paris, 1892), pp. 457-459.

in this essay with determining this significance and its effect upon the total meaning of the play. My analysis of the three symbols in their relationship to the theme, the characters, and the action will be based upon several broad assumptions which reflect views of Ibsen's concepts and methods implied or expressed by a number of previous commentators: 1) In *Hedda Gabler,* Ibsen examines the possibility of attaining freedom and fulfillment in modern society. 2) Hedda is a woman, not a monster; neurotic, but not psychotic. Thus, she may be held accountable for her behavior. But she is spiritually sterile. Her yearning for self-realization through exercise of her natural endowments is in conflict with her enslavement to a narrow standard of conduct. This conflict is complicated by her incomplete understanding of what freedom and fulfillment mean and how they may be achieved. She fails to realize that one must earn his inheritance in order to possess it, and she romanticizes the destructive and sensational aspects of Dionysiac ecstasy without perceiving that its true end is regeneration through sublimation of the ego in a larger unity. 3) Ibsen, as an experienced artist, was aware of the impact of *minutiae* and the need for integrating these with the general impression to be projected; therefore we may regard his descriptions, his stage directions, and his properties, no less than his dialogue,[5] as means whereby intention and significance are conveyed.

While all the other characters in *Hedda Gabler* are implicitly compared to Hedda and serve, in one way or another, to throw light upon her personality, Thea Elvsted is the one with whom she is most obviously contrasted. Furthermore, their contest for the control of Lövborg is the most prominent external conflict in the play. The sterility-fertility antithesis from which central action proceeds is chiefly realized through the opposition of these two. Hedda is pregnant, and Thea is physically barren. But in emotionally repudiating her unborn child, Hedda rejects what Ibsen considered woman's opportunity to advance the march of progress.[6] The many other symptoms of her psychic sterility need little enlargement. Unwilling to give or even share herself, she maintains her independence at the price of complete frustration. Ibsen uses Thea, on the other hand, to indicate a way to freedom which Hedda never apprehends. Through her ability to extend herself in comradeship with Löv-

---

[5] All citations are from the translation by Edmund Gosse and William Archer, *The Collected Works of Henrik Ibsen,* ed. by William Archer (13 vols., New York, 1906-1928), Vol. X.

[6] Cf. Ibsen's speech to the Norwegian Women's Rights League (1898): "It is women who are to solve the social problems. As mothers they are to do it. And only as such can they do it. Here lies a great task for woman" (*Speeches and New Letters of Henrik Ibsen,* trans. by Arne Kildal [Boston, 1901], p. 66).

borg, Thea not only brings about the rebirth of his creative powers, but merges her own best self with his to produce a prophecy of the future, conceivably of the "Third Kingdom," in which Ibsen believed that the ideals of the past would coalesce in a new and more perfect unity.[7] Having lost herself to find herself, she almost instinctively breaks with the *mores* of her culture in order to ensure continuance of function. Despite her palpitating femininity, she is the most truly emancipated person in the play. And it is she who wins at least a limited victory in the end. Although Lövborg has failed her, her fecundity is indefatigable; as Hedda kills herself, Thea is busily preparing to recreate her "child" with Tesman, thereby at once enabling him to realize his own little talents, and weakening even further the tenuous bond which ties him to Hedda.

The contrast outlined above is reinforced by the procreative imagery of the play. The manuscript is Lövborg's and Thea's "child," the idea of progress born of a union between individuals who have freed themselves from the preconceptions of their environment.[8] This manuscript the sterile Hedda throws into the fire at the climax of her vindictive passion. Her impulse to annihilate by burning is directed both toward Thea's "child" and toward Thea's hair and calls attention to the relationship between them. Even without other indications that Ibsen was using hair as a symbol of fertility, such an inference might be made from the words which accompany the destruction of the manuscript:

Now I am burning your child, Thea! Burning it, curly-locks! Your child and Eilert Lövborg's. I am burning—I am burning your child.

There is, however, considerable evidence, both before and after this scene, that Thea's hair is a sign of that potency which Hedda envies even while she ridicules and bullies its possessor. Ibsen, of course, had ample precedent for employing hair as a symbol of fertility. Perhaps the best support for the argument that he made a literary adaptation of this well-known, ancient idea in *Hedda Gabler* is a summary of the instances in which the hair is mentioned.

Although Ibsen's unobtrusive description of the hair of each of these women at her initial entrance may seem at the time only a casual stroke in the sketch, it assumes importance in retrospect. Hedda's hair is "not particularly abundant," whereas Thea's is "unusually abundant and wavy." Hedda's strongest impression of Thea is of that abundance:

---

[7] See *Emperor and Galilean, passim,* and *Speeches and New Letters,* pp. 56-57.

[8] Cf. Ibsen's statement: "I firmly believe in the capacity for procreation and development of ideals" (*Speeches and New Letters,* p. 57).

she recalls her as "the girl with the irritating hair, that she was always showing off." Moreover, Thea fearfully recollects Hedda's school-girl reaction to it: ". . . when we met on the stairs you used always to pull my hair. . . . Yes, and once you said you would burn it off my head." When Thea and Lövborg first meet in the play, Hedda seats herself, significantly, between them; the brief exchange of questions and answers which ensues is notable for its overtones: "Is not she [Thea] lovely to look at?" Lövborg asks. Hedda, lightly stroking Thea's hair, answers, "Only to look at?" Lövborg understands the innuendo, for he replies, "Yes. For we two—she and I—we two are real comrades." Later, when the women are alone, Hedda, now fully informed of the extent to which Thea has realized her generative powers, laments her own meager endowment and renews her threat in its adolescent terms:

> Oh, if you could only understand how poor I am, and fate has made you so rich! [*Clasps her passionately in her arms.*] I think I must burn your hair off after all.

Hedda's violent gesture and Thea's almost hysterical reaction ("Let me go! Let me go! I am afraid of you, Hedda!") indicate the dangerous seriousness of words which otherwise might be mistaken for a joke; the threat prepares us for the burning of the manuscript, which follows in Act III. In the last tense scene of the play Hedda twice handles Thea's hair. The reader's imagination readily constructs the expressions and gestures whereby an actress could show Hedda's true attitude toward the hair which Ibsen directs her to ruffle "gently" and to pass her hands "softly through." The first gesture follows immediately upon an important action—Hedda has just removed the pistol to the inner room. The second accompanies dialogue which for the last time emphasizes Hedda's association of the hair with Thea's fertility and which brings home to Hedda her own predicament:

> *Hedda* [*Passes her hands softly through Mrs. Elvsted's hair*]. Doesn't it seem strange to you, Thea? Here you are sitting with Tesman—just as you used to sit with Eilert Lövborg?
> *Mrs. Elvsted.* Ah, if I could only inspire your husband in the same way!
> *Hedda.* Oh, that will come too—in time.
> *Tesman.* Yes, do you know, Hedda—I really think I begin to feel something of the sort. But won't you go to sit with Brack again?
> *Hedda.* Is there nothing I can do to help you two?
> *Tesman.* No, nothing in the world.

These scenes in which the hair plays a part not only call attention to Hedda's limitations but show her reaction to her partial apprehension of them. In adapting a primitive symbol, Ibsen slightly altered its conventional meaning, substituting psychic for physical potency. Its primitivistic associations nevertheless pervade the fundamental relationships between the two women. The weapons Hedda uses against Thea are her hands and fire. The shock of the climactic scene results chiefly from seeing the savage emerge from behind her veneer of sophistication—the Hedda who feeds the manuscript to the flames is a naked woman engaged in a barbaric act. In contrast, the Hedda who handles her father's pistols is self-consciously cloaked in illusions of her hereditary participation in a chivalric tradition.

The pistols, like many other symbols used by Ibsen, quite obviously are not merely symbols, but have important plot function as well. Moreover, their symbolic significance cannot be reduced to a simple formula, but must be thought of in the light of the complex of associations which they carry as Hedda's legacy from General Gabler. Through Hedda's attitude toward and uses of the pistols, Ibsen constantly reminds us that Hedda "is to be regarded rather as her father's daughter than as her husband's wife." [9] Clearly the pistols are linked with certain values in her background which Hedda cherishes. Complete definition of these values is difficult without a more thorough knowledge of Ibsen's conception of a Norwegian general than the play or contemporary comment on it allows. Perhaps, as Brandes said, nineteenth century audiences recognized that Hedda's pretensions to dignity and grandeur as a general's daughter were falsely based, "that a Norwegian general is a cavalry officer, who as a rule, has never smelt powder, and whose pistols are innocent of bloodshed." [10] Such a realization, however, by no means nullifies the *theoretical* attributes and privileges of generalship to which Hedda aspires. Possibly Ibsen intended us to understand that Hedda is a member of a second generation of "ham actors" [11] who betray their proud tradition by their melodramatic posturings. But it is this tradition, however ignoble its carrier, to which the pistols and Hedda (in her own mind) belong, and it is, after all, the general only as glimpsed through his daughter's ambitions and conceptions of worth that is of real importance in the play. These conceptions, as embodied in Hedda's romantic ideal of manhood, may be synthesized from the action and dialogue. The aristocrat possesses, above all, courage and self-control. He expresses himself through direct

---

[9] *The Correspondence of Henrik Ibsen*, trans. & ed. by Mary Morison (London, 1905), p. 435.

[10] Georg Brandes, *Henrik Ibsen. Björnstjerne Björnson. Critical Studies* (New York, 1899), p. 94.

[11] Ehrhard, *op. cit.*, p. 445, uses the term *cabotine.*

and independent action, living to capacity and scorning security and public opinion. Danger only piques his appetite, and death with honor is the victory to be plucked from defeat. But the recklessness of this Hotspur is tempered by a disciplined will, by means of which he "beautifully" orders both his own actions and those of others on whom his power is imposed. Such a one uses his pistols with deliberation, with calculated aim. He shoots straight—to defend his life or his honor, and to maintain his authority. Pistols, however, have an intrinsic glamor. Of the several possible accoutrements of a general, his pistols are those least likely to evoke thoughts of chivalric principles and most likely to recall the menace of the power vested in him. And such power, as *Hedda Gabler* shows us, delivered into the hands of a confused and irresponsible egotist, brings only meaningless destruction to all who come within its range.

The manipulation of the pistols throughout the play is a mockery of their traditional role. Except at target practice, Hedda does not even shoot straight until her suicide. Her potential danger is recognized by both men whom she threatens, but both understand (Brack, immediately; Lövborg, in Act II) that her threat is a theatrical gesture, and that she has no real intention of acting directly, in defiance of the conventions which bid her "go roundabout." Her crass dishonesty in her sexual encounters is highlighted by this gun play. She uses the pistols, to be sure, to ward off or warn off encroachments upon her "honor." This honor, however, is rooted in social expedience rather than in a moral code. Having indirectly encouraged Lövborg by a succession of intimate tête-à-têtes, she poses as an outraged maiden when he makes amorous advances, thereby, as she later hints, thwarting her own emotional needs. Subsequently she sells her body to Tesman as cynically as (and far less honestly than) Madame Diana sells hers, then deliberately participates in the form, if not the substance, of marital infidelity with Brack in order to relieve her boredom. Both Hedda and Brack become aware of the cold ruthlessness of the other and the consequent danger to the loser if the delicate equilibrium of their relationship should be disturbed. But until the end Brack is so complacently convinced that Hedda is his female counterpart that he has no fear she will do more than shoot over his head; even as she lies dead, he can hardly believe that she has resorted to direct action —"People don't do such things."

The part the pistols play in Lövborg's death makes a central contribution to our understanding of the degree to which the ideals they represent are distorted by the clouded perspective from which Hedda views them. She has no real comprehension of, nor interest in, the vital creative powers Thea helps Lövborg to realize. Instead, she glorifies his weaknesses, mistaking bravado for courage, the indulgence of physical appetites for god-like participation in "the banquet of life," a flight from reality for a heroic quest for totality of experience. Even more important is the fact that as she inhibits her own instinctive urge for fulfillment, she romanticizes its converse. Thus, having instigated his ruin, she incites Lövborg to commit suicide with her pistol. This radical denial of the will to live she arbitrarily invests with the heroism and beauty one associates with a sacrificial death; Hedda is incapable of making the distinction between an exhibitionistic gesture which inflates the ego, and the tragic death, in which the ego is sublimated in order that the values of life may be extended and reborn.

Her inability to perceive the difference between melodrama and tragedy accounts for the disparity between Hedda's presumptive view of her own suicide and our evaluation of its significance. Ibsen with diabolical irony arranged a situation which bears close superficial resemblance to the traditional tragic end. Symbolically withdrawing herself from the bourgeois environment into the inner chamber which contains the reliques of her earlier life, Hedda plays a "wild dance" upon her piano and, beneath her father's portrait, shoots herself "beautifully" through the temple with her father's pistol. She dies to vindicate her heritage of independence; with disciplined and direct aim she at last defeats the Boyg, which hitherto she has unsuccessfully attempted to circumvent. So Hedda would see her death, we are led to believe, could she be both principal and spectator; and no doubt she would find high-sounding phrases with which to memorialize it. But of course it is Brack and Tesman who have the curtain lines, and these lines show how little of her intent Hedda has conveyed to her world. And we, having the opportunity to judge the act with relation to its full context, may properly interpret it as the final self-dramatization of the consistently sterile protagonist. Hedda gains no insight; her death affirms nothing of importance. She never understands why, at her touch, everything becomes "ludicrous and mean." She dies to escape a sordid situation that is largely of her own making; she will not face reality nor assume responsibility for the consequences of her acts. The pistols, having descended to a coward and a cheat, bring only death without honor.

It would appear, then, that the symbols, while they do not carry the whole thematic burden of *Hedda Gabler,* illuminate the meaning of the characters and the action with which they are associated. As Eric Bentley has suggested, the characters, like those in the other plays of Ibsen's last period, are the living dead who dwell in a waste-land that resembles T. S.

Eliot's. And, like Eliot later, Ibsen emphasized the aridity of the present by contrasting it with the heroic past.[12] Indeed, *Hedda Gabler* may be thought of as a mock-tragedy, a sardonically contrived travesty of tragic action, which Ibsen shows us is no longer possible in the world of the play. This world is sick with a disease less curable than that of Oedipus' Thebes or Hamlet's Denmark. For its hereditary leaders are shrunken in stature, maimed and paralyzed by their enslavement to the ideals of the dominant middle-class. With the other hollow men, they despise but nonetheless worship the false gods of respectability and security, paying only lip-service to their ancestral principles. Such geniuses as this society produces are, when left to themselves, too weak to do more than batter their own heads against constricting barriers. They dissipate their talents and so fail in their mission as prophets and disseminators of western culture; its interpretation is left to the unimaginative pedant, picking over the dry bones of the past. Women, the natural seminal vesicles of that culture, the mothers of the future, are those most cruelly inhibited by the sterilizing atmosphere of their environment. At one extreme is Aunt Julia, the genteel spinster, over-compensating for her starved emotions with obsessive self-dedication. At the other is Diana, the harlot. Even Thea, the progenitive spirit, the girl with the abundant hair, is a frail and colorless repository for the seeds of generation. Her break with convention when it threatens her maternity is shown to be the one mode of escape from the fate that overtakes the others. But Ibsen gives her triumph, too, a ludicrous twist. Hardly having begun the mourning song for her Adonis, she brings forth her embryonic offspring from her pocket and proceeds to mold it into shape with the aid of a Tesman—an echo of the classic death and rebirth, to be sure, but one not likely to produce the glorious Third Kingdom of which Ibsen dreamed. And appropriately holding the center of the stage throughout is Hedda, in whom the shadows of the past still struggle in a losing battle with the sterile specter of the present. Her pistols are engraved with insignia which the others understand not at all and which she only dimly comprehends. Her colossal egotism, her lack of self-knowledge, her cowardice, render her search for fulfillment but a succession of futile blunders which culminate in the supreme futility of death. Like Peer Gynt, she is fit only for the ladle of the button-molder; she fails to realize a capacity either for great good or for great evil. Her mirror-image wears the mask of tragedy, but Ibsen makes certain that we see the horns and pointed ears of the satyr protruding from behind it.

[12] *The Playwright as Thinker* (New York: Reynal and Hitchcock, 1946), p. 59.

Henrik Ibsen:
Motifs in the Realistic Plays

by Leo Lowenthal

In the latter half of the nineteenth century, the institutions as well as the mores of society have come completely under the control of the middle class, and its ethos is challenged only by a handful of European artists and intellectuals. English utilitarianism now states this ethos of unmitigated progress in the most optimistic form conceivable: the good of the individual is identical with the good of society.

Ibsen is a true liberal. Nonetheless he emerges as one of the most severe critics of his age. He followed Lessing's advice to make the theater a moral testing ground, but while Lessing had used his esthetic precepts to advocate social conditions which would permit the freer development of the individual, Ibsen, a century later, used the same principles to question whether these conditions had been met. The stage becomes a tribunal in which society is defended by its ideology and prosecuted by its reality. The characters (dynamic often to the point of self-contradiction) try by every available means to achieve the success and happiness that liberalism has promised them. The outcome of the trial is unequivocal: the sentence is to be found in the social meanings of the defeats the protagonists suffer.

This indictment and trial were intentional. Ibsen wrote in one of his letters:

> . . . a man shares the responsibility and the guilt of the society to which he belongs . . . to *write* is to summon one's self, and play the judge's part.[1]

"Henrik Ibsen: Motifs in the Realistic Plays" by Leo Lowenthal. (Original title: "Henrik Ibsen".) From *Literature and the Image of Man* by Leo Lowenthal (Boston: Beacon Press, 1957). Copyright © 1957 by Leo Lowenthal. Reprinted by permission of Leo Lowenthal and the Beacon Press.

[1] Letters of Henrik Ibsen, tr. by J. N. Laurvik and Mary Morison (New York, 1905), p. 334 (6/16/80). All quotations from Ibsen's plays and drafts of plays are taken from the William Archer "Viking Edition," *The Works of Henrik Ibsen* (New York, 1911-1912) 12 vols., by permission of Charles Scribner's Sons.

The concern of writers with the relation of the individual to society had for some time been deliberately invoked as a weapon—first of defense, and then of attack—against the aristocracy and reactionary monarchies which at least until 1848 remained a threat in Europe. But now this social consciousness is used to examine and judge the middle-class world itself.

Private Life and Social Forces

Liberalism conceives of society as a more or less elastic system whose function is to make possible the individual's pursuit of happiness. Ibsen appears to share this attitude. He does not write "social drama." Specific social, political or economic questions are touched upon only occasionally, as in *An Enemy of the People,* or *Pillars of Society.* Hardly ever does a policeman, soldier or other public official appear. The state seems to be reduced to the role of a night watchman. Official institutions appear only in such incidental business as the report of the prison sentence of old Borkman in *John Gabriel Borkman,* or as the threats of Dr. Wangel to call in the authorities against the Stranger in *The Lady from the Sea.* The scenes of Ibsen's plays are usually laid in the home, and the dialogue tends to be limited to the problems of the private person.

Here, however, we find the key to Ibsen's social concepts. He indicts society in the area of its strongest claims by allowing the prevailing social philosophy every opportunity, especially in the field likely to be most conducive to a favorable judgment: in the sphere of private life where the individual can reveal himself freely. And this revelation shows man as the focal point for contradictions that originate in the society.

Public and private interests of the protagonists are portrayed as being inevitably irreconcilable. Energies available for use in public affairs deteriorate as soon as private needs and desires come into play. Solness, the Master Builder of churches and settlement houses, finds his only happiness in friendship with a young girl, whereupon he becomes completely lost in his dreams. The sculptor Rubek confesses to an emotional crisis when

> all the talk about the artist's vocation and the artist's mission and so forth began to strike me as being very empty, and hollow, and meaningless at bottom . . . Yes, is not life in sunshine and in beauty a hundred times better . . . ?[2]

Allmers (in *Little Eyolf*) abandons his book, his great calling, to dedicate himself to the education of his son, little Eyolf, in order to "perfect all

[2] *When We Dead Awaken,* Act II (Vol. XI, p. 429).

the rich possibilities that are dawning in his childish soul." [3] These either-or attitudes are products of the isolation of the spheres of life. Not only does the pursuit of happiness in one realm require neglect of human obligations in every other, but even voluntary withdrawal from society cheats the individual of the happiness he seeks. The Master Builder never erects his dream castle but falls to his death from a real tower. The sculptor Rubek's (in *When We Dead Awaken*) original zest for life and art is lost in the tedium of a banal marriage. Eyolf's father is tortured by his unproductive existence, as well as by the jealousy of his wife and finally by the death of his child. Whether man turns to private or public life, as soon as he begins to develop his potentialities in one he runs into conflicts and frustrations in the other.

Ibsen's portrayals thus follow a pattern. A person starts out with the expectation of fulfillment. Then he finds himself involved in a series of conflicts and troubles which almost always bring ruin to him and force him to injure others. The result is solitude, death, or worse still, the announcement of social programs that have been thoroughly discredited by what has gone on before. Mankind is trapped in a cycle of unattainable hopes and real suffering.

Ibsen's dramas display a virtual catalogue of failure—in daily life, in the professions, in the arts, in marriage, in friendship, and in communication between the generations. Either the person cannot make an adjustment to these relationships, or he develops some of his powers at the expense of certain others or at the expense of his fellows. The discrepancy between the apparent wealth of potentialities and the narrow range of their fulfillment is a steadily recurrent motif.

THE COMPETITIVE PERSONALITY

For Ibsen, Molière's advice—that the road to happiness lay in observation, adjustment, and moderation—would have been irrelevant, if not absurd. Goethe had foreseen that the individual would come to feel increasingly the limitations caused by adjustment to social conditions, but he had not anticipated the frustrations demonstrated by Ibsen. The individual can no longer merely renounce certain claims in order to preserve others. He must, to adjust, develop certain sides of his being to a point where the whole man ceases to exist. Competition has now entered a new field, private life. In *Pillars of Society*, Consul Bernick can conduct his financial transactions successfully only at the price of slandering

[3] *Little Eyolf*, Act I (Vol. XI, p. 49).

his brother-in-law and suppressing his love for his future sister-in-law. The merchant Borkman sacrifices the love and happiness of two women to his ambition to expand his industrial enterprises. Solness pays for the success of his real-estate development with the inner peace of his wife and the lives of his children. Rubek drives a woman crazy in order to complete his masterpiece.

In claiming the right of individuality for themselves, the characters often justify the damage they cause to those near them by claiming that they have created happiness, instead, for the many.

> *Borkman.* I have loved power . . . The power to create human happiness in wide, wide circles around me!
> *Mrs. Borkman.* You had once the power to make me happy. Have you used it to that end?
> *Borkman.* Some one must generally go down in a shipwreck.[4]

> *Solness.* That I might build homes for others, I had to forego . . . the home that might have been my own. I mean home for a troop of children—and for father and mother, too . . . But her [Solness' wife's] vocation has had to be stunted, and crushed, and shattered—in order that mine might force its way to—to a sort of great victory.[5]

Competition turns out to be not only a struggle for social and economic success among various individuals; it is also an inner struggle in which the individual must drastically curtail certain sides of his own being, his personality, in order to realize his particular ambitions. There arises a sequence of guilt and retribution. Bernick's projects lead him to the verge of collapse; Borkman ends in economic and social ruin; the Master Builder's plans are surpassed by those of younger men; the sculptor's creative power is exhausted. Consul Bernick's lies do not, moreover, save him from melancholia; Borkman pays for his ambition with bitter misanthropy; the Master Builder succumbs to his guilt; Rubek flounders in discontent bordering on despair.[6]

Ibsen formulates the predicament of the modern individual: he is fated to become an exaggerated, one-sided being no matter what he chooses to do. The very concept of adaptation has acquired a new meaning from the one Goethe implied—to say nothing of Molière. What once was a bearable degree of anxiety about fitting oneself to new conditions has become veritable anguish; life becomes a game that one hopes to win by achieving

---

[4] *John Gabriel Borkman*, Act III (Vol. XI, pp. 296-297).
[5] *The Master Builder*, Act II (Vol. XX, pp. 350-353).
[6] The plays referred to are *Pillars of Society, John Gabriel Borkman, The Master Builder,* and *When We Dead Awaken,* respectively.

success, only to find that the specialization and exertion required for this success add up, after all, to failure.

MARRIAGE AND THE FAMILY

Failure manifests itself right in the very center of private life, in marriage. For the eighteenth century novelists the home was a stabilizing force in a mobile world. For Molière, marriage was the happy end, whatever the conflict. It was the impossibility of marriage that occasioned the suicide of Werther. Ibsen's plays, however, do not stop at the threshold of family life; on the contrary, it is precisely there that they begin.

In almost every case, the characters or interests of the partners are at variance and bring marriage to defeat or frustration. Weak husbands such as Tesman, Alving, Helmer, or Allmers fail their wives and drive them to distraction.[7] Ibsen is not partial to either of the sexes; weak wives like Aline Solness, Irene Rubek, or Gina Ekdal have a similar effect.[8] Marriages may be ruined by love for a third person (*Hedda Gabler* and *Master Builder*), by an unbridgeable rift between parents and children (*John Gabriel Borkman*) or between the parents on account of the children (*Little Eyolf*), and by increasing boredom (in nearly every play).

Consul Bernick and Borkman marry women whom they do not love, and the insincerity of the relationships brings feelings of guilt to the husbands and of inadequacy to their wives. Rubek marries a woman inferior to him as a personality and pays with nervous restlessness; she in turn, to avenge herself, deserts him. Ellida, in *The Lady from the Sea,* seems fated to stagnate in a marriage she had contracted merely to escape from an unbearable environment. Nora, in *A Doll's House,* breaks off a relationship in which husband and wife could educate neither each other nor the children to live together equably. In *Little Eyolf* the husband conveys to his wife his decision to concentrate on the education of his son; the ensuing dialogue illustrates vividly the manner in which the law of competition operates within the intimacy of the family.

Rita. Now you have given yourself up to something worse.
Allmers. Worse! Do you call our child something worse?
Rita. Yes, I do . . .
Allmers. I am often almost afraid of you, Rita.
Rita. I am often afraid of myself. And for that very reason you must not awake the evil in me.

[7] We refer to *Hedda Gabler, Ghosts, The Wild Duck,* and *Little Eyolf,* respectively.
[8] See, *The Master Builder, When We Dead Awaken,* and *The Wild Duck,* respectively.

Allmers. Why, good heavens, do I do that?

Rita. Yes, you do—when you tear to shreds the holiest bonds between us.

Allmers. . . . it is of no use demanding anything. Everything must be freely given . . . I must divide myself between Eyolf and you.

Rita. But if Eyolf had never been born? What then?

Allmers. Oh, that would be another matter. Then I should have only you to care for.

Rita. Then I wish he had never been born . . . I will live my life—together with you—wholly with you. I cannot go on being only Eyolf's mother . . . I will not, I tell you! I cannot! I will be all in all to you. To you, Alfred! [9]

The family does not live up to the function of being a sanctuary where the hurt suffered in public life can be healed. Even the relationship between the two generations is one of interference, not of help. The death of the Allmers' child terminates the father's interest in education, which from the beginning was not rooted in generic sympathy for the younger generation. This is, briefly, the life of the Allmers family: incompatibility between public and private life, neglect of the wife because of the husband's preoccupation with the child, dull pressure on the husband's life from lack of confidence in his productivity, general spiritual disorder.

The atmosphere in Consul Bernick's house is similarly unpleasant. Bernick tries to justify his social and personal machinations with the claim that he is seeking to provide his son with a life-work.[10] His eventual self-reproach disavows his previous life and program which had brought about a hypocritical mentality in himself, an inner impoverishment of his wife, and a guilt-ridden relationship toward his son.

Ibsen's characters voice dubious educational doctrines which actually conceal antagonism and competition. When John Gabriel Borkman's proposal that he and his grown son should build a new life together is coldly rejected, he has earned the same fate as Bernick and for similar reasons. The aging Master Builder is bitter against the younger generation:

Some one or other will take it into his head to say: Give me a chance. And then all the rest will come clamouring after him, and shake their fists at me and shout: Make room—make room . . . presently the younger generation will come knocking at my door . . . Then there's an end of Halvard Solness.[11]

It is left uncertain how heavily the death of Solness's children lay on his conscience. Ideally, the long experience and the mature wisdom of an

[9] *Little Eyolf*, Act I (Vol. XI, pp. 61-63).
[10] See *Pillars of Society*, Act IV (Vol. VI, p. 457).
[11] *The Master Builder*, Act I (Vol. X, p. 284).

aging man should invest him with a higher humanity, the benefits of which he could pass on to the younger generation. Instead, the sheer biological difference in age becomes a source of hostility. Biology itself is incorporated into a category of property, and the limitations of old age appear as a loss of property, a loss that has no compensations.

SOCIAL NATURE OF PERSONAL CONFLICTS

Social relationships intimately permeate the personal disasters Ibsen portrays. In all the plays someone stands in the way of another's needs or the protagonist frustrates his own needs by the nature of the activity he has selected. The characters themselves explain these conflicts on the grounds of inner necessity: they cannot change their natures.[12] This explanation, however, leaves out of account the social connections which are clearly established. Ellida, the Lady from the Sea, finds life unbearable after she recognizes that her marriage actually rests on a sales transaction, and the tawdry yet expedient middle-class career marriages of Bernick, Tesman, Allmers, and Borkman signify that we are concerned with something else than innate human nature. In other instances human problems develop which seemingly do not have any connection with material questions or broader social relationships, yet they are described in almost the same language as that which is used to describe instances of business and professional competition.

> Oh, it all seems to me so foolish. . . . Not to be able to grasp at your own happiness—at your own life! Merely because some one you know happens to stand in the way! [13]

Indeed, this remark from Hilda, the Master Builder's friend, is close to the Master Builder's own language when he feels threatened by his competitors. The professional pattern in which the success of one means the failure of another has penetrated intimate relationships. The aggressiveness of the Master Builder is matched by that of Hedda Gabler. Rubek must use the same force and drive to succeed in the art world that Borkman or Solness uses in the world of business and industry.

ACCLIMATIZATION AND SPECIALIZATION

Like Cervantes and Shakespeare, Ibsen often puts truths into the mouths of marginal figures. Ballested, jack-of-all-trades and master of

---

[12] See, for example, *The Master Builder*, Act I (Vol. X, p. 258), *When We Dead Awaken*, Act II (Vol. XI, p. 450), *Little Eyolf*, Act II (Vol. XI, p. 117).
[13] *The Master Builder*, Act III (Vol. X, p. 402).

none in *The Lady from the Sea,* declares that man can and must "acclimatize" himself, that he must adapt himself to the "facts."

The men in Ibsen always respect the facts of their world: eliminating competitors, cheating partners, playing ball with public authorities—these are realistic and profitable activities. If these people seem to be crushed by a blind fate, it is because they live their social roles in their private lives but fail to see them for what they are, namely, as the struggle to succeed, to obtain more, and to treat all things in an acquisitive manner. The protagonists may prefer one lover to another, one generation to another, or one side of their own nature to another, but in every case the choice is pursued with a restlessness and tenacity identical to that by which they forward their careers. As their social roles are extended to private relations, they almost inevitably miss happiness in the very act of energetically pursuing it. The schema of utilitarianism backfires.

An outstanding characteristic of almost all of Ibsen's persons is that they are, in one form or another, specialists. Only a few escape the isolation resulting from a high degree of specialization, and even those who do pay a heavy penalty. The good-for-nothing Ballested is a painter, actor, decorator, hairdresser, dancing master, and music teacher all in one; he is, of course, a failure. The identity of self-interest and social interest proves to be a misstatement of reality. Selective, self-centered activity is the requirement for effective social participation; the alternative is to become an ineffectual jack-of-all-trades. It is true irony that advice to conform should be put into the mouth of a man who fails to conform.

The social trait of specialization afflicts Ibsen's people in their private lives. The position of husband, wife, friend, father, or mother is seen as a form of existence at odds with the prerogatives of the individual himself as well as with those of the other members of his family. Hedda, who has managed for a while to assert her integrity in spite of a banal environment, tells a friend about the disappointments of her honeymoon, which have become the leitmotif of her marriage. She says:

Tesman is a specialist . . . and specialists are not at all amusing to travel with. Not in the long run, at any rate.[14]

When the friend asks, "not even the specialist one happens to love?" she makes a bitter reply.[15] The episode is particularly significant because Tesman is not unattractive to women and his profession (he is a scholar)

[14] *Hedda Gabler,* Act II (Vol. X, p. 92).
[15] *Loc. cit.,* pp. 92-93.

is hardly repelling. Far removed as he may seem from the average pattern of commercial activity, he still remains caught by a web of narrow specialization.

Gunhild Borkman's hatred of her husband is a reaction to his view of life which centers its emphasis on the sound business reputation of the family. Aline Solness's tolerance of her husband and his friend Hilda is not born of a limitless feminine capacity for love but only of the naïve, dutiful desire to assist her husband's business and to maintain a conventional family life. The asceticism of Pastor Manders has more to do with his own bigotry than with morality. Helmer's ethical pretensions spring from his anxiety to retain directorship of the bank rather than from conscience and remorse.

Although Ibsen states in various forms the view of Dr. Stockmann that he who stands alone is most powerful, nevertheless his dramatic work illustrates again and again that the enforced self-dependence of man leads to solitude and loss of vitality. The pursuit of special self-interest spells ruin, and not fulfillment. Such is the fate not only of his less engaging characters, for instance the overbearing merchants Bernick and Borkman, but also of the likable ones. The latter—like Helen Alving, Hedda Gabler, Rosmer, and Rubek—finally go to pieces in the complete isolation into which they have been driven; the pressure of outside interests pursues them even when they seek to withdraw into themselves.

The Dilemma of Freedom and Necessity

LOVE AND ANXIETY

Men face each other as strangers. When Ibsen's characters speak of love they often tremble—a phenomenon which proves on examination to be historical and social in its origins. The division of the individual into a professional self and a private self frightens the wife lest her beloved turn out to be someone vastly different from the man she knows; he may even be different from the man he thinks he is. The man who binds himself for life to a woman—to a member of the sex which, in Ibsen's day, society still confined to an existence within conventional marriage—may also expect disappointment. An order of life in which husbands and wives are specialized beings intensifies the anxiety that in any case goes with love.

When his wife asks him what his first sensation had been upon meeting her, Allmers replies quite frankly: "Dread." [16] Wangel admits that "the

[16] *Little Eyolf*, Act II (Vol. XI, p. 117).

terrible" plays a dominant role in his relationship with his wife.[17]
Madly in love with the childish Hilda, Solness sees his world full of
devils: "If only you could always tell whether it is the light or dark
one that have got hold of you!" [18] Ellida indicates what is problematic in
her love in these words:

> Oh, there are times, you may be sure, when I feel as though there would
> be safety and peace in clinging close to you, and trying to defy all the
> powers that frighten and fascinate me. But I cannot do it. No no,—I can-
> not do it! [19]

Personal relationships are more fearful than comforting. "She must
bear it all alone." [20] Love cannot efface this insecurity, and Allmers, who
has tried to break away from public life completely, finds no peace.

> *Allmers.* There is something horrible in being alone. The thought of it runs
>   like ice through my blood—
> *Asta.* O, but Alfred, you are not alone.
> *Allmers.* There may be something horrible in that, too, Asta.[21]

Several of Ibsen's plays seem to suggest that he nonetheless believed in
the possibility of realizing a genuine human relationship within and
despite the prevailing social aura. But while there are glimmers here and
there of such hope, by and large, where true love seems about to be
realized, it is only at the point of death. Solness, Hedda Gabler, Rubek,
and Irene die at the very moment overpowering emotion tears these
people from their self-preoccupation. Solness, we are told, is too frightened to mount a scaffold, but he clambers to the top of a new house the
first time he feels truly and warmly human, and [falls] off. Accustomed to
a soft life, Rubek climbs the most forbidding mountains when he meets
the mate who stands beyond all conventional conceptions of life, whereupon an avalanche buries them both. Hedda Gabler, tied down by a
mediocre marriage, exults in the suicide of her friend as an expression of
freedom and the beauty of life, and she confesses that she feels alive for
the first time just before she shoots herself. Death climaxes the will to life
of all these people. It stands in somber contrast to the complacent self-
confidence of Molière, for whom suicide was absurd and ridiculous. The
disparity between Molière's and Ibsen's resolutions illustrates the decline
of the curve of middle-class optimism.

[17] *The Lady from the Sea,* Act IV (Vol. IX, p. 368).
[18] *The Master Builder,* Act II (Vol. X, p. 367).
[19] *The Lady from the Sea,* Act V (Vol. IX, p. 380).
[20] "Notes for a Modern Tragedy" [Draft of *A Doll's House*], (Vol. XII, pp. 91-92).
[21] *Little Eyolf,* Act III (Vol. XI, pp. 140-141).

THE IMAGINATION AND ART

Ibsen is obsessed by the dilemma of how to maintain the integrity of the individual under the impact of the prevailing social atmosphere:

> The fault lies in that all mankind has failed. If a man claims to live and to develop in a human way, it is megalomania.[22]

> So to conduct one's life as to realize one's self—this seems to me the highest attainment possible to a human being. It is the task of one and all of us, but most of us bungle it.[23]

The sum total is mostly negative. Face to face with the injury he has done to himself and to others, Solness condemns his professional accomplishments:

> See, that is the upshot of the whole affair, however far back I look. Nothing really built . . . Nothing, nothing! The whole is nothing! [24]

What remains is loneliness without hope.

Even individual fantasy and artistic imagination—which ordinarily we would think of as the last strongholds against the inroads of the world—do not transcend social reality but merely reflect it. Wishdreams, for example, without ever being translated into action, are consummated in events that injure and kill. Solness wants his old house to burn; when his wish comes true, the fire destroys his children. Rebekka West (in *Rosmersholm*) desires the love of the married pastor, only to feel eventually that her innermost wishes were responsible for the death of his wife. Rita Allmers confesses her jealousy of her child and would rather it had never been born than that it detract from her husband's love for herself; the child dies.

Art, too, is engulfed by this process. At the beginning of the liberal era, music sang triumphantly of joy and solidarity; in Ibsen's work the tune has changed to one of suffering and isolation. Hedda Gabler plays the piano in a moment of supreme distress, and she draws out, according to stage direction, notes of despair. In *When We Dead Awaken* Ibsen introduces the plastic arts. A comparison with the Greek legend might help to point up the character of Rubek, the sculptor. The ancient story tells how Pygmalion fell in love with his statue of a young girl, how then a goddess endowed her with life, and how finally Pygmalion married the product of his own creation. In this tale, inanimate material is released

---

[22] Draft for *Ghosts* (Vol. XII, p. 186).
[23] *Letters*, p. 359 (8/8/82).
[24] *The Master Builder*, Act III (Vol. X, p. 426).

for the development of a human being, but Ibsen's drama displays a reverse process: the artist sees in his wife only the model. The egoism of the artist, on a special plane to be sure, is as boundless as the egotism of the business and professional man. He transforms human relations and men themselves into objects to be used for his own purposes; they have value for him only when they serve his ambitions.

IDEALISM DISENCHANTED

For the Wilhelm Meisters, the language in which idealism set forth its values—truth, freedom, responsibility, and duty—was a meaningful part of the emancipation of the middle classes. Now, however, when these same words are pronounced by a Rubek, who is imprisoned in his egoism, or by a Bernick, whose whole life has been based on the deception and repression of his fellow men, or by an Allmers, whose weak soul can escape conventional norms only at rare moments, they have ceased to provide a genuine motivation for creative acts.

Two parallel themes run throughout Ibsen's works: the one shows an effort to live up to established social values and ideals only to meet with defeat, and the other shows the defeat of those who reject these values and have nothing to put in their place. Ulrik Brendel, a vagabond and down-at-the-heel writer, is a spokesman for such pointless disillusionment. The first time he visits his former pupil, Rosmer, to arrange for lectures on human freedom, he begs for some cast-off clothes. The plan for the lectures is abandoned when he becomes aware of the apathy and cynicism in the town. He visits Rosmer once more before leaving, and this time begs for "one or two cast-off ideals." [25] He announces cynically that life can be mastered only by men like Mortensgaard, an unscrupulous climber "capable of living his life without ideals." "And that," he adds, ". . . is just . . . the sum of the whole world's wisdom." [26] Again a marginal figure has formulated a basic feature of society. A world of ideals is invoked to dignify the relentless pursuit of material advantage, and they dissolve as soon as their consequences are considered; man's life runs its course between the pursuit of material goods and the worship of powerless ideas.

Of values implicit in the categorical imperative, duty had struck a particularly militant note; the equal commitment of all men to duty aimed at the elimination of hereditary privilege. In Ibsen's drama, how-

[25] *Rosmersholm,* Act IV (Vol. IX, p. 183).
[26] *Loc. cit.* (pp. 184-185).

ever, this concept becomes self-defeating. Pastor Manders' life is governed by wholesale acceptance of moral and sexual conventions, and his every action and word are confounded by the mirror of truth that Helen Alving holds up to him. Yet this man, wallowing in the comforts gained by submitting to conformity, preaches duty to Helen Alving when she confesses her unhappiness:

> What right have we human beings to happiness? We have simply to do our duty, Mrs. Alving! And your duty was to hold firmly to the man you had once chosen, and to whom you were bound by the holiest ties.[27]

He says to this woman whose life has been wretched and whom he had humiliated when she revealed her love for him:

> And what a blessing has it not proved to you, all the days of your life, that I induced you to resume the yoke of duty and obedience! [28]

When the curtain has fallen and the audience strikes a balance, it is found that "duty" has brought Chamberlain Alving and his son to a terrible end, shattered the life of Mrs. Alving, brought about the degradation of her husband's illegitimate daughter, helped establish a sailor's brothel, and destroyed an orphanage. This is the reality. The pastor's sermon is an insipid moral recipe.

Aline Solness, too, is a victim of official morality. Ruled by a domineering and unreliable husband, robbed of her children by a terrible accident, restricted to a narrow circle of gossipy companions, she clings to the doctrine that all that matters is duty. All she gets for her faith in this moral dictum is mockery from her successful rival, the Master Builder's young friend:

> *Hilda.* She said that she would go out and buy something for me, because it was her duty. Oh I can't bear that ugly, horrid word!
> *Solness.* Why not?
> *Hilda.* It sounds so cold, and sharp, and stinging. Duty—duty—duty. Don't you think so, too? Doesn't it seem to sting you? [29]

Time and again Ibsen's people sacrifice themselves and do what they believe to be their duty, only to achieve negative results. Sacrifice of human lives becomes absurd, unless it is linked with a value that transcends those lives. It is a sheer perversion of the idea of self-sacrifice when sickly and childish Hedvig Ekdal commits suicide to satisfy the

---

[27] *Ghosts*, Act I (Vol. VII, p. 255).
[28] *Loc. cit.* (p. 256).
[29] *The Master Builder*, Act II (Vol. X, p. 335).

pathological ideas of Gregers Werle and the inner instability of the man she believes to be her father. When Rebekka West joins Rosmer in death to satisfy the feeling of guilt he has projected upon her, the result is only the heaping of human destruction upon destruction. Even Nora's renunciation of her home has something of the sadness of a futile sacrifice.

THE ROLE OF WOMEN

Ibsen once wrote to his friend Georg Brandes:

> What will be the outcome of this mortal combat between two epochs, I do not know; but anything rather than the existing state of affairs—so say I.[30]

The standards for a life superior to the "existing state" are set by women in Ibsen's plays. Although for them it is not hunger and other material privations that indict society, their frustrations are allied nonetheless to the present "epoch." Ibsen occasionally links the situation of women in his time to that of the workers. He insists on the nobility of character as superior to the privileges which come with property, and adds:

> This nobility . . . will come to us from two sources . . . from our women and from our workingmen.
> The reshaping of social conditions which is now under way out there in Europe is concerned chiefly with the future position of the workingman and of woman.
> That it is which I hope for and wait for; and it is that that I will work for, and shall work for my whole life so far as I am able.[31]

Ibsen again turns to a minor character for the formulation of an important problem. In *The Lady from the Sea*, Boletta, an elderly, dry, prosy woman, asks the sculptor Lyngstrand, who is declaiming that the wife must accommodate herself to her husband:

> Has it never occurred to you that perhaps a husband might be absorbed in the same way into his wife? Might come to resemble her, I mean. . . . But why not the one as well as the other? [32]

Women fare badly in a society where economic and social functions are almost exclusively male prerogatives. They represent, in a sense, incomplete men. They must not only suffer from the pressures of society,

---

[30] *Letters*, p. 234 (4/4/72).
[31] "Speech to the Workingmen of Trondhjem" (6/14/85). In: *Speeches and New Letters*, tr. by Arne Kildal (Boston, 1910), p. 54.
[32] *The Lady from the Sea*, Act IV (Vol. IX, p. 334).

they must also serve and seek the approval of the men. Or, as Ibsen himself says:

> A woman cannot be herself in the society of the present day, which is an exclusively masculine society, with laws framed by men and a judicial system that judges feminine conduct from a masculine point of view.[33]

"Modern society is not a human society; it is only a society of males." [34]

But the disenfranchisement of women has positive as well as negative results. Thanks to the fact that public life is ruled by men, women retain traces of another kind of existence; they are at least capable of expressing true human traits. Their greater distance from public life does not free them entirely from social pressures (the latter are, as we have seen, too omnipresent for that), but it does allow them at times to transcend these limitations.

Insofar as women have any business life in Ibsen's plays, they are helpless, faltering and perverse—with the exception of essentially innocuous characters like Gina Ekdal, who do have some practical ability. Nora forges a note with almost touching clumsiness and carelessness. Helen Alving is persuaded by Pastor Manders' spurious arguments not to insure her orphanage. But this removal of women from men's work serves in the end to protect them from complete surrender to social and economic pressures.

The unique human quality women retain is the steadfastness with which they cling to the truth as an absolute value. It is man, ready to combat others for his own success, who preaches the ideals of progress, humanity, duty—the ideals that are undermined by the conduct of his life. Ibsen's male protagonists almost never live up to what they preach, and they never admit the one principle by which they in fact do live, the materialism of personal profit. Women are also materialistic, but their materialism is significantly different and outspoken. It is dramatic irony that egoists preach morality and moralists egoism; Ibsen's women often say that desire for personal happiness is their only true goal, but, in fact, they love to the point of self-sacrifice. Not once does Ibsen honor a man by allowing him to come forth as a witness to the humanly desirable. Only women such as Ellida, Hedda, Nora, Irene, Mrs. Rentheim, and Rita Allmers defend that faith. Ibsen remarks of his own wife that

[33] Draft for *A Doll's House* (Vol. XII, p. 91).
[34] Ibsen, *Nachgelassene Schriften*, ed. by J. Elias and H. Koht (Berlin, 1909), Vol. I, p. 206.

she never succumbed to the temptation of inertia in the present society.[35]

The clash between the self-seeking world of men, and love and humanity, represented by women, is crucial in Ibsen's drama. Rubek, perhaps the most talented character in Ibsen's works, abounds in creative ability, passion and a feeling for nuance. His wife, Irene, has neither the intellectual superiority of a Helen Alving, the zest of a Hedda Gabler nor the healthy directness of a Hilda. In this instance, the husband towers above the male average, while the wife fails to reach the level of several other women in Ibsen's dramas. It is in this relationship, however, that the mutually exclusive principles become most clear: adjustment to the "fact" on the one hand, and unconditional love on the other. Rubek, as the youthful sculptor, pursued the ideal of symbolizing, in the form of a young woman, the awakening of mankind from its present state. Later, having "learned worldly wisdom in the years that followed," he placed this single figure far in the background and transformed the central theme of the work into an allegory of life with "men and women with dimly-suggested animal faces." Irene tells him: "There you uttered your own doom."[36] The sculptor has betrayed the promise of his youth; he has achieved material success by turning out works that did not come sincerely from his own humanity; and because of his guilt he represents himself in his sculpture as a penitent who indeed has forfeited his life. On the other side, Irene's steadfast love for Rubek signifies a humanity which any number of shocks and depressions could not weaken; it holds out against every difficulty, disappointment and convention. For Hilda, no outside world—neither reputation nor family—exists when she wants to erect her castle with the Master Builder. Hedda Gabler goes to her death without giving up her faith in beauty as the only worthy aim of life.

In male idealism, truth becomes mere talk. In feminine egoism, on the other hand, there is an element of truth, for desires are consciously recognized and defended. Helen Alving opposes the sermonizing call to duty by men with the idea of "joy." She says to her son:

A little while ago you spoke of the joy of life; and at that word a new light burst for me over my life and everything connected with it.[37]

In the same vein, Irene's love casts light on Rubek's confusion, just as Hilda's need of happiness exposes the Master Builder's disorganized existence. Hedda Gabler's contempt for the world of the specialist shows the abyss between the latter and a total human existence.

[35] See *Letters*, p. 199 (10/28/1870).
[36] *When We Dead Awaken*, Act II (Vol. XI, pp. 447-449).
[37] *Ghosts*, Act III (Vol. VII, p. 336).

By their intransigence, Ibsen's women uncover the rationalizations of men: the architectural ambitions of Solness, the artist's egoism of Rubek, the conceited scholarship of Tesman, and the pomposity of Bernick and Borkman. In fact, the relation between men and women can be compared to that of the neurotic and the psychoanalyst. The men say everything that comes into their heads; they express guilt feelings, justifications and accusations. In contrast women represent the ego-ideal of a structured, realistically grounded existence. As in the analytic session, everything is restricted to the field of conversation and there is no lecturing. But the comparison ends here. True, Ibsen studies the psychological effects of society upon the individual, but his work does not proclaim that the mere understanding of psychological difficulties will cure the social ills which are at the bottom of personal misery.

Ibsen's women are not judged by specific "good" actions as opposed to "bad" ones, but rather, by the good faith they bring to their acts. Their attitude toward sex illuminates their struggle for happiness. The men generally declare sensual pleasure inferior to more ideal varieties. Those of the women who are endowed with the greatest critical clarity and energy are also the most sensual, and they admit it themselves. Against weaklings like Rosmer, or the vacillating Allmers, the colorless Tesman, or cowards like Manders, or the thoroughly beaten Rubek, all of whom flee from women in pursuit of their ideals, Ibsen opposes women who admit their demand for sexual happiness with the same candor as that with which they berate compromises demanded by the world. True, Rosmer, Rubek, and Allmers have traces of the rebel, but their ideals express dissatisfaction only with certain facets of prevailing society. Their female partners, however, say "no" to the claims and pressures of society as a whole, and hence to the weak principles of their men.

THE ROLE OF THE ARTIST

The naturalistic school, of which Ibsen was a leading figure, expressed an increasing conviction that esthetic purism—art for art's sake—must give way to the artist's concern with the concrete problems of men. Ibsen's critique of the ideals of modern society did not derive from a philosophy of relativism but from a desire to relate these ideals to the social struggle. He expressed the idea that the subdivision and independent existence of different spheres of life—the seemingly unconnected separation into economics, politics, and culture—are transitory, and once wrote:

I believe that the time will soon come when political and social conceptions will cease to exist in their present forms . . . I believe that poetry, philosophy, and religion will be merged in a new category and become a new vital force.[38]

In challenging the purely esthetic approach, Ibsen tried to avoid specialization and isolation, which he had stigmatized in his dramas as a danger to human development. While traveling in Italy, he wrote to Björnson:

> If I were asked to tell you at this moment what has been the chief result of my stay abroad, I should say that it consisted in my having driven out of myself the aestheticism which had a great power over me—an isolated aestheticism with a claim to independent existence. Aestheticism of this kind seems to me now as great a curse to poetry as theology to religion. . . . Is it not an inexpressibly great gift of fortune to be able to write? But it brings with it great responsibility; and I am now sufficiently serious to realize this and to be very severe with myself.[39]

Yet, much as he tried to throw off the limitations set upon him by his milieu—by sharing "the responsibility and the guilt of the society" to which he belonged—he nevertheless displayed traits characteristic of the society he criticized.[40] Although his female protagonists speak of freedom and joy as goals that are incompatible with prevailing conditions, still the manner in which they express their desires is often reminiscent in terms and tones of the austere language of the professed idealism of the male; it remains part and parcel of the value system they themselves protest.

Austerity lives closely with misanthropy and arrogance. Dr. Stockmann, the enemy of the people, rejects the world in a pronunciamento of truculent self-sufficiency. Rubek imperiously lashes the mob for its lack of appreciation. Rosmer prefers to take his program for nobility to the grave rather than make it public. Ibsen himself possessed traces of the misanthropy displayed by these characters. He wrote in a letter to Georg Brandes:

> What I chiefly desire for you is a genuine, full-blooded egoism, which shall force you for a time to regard what concerns you yourself as the only thing of any consequence, and everything else as non-existent . . . I have never really had any very firm belief in solidarity; in fact, I have only accepted it as a kind of traditional dogma. If one had the courage to

---

[38] "Speech at the Banquet in Stockholm (9/24/87)," *Speeches*, pp. 56-57.
[39] *Letters*, p. 86 (9/12/65).
[40] See his letter of June 16, 1880.

throw it overboard altogether, it is possible that one would be rid of the ballast which weighs down one's personality most heavily.[41]

Suggestions of pessimism also may be found in the use of dumbness in his plays. He could have said with Goethe: "Silence befits the man who does not feel himself to be fully rounded. Silence also befits the lover who cannot hope to be happy." [42] In any case silence is the answer whenever men are giving up the confidence that they can lead their lives, as Wilhelm Meister had hoped for, in the direction of "a harmonious cultivation" of their nature. Silence comes over many of Ibsen's persons when they find they do not know how to break through the hard shell of their environment. Ellida, the Lady from the Sea, cannot communicate what she calls the "incomprehensible" in her life. Similarly, Hedda Gabler engages in an abruptly muted conversation:

> *Brack.* Why should you not, too, find some sort of vocation in life, Mrs. Hedda?
> *Hedda.* A vocation—that should attract me?
> *Brack.* If possible, of course.
> *Hedda.* Heaven knows what sort of vocation that could be. I often wonder whether—(*breaking off*). But that would never do either.[43]

Irene confesses that in her youth she had hated Rubek but loved his work, and had kept quiet on the subject. Silent hatred and silent love, the aging woman's recollection of her earlier dumbness, these are signs of actual human isolation.

In Ibsen's plays the societal concept of man reaches a climax: his inner life appears at once as a reaction to social forces and a reflection of them; social forces continue to live inside the individual, and thus to control him. In this context, nature as the symbol of freedom becomes a significant issue: many of his figures dream of natural space as a counter-image to society. Ellida longs for the great open sea, Rubek and Irene have faith in the redemptive power of the mountains, the parents of Little Eyolf turn to the peaks and the stars. Even Oswald Alving's longing for Paris ("light and sunshine and glorious air") and the ecstasy of Solness and Hilda over their air castles imply a renunciation of the possibility of human fulfillment in society, and a surrender to the demiurge of nature.

---

[41] *Letters*, p. 218 (9/24/71).
[42] Goethe, *Der Sammler und die Seinigen. Sämtliche Werke*, vol. 33, p. 182.
[43] *Hedda Gabler*, Act II (Vol. X, p. 105).

The Unexpected Visitor
in Ibsen's Late Plays

by Richard Schechner

C. G. Jung, although not writing about Ibsen, makes several observations in his "Phenomenology of the Spirit in Fairy Tales" which provide us with an enriching insight into those mysterious late plays: *The Lady from the Sea, Little Eyolf, The Master Builder, John Gabriel Borkman,* and *When We Dead Awaken.*

> The old man always appears when the hero is in a hopeless and desperate situation from which only profound reflection or a lucky idea—in other words, a spiritual function or an endopsychic automatism of some kind—can extricate him. But since, for internal and external reasons, the hero cannot accomplish this himself, the knowledge needed to compensate for the deficiency comes in the form of a personified thought. . . .[1]

> To the man of enlightened intellect it seems like the correction of a fallacy when he recognizes that what he took to be spirits is simply the human spirit and ultimately his own spirit. All the superhuman things, whether good or bad, that former ages predicted of the *daimonia,* are reduced to "reasonable" proportions as though they were pure exaggeration, and everything seems to be in the best possible order. But were the unanimous convictions of the past really and truly only exaggerations? If they were not, then the integration of the spirit means nothing less than its daemonization, since the superhuman spiritual agencies that were formerly tied up in nature are introjected into human nature, thus endowing it with a power which extends the bounds of personality ad infinitum, in the most perilous way.[2]

"The Unexpected Visitor in Ibsen's Late Plays" by Richard Schechner. From *Educational Theater Journal*, XIV, 2 (May 1962), 120-127. Copyright © 1962 by *Educational Theater Journal*. Reprinted by permission of the author and *Educational Theater Journal*.

[1] C. G. Jung, "The Phenomenology of the Spirit in Fairy Tales." Reprinted in *Psyche and Symbol* (Garden City, New York, 1958), pp. 72-3.

[2] *Ibid.*, pp. 110-11.

The central figures of these late plays (with the possible exception of Rita and Allmers in *Little Eyolf*)—Ellida, Solness, Borkman, Rubek— are people who have already passed through the great experience of their lives. Solness, Borkman, and Rubek are old men each seeking meaning for their lives in the form of a new grandeur which will somehow externalize the immensity of their souls' vision. Each central character is at an impasse. Ellida is not happy with Wangel; Rita and Allmers are unable to live together in the presence of Eyolf; Solness is building his new house, but it does not satisfy him; Borkman realizes that the world will not seek him out; and Rubek, who had one moment of supreme creation, is searching for something in his art which will equal and then surpass "The Day of Judgment." At the moment of supreme frustration, Jung's "old man" materializes in the form of the Stranger, the Rat-Wife, Hilde, Ella, and Irene. Each of these figures (with, again, the possible exception of the Rat-Wife from *Little Eyolf*) is a person from the past. Each of them, too, is a promise unkept. These people come to demand something of the heroes—and whether this demand be running off to sea, clearing the rats out of the house, wreathing the highest spire, climbing "up into the light, where glory shines," or the voice which prophesies that "you will never ride triumphant into your cold kingdom"—they drive the hero to his final achievement, and in the cases of Solness, Borkman, and Rubek, to death. Undoubtedly these unexpected visitors are, as Jung has it, "personified thoughts." They are those sectors of the hero's mind which cannot be faced directly. These "trolls"—fairy-tale people—condense out of the past to haunt the decisive days of the hero's life. The trolls drive Borkman to his peace-in-death, and Solness and Rubek to their victory-in-death: their tragic knowledge.

These mysterious "thoughts" are fully realized in *The Lady from the Sea, The Master Builder,* and *When We Dead Awaken.* They are less mature in *Little Eyolf* and *John Gabriel Borkman.* One may even see something of the daemonic personified in Lövborg of *Hedda Gabler.* These figures, recurring throughout the late plays, are all the more important to an understanding of Ibsen's dramaturgy because no counterpart to them appears in the realistic plays written before *The Lady from the Sea.* We must go all the way back to Gerd of *Brand* (1865) to find a character like them. Although I shall not discuss *Brand* here, it is interesting to note that the end of that monumental play is strikingly similar to the end of *When We Dead Awaken.* A close investigation of these two plays would disclose other similarities both in form and theme: the child image, the ascent up the mountain, the renunciation of life for art or duty. We may recall that it was with the writing of *The Lady from the Sea* in 1888 that Ibsen said to Georg Brandes, "Now I shan't write any more polemical plays." [3] We may be sure, then, that Ibsen was indeed very conscious of the new turn his work was taking.

The Lady from the Sea, the first of the non-polemical plays, shows us clearly what Ibsen intended in his late work, and how close his intention matches Jung's observations. After the Stranger first appears, Wangel is talking to Arnholm:

> *Wangel.* My dear friend, there are aspects of this case which cannot be explained.
> *Arnholm.* You mean it's something that's beyond rational explanation?
> *Wangel.* Yes. For the time being anyway.

Later Ellida is explaining to Wangel what the Stranger means to her:

> *Wangel.* What do you know about him? Nothing. Not even who he is—or what he is.
> *Ellida (To herself).* I know. It's just that that is so—demonic.
>
> *Wangel (Comes closer to her).* Ellida, what exactly do you mean by demonic?
> *Ellida (Pauses).* The demonic—is something that appals—and attracts.
> *Wangel.* Attractive too?
> *Ellida.* More than anything, I think.

Finally, when Wangel offers to protect Ellida against the Stranger, she reacts sharply:

> Protect me? What is there to protect me against? There is no power or force outside me that threatens me. The root of that fascination lies in my own mind. What can you do against that?

If the scene had been written by Jung to explain what he meant by the "old man" he could not have done better. The Stranger is clearly the externalized thought which comes materialized as a person to threaten Ellida. Ellida, like modern man, recognizes that this "person" is within her own mind. She fights against him and finally triumphs over him. With this triumph she is, for the first time, able to feel loved and at home with Wangel. She recognizes that the Stranger typifies her own wishes:

> But my mind—my thoughts—my dreams and longings—those you [Wangel] cannot imprison. They strain to roam and hunt—out into the unknown—which I was born for—and which you have locked me away from.

When Ellida confronts the Stranger for the last time she is for the first time fully confronting herself. Her ability to withstand the Stranger's

[3] Quoted by Michael Meyer in his introduction to *The Lady from the Sea* in *When We Dead Awaken and Three Other Plays* (Garden City, New York, 1960), p. 4.

seductiveness means that she has conquered her daemonic urge to wander. Therefore her dramatic shift in attitude toward Wangel is comprehensible. She faces the Stranger, rejects him, and immediately he becomes for her "a dead man washed up by the sea. . . . I no longer fear you. I no longer want you." In terms of such a rejuvenation, Ellida's acceptance of Wangel is entirely plausible. Theatrically it may seem forced; psychologically it is credible.

A similar action is repeated in *Little Eyolf*. Here the Rat-Wife lures Eyolf to his death. The boy is the object of Rita's and Allmer's hate and the Rat-Wife is the personification of that hate. Through Eyolf's sacrifice his parents are able to find love again. The Rat-Wife performs the purgative function for Rita and Allmers. As she leaves, the Rat-Wife says:

> If your ladyship should find that there's anything here that keeps nibbling and gnawing, creeping and crawling, then just see and get hold of me . . .

The "creeping and crawling" thing which disrupts the household is, of course, Eyolf himself, the cripple-child who is the living reminder of Rita and Allmer's sin, and, therefore, the object of their hate and the cause of their inability to live in love with one another. Little Eyolf is literally "wished" to death by his parents and the Rat-Wife materializes to lead the boy out of the house and to his watery graveyard. Once he is gone, Rita and Allmers can begin their lives anew. The Rat-Wife is not so fully developed in terms of the entire play as the Stranger in *The Lady from the Sea,* but she shares his daemonic qualities and performs the same function within the play.

In *John Gabriel Borkman,* Borkman is a character who approximates the grandeur of Solness and Rubek. Here Ibsen combines the daemonic externalized thought with the perilous inclusion of that thought within the hero himself. Ellida is so much two people that she can fully reject one part of herself and live happily after this purgation. Rita and Allmers' guilt has been thrust onto Little Eyolf and with his death they are free. But Borkman bears his own cross.

Jung's second statement helps us understand the daemonic natures of Solness, Borkman, and Rubek. Indeed, as each play proceeds, the heroes seem "possessed." In *The Master Builder* Mrs. Solness thinks her husband is insane. Similarly, Borkman's vision of

> . . . those veins of iron ore, stretching their twisting, branching, enticing arms toward me . . . I love you, treasures that crave for life, with your bright retinue of power and glory. I love you . . .

is a superhuman one, as is Rubek's last vision on the mountaintop. In other words, as each play unfolds, the daemonic is integrated into the personality of the hero—"introjected into human nature"—with a subsequent "power which extends the bounds of personality ad infinitum, in the most perilous way." Knowledge of the daemonic, possession of it, or by it, kills.

These last plays focus on the artist because it is the artist who encloses the daemonic within him, only to let it loose in disciplined form upon the world in terms of his work. It is as if Jung's wild archetypal forces were enchained by the artist, taken to the workshop of the soul, broken in, and then put out in the world as a tamed art-work. While parading through books, in museums, or as a building of great beauty, the art-work can do no harm to those who see it. However, the process of break-ing-it-in lets loose havoc within the artist's soul. It is indeed "perilous" work.

This havoc of the artist is not restricted to his own psyche, though it is there that the most damage is done, but radiates out to those who love the artist. The great human crime of which Solness, Borkman, and Rubek are all guilty is the crime which each true artist must answer for:

> *Ella* (*Moving closer to him*). You are a murderer! You have committed the mortal sin!
> *Borkman* (*Retreats towards the piano*). You are raving, Ella!
> *Ella.* You have killed love in me! (*Goes toward him*) Do you understand what that means? The Bible speaks of a mysterious sin for which there is no forgiveness. I've never understood what that meant before. Now I understand. The sin for which there is no forgiveness is to murder love in a human being.

In making art, the soul must suffer. As we examine the action of these plays we realize that there is a circle of sterility surrounding each man. Mrs. Solness is not grieving over her children, but over her lost love and the innocence she knew as a child: this is the meaning of her dolls. Borkman remains pacing upstairs isolated from everything but delusion (Old Foldal) and art (the music of Frida). Rubek explains it to Maja:

> I live so fast, Maja. We live like that, we artists. I have lived through a whole lifetime in the few years we two have known each other. And I've come to realize that it's not within my power to find happiness in idleness and soft living. Life is not shaped like that for me and my kind.

Furthermore, when Irene accuses Rubek of killing her she is saying that he has killed love in her, the essence of her humanity. It is the common sin of all three heroes: Borkman, Solness, and Rubek; a sin which is inherent in the shape of the life an artist lives.

However, *John Gabriel Borkman, The Master Builder,* and *When We*

Dead Awaken do not stand in equal relation to the problem of the artist. *When We Dead Awaken* comes closest to giving us Ibsen's definitive statement on the artist and therefore demands, in this regard, special attention. Irene—who is closer to Rubek than Ella is to Borkman or Hilde to Solness—continually emphasizes two things: her nakedness and her murders. And her great outcry against Rubek is forthrightly stated:

> I stripped myself naked for you to gaze at me. (*More quietly*) And you never once touched me.

This is the heart-piercing rage of humanity against the artist. For Irene here represents the human soul which is laid bare by the artist and she despairingly resents the fact that the artist does not love, but like God himself, ascetically creates. In these lines are the mysteries of art, which takes to itself, uses all that is most human but which cannot itself enter into the quintessential human condition: love. Rubek answers Irene's cry:

> Irene, didn't you understand that your beauty often drove me almost out of my mind? . . . [But] before all else, I was an artist. And I was sick— sick with a longing to create the one great work of my life.

And since Irene is the personified thought of Rubek himself, his cry is against life itself which is beautiful and drives the artist near out of his mind for longing, but which he cannot touch. It is the work—the creation of the artist—which is his "child," as Rubek notes: the hard, self-formed, immortal art-work. The relationship between Rubek and his sculpture is the only love relationship there can be for him. And this love is, at best, metaphorical. When man becomes God he surrenders his humanity or, if you prefer, rises above it. Yet the memory of his humanity—Irene—continually haunts him and finally comes to take what it owns in the final act of his life.

I mentioned before that the havoc which the artist creates within himself inflicts itself upon those who love him. It is this havoc which is symbolized by Irene's murders. We are not asked to believe that she actually killed others. Rubek has killed the soul in her and therefore anyone who loves her is damaged in turn. The disease of art, although neutralized in the art-work, passes on from person to person. The "fine, sharp dagger" which Irene always takes to bed with her and with which she almost kills Rubek is the psychical memento of Rubek's art: the death of love, of the soul.

In *The Master Builder, John Gabriel Borkman,* and *When We Dead Awaken* the artist is in contention with himself, with his vision. What Ibsen saw, and reflected dramatically, is the titanic isolation of the artist: alone with himself and those ideas which mirror him. The artist recognizes this isolation and deplores it. He shuns his daemonic ideas and tries to give up art for the sake of his humanity. He vows to build homes for human beings, to do striking likenesses which are at heart nice domestic animals, or to wait for the world to call him to practical leadership.

But, finally, the artist realizes that this lower road is not for him. He returns to the mountain of his vision—the tower of his superhuman aspiration where he must face in all its nakedness the pure power and beauty of the clear, cold transcendental truth. It is not by accident that these three plays all end in high, cold, and lonely places. Jung suggests that "the mountain stands for the goal of the pilgrimage and ascent, hence it often has the psychological meaning of the self." [4] And, indeed, it is on high that Solness, Borkman, and Rubek all ultimately face what they are: artists. Prodded by his daemonic ego, atop his peak, the artist catches a last glimpse of the immutable and ineffable. Realizing that it is just so—he sees, knows, and dies. Below him, the institutions of man with their righteous strait-jackets and their codes that work utter a forgiving and perhaps worshiping *Pax Vobiscum!* Those who cannot understand—the great mass of individual human beings—sing on merrily that they are free—"from further down the mountainside."

It is clear that these daemon characters fall into three groups: The Stranger and the Rat-Wife; Ella and Hilde; and Irene. The Stranger and the Rat-Wife are explicitly designed as "mysterious" people. They bring no past with them: they appear, act, and disappear. The Rat-Wife is a pied-piper who lures the evil she loves out to its death in the sea. Once her duty has been done, we never see her again. Ibsen makes no attempt to relate her closely to the other characters on stage. She is a pariah in the town and in the play. The Stranger has only his former brief union with Ellida to tie him to the action of the play. He comes, does what he must do, fails to seduce Ellida, and is thereafter "dead." Paradoxically, although the Stranger is the most self-contained character of the unexpected visitors, he is the most purely daemonic figure of all. He is pointedly described as Ellida's haunting dreams and fears; he is recognized as the harbinger of something "beyond rational explanation." However, this psychical function does not change the fact that on stage he is, like the Rat-Wife, a person all to himself, complete and mysterious.

Ella and Hilde each live two half-lives. They are more or less normal people to everyone except Borkman and Solness. Ella has a clearly defined relationship to both Gunhild and Erhart. She has a past which is well-known to the persons within the play. She is a daemon to Borkman; but she is a sister to Gunhild and an aunt to Erhart. Hilde, too, has a past. But this past is a strange one existing only within her mind and, finally, within Solness's mind. Like Ella, Hilde taunts her man with the promise he has made. But this promise is, perhaps, an imaginary one: made only within Solness's own mind, never verbalized—or, as Solness himself says, "willed" into reality.

> I must have thought all this. I must have wanted it—wished it—desired it. So that— Couldn't that be an explanation? (*Hilde remains silent. Solness bursts out impatiently*) Oh, damn it! Have it your own way—say I *did* it!

> *Solness.* Don't you think, Hilde, that there are people singled out by fate who have been endowed with grace and power to wish for something, desire it so passionately, *will* it so inexorably that, ultimately, they must be granted it? Don't you believe that?
> *Hilde (With an enigmatic expression in her eyes)*. If that is so, the time will come when we shall see if I am one of them.
> *Solness.* No man can achieve such things alone. Oh, no—there are helpers and servants—who must be at our side if we are to succeed. But they never come of their own accord. One must call on them with all one's strength. Silently, you understand.

Later Solness realizes that Hilde, like himself, "has the troll" in her. He slowly comes to the awareness that he has summoned Hilde, silently: she is his helper and servant, the daemon which is finally introjected into his psyche so that his personality is extended ad infinitum—he tries the impossible: to wreathe the tower—and he plunges to his death. However, to the other characters in the play, Hilde is a light-hearted and even compassionate human being. Mrs. Solness, first resenting her, finally confides to Hilde the deepest secrets of her heart—the story of the dolls and the fire. Ironically, Hilde is so well-trusted that she is given the mission of dissuading Solness from his spire-wreathing. This is, of course, the last thing she would think of doing.

Irene is the most fully realized character of them all. She combines the total daemonism of the Stranger and the Rat-Wife with the total introjection into the hero's mind of Hilde. Except for a few words to Maja, she never speaks to any character but Rubek. When Rubek talks of her to Maja, he is describing his own psyche, his inspiration, his renewed call to art:

> *Rubek (Hesitantly)*. What I feel so keenly—almost painfully—is the need of someone who is really close to me—
> *Maja (Interrupts)*. Aren't I, Rubek?
> *Rubek.* Not in that way. I must live with someone who can make me com-

plete—supply what's missing in me—someone who is with me in everything I strive for. . . .

Maja. It was that pale lady you were thinking of, wasn't it?
Rubek. Exactly; of her. . . .

Maja (Calmly). Does that mean, in plain words, that you've grown tired of me?
Rubek (Vehemently). Yes, that is what it means! I've grown bored, intolerably bored and tired of living with you; it's drained all my vitality. Now you know! *(Controls himself)* Those are hard and ugly words. I know that well. And you are not to blame. It's only in me that this change, this revolution has occurred. *(Half to himself)* This awakening to the life that is really mine. . . .

Rubek (Taps himself on the chest). In here, Maja—in here I keep a small casket, with a lock that cannot be picked. In that casket, all my visions lie. But when she left me, and vanished from my life, the lock of that casket snapped shut. She had the key, and she took it with her. You, my poor Maja, you had no key. So everything in it lies unused. And the years pass —and all that wealth lies there—and I cannot touch it!

In these selections from Act II of *When We Dead Awaken* we see clearly that Irene is Rubek's alter-ego: one with him in everything he strives for. I have shown previously how Irene represents the human-in-the-artist within Rubek. Here she represents the inspiration-of-the-artist within him. The combination of facets makes her a complete alter-ego, a total introjection, personifying the colossal struggle within Rubek's tortured soul between life and art; an antagonism which can only be resolved, fused, at the moment of supreme vision and death on the mountaintop. Irene returns to Rubek at the precise moment and place where she can do the most good, or harm—depending on your point of view. The action of *When We Dead Awaken* shows Rubek casting off everything and everyone except Irene. Alone with her—alone with himself—he goes to face his fate.

I may now draw these ideas together. First let me note again that Jung's statements are not in themselves a definitive piece of literary criticism. They were not written with Ibsen in mind. What they do for us is to provide a key to a deeper understanding of the plays. We must not try to force these plays into a strait-jacket. They demand opening up, not closing. Their very power grows out of the richness and multiplicity of their connotations. My reading of them here is intended to be neither complete nor exclusive. I have used Jung simply because his observations about fairy tales are fraught with radiating hints.

If these hints are accurate and these daemonic characters are at once personified thoughts of the hero and pure daemonization introjected into the hero's psyche, what effect does this have on their theatrical effectiveness? How do they work on stage?

On stage these "personified thoughts" lead an uneasy and not altogether satisfactory life. The Stranger and the Rat-Wife are clearly "mysterious people" and we accept them as such. However, Ibsen attempts to maintain the façade of fourth-wall reality in *The Lady from the Sea* and *Little Eyolf* and there is such a jarring disparity between the language and manners of the introjected thought-people and the other, normal, persons on stage that the plays tend to fall apart. At one moment we are asked to accept what is happening as conventional "reality"; at the next we are shown a daemon rising up full-blown from the depths of the mind. It is this *theatrical* disparity which makes us uneasy over Ellida's rejuvenation in *The Lady from the Sea* and which turns the Rat-Wife into a quasi-comic figure. Such an unintended reaction is due to the fact that the Stranger and the Rat-Wife project themselves beyond the limits of the conventions Ibsen uses during most of the two plays. The daemon characters are outside of the action; they are not woven into the fabric of the world of those people they affect. Onto a stage peopled with rounded characters walks an idea, and we are understandably shocked.

In *The Master Builder* and *John Gabriel Borkman*, Ibsen tries to solve this problem of stage credibility by giving Ella and Hilde objective contact points with persons other than Solness and Borkman. This solution also proves somewhat unsatisfactory on stage. How are we to play Hilde? Is she a daemon in disguise when she is speaking to Mrs. Solness and Dr. Herdal? Is she really two people? When is the mask on and when is it off? The same questions may be asked of Ella, although her previous relationship with Borkman and her position within the family make her more believable on stage. If this split in character were due to the special vision of Borkman and Solness it would, perhaps, succeed. But Ella and Hilde actually talk a different kind of language to their heroes than they do to the other people in the plays. What Ibsen has done is to integrate them into the heroes' consciousness, while leaving them "themselves" to everyone else. This solution violates the surface reality of Ibsen's constructs. By trying to have the best of the real and symbolic worlds, he vitiates both.

In *When We Dead Awaken,* Ibsen at last succeeds in fully realizing the personified thought on stage. Irene is completely integrated into Rubek's psyche. His language and hers are in harmony. She speaks to no one else. He finds it increasingly difficult to talk to anyone but her.

She becomes part of him. In this, his last play, Ibsen finally breaks whole-heartedly with the fourth-wall reality which was, more or less, part of his stock-in-trade in every play after *Peer Gynt* and *Brand*. The private language of the soul *is* the language of the play. Rubek's climb to self-knowledge is a pilgrim's progress frankly presented as such. The other characters play their roles in the hierarchy of perception without a flaw: the animalistic Ulfhejm; the bourgeois Inspector; the fascinated-with-art but truly life-loving Maja. Even the shadowy nun—the chronicler of Rubek's-Irene's pilgrimage—is acceptable on stage because Ibsen does not ask us to believe that his passion-play of the artist is "real."

In these last plays Ibsen is struggling with form as he had not struggled since *Peer Gynt* and *Brand*. He thought he could isolate his daemons in *The Lady from the Sea* and *Little Eyolf*. This proved intellectually false and theatrically disquieting. Then, in *John Gabriel Borkman* and *The Master Builder* Ibsen tried to integrate the daemons into the consciousness of the heroes without affecting the daemons' "normal" relationships with other people. Although this solution was somewhat more palpable theatrically, the resulting ambivalence of character was unsatisfactory. Only in *When We Dead Awaken* did Ibsen arrive at a form free enough to suit the idea: a fully integrated daemon in a frankly symbolist play peopled with aspectival characters.

The World of Ibsen

by Stephen Whicher

We notice first the landscapes. A tremendous range of mountains looms through the rain behind the home of the Alvings in *Ghosts*. In the last scene the sun touches a far-off peak as the curtain drops. The mountains tower so close over Brand's home—which the sun reaches only three weeks in the year—that avalanches will pass harmlessly *over* the house. Waterfalls are everywhere; throughout *Rosmersholm* we hear the rush of the stream that has taken Beata and will take Rosmer and Rebekka. In the other direction a narrow, bottomless fjord winds out of sight to the distant ocean.

That life can be hard in this vertical world goes without saying. Even the towns offer little relief, absorbed as they are in local affairs, small-minded places where neither idealism nor joy in life can find air to breathe. Yet Ibsen's plays do not weigh down the spectator in the manner, for instance, of Strindberg's *Dance of Death*. The closed world of dark fjords and heavy middle-class interiors that repels Ibsen's casual readers opens, on greater acquaintance, into deeper and deeper vistas in every direction, upward, outward, and downward. If the grand landscape crushes in, it also draws out, and always does both with maximum force.

Outward there is first the sea, "the terrible that attracts and repels," as Ellida Wangel defines it in *The Lady from the Sea*. For her its lure is embodied in the Stranger from the North. Rebekka West in *Rosmersholm* also comes (by sea) from the extreme North, where the pagan Viking spirit of old Norway made its last stand. The North enters other plays like a wind from the sea.

Beyond the sea lies the great world, where Ibsen himself found emancipation. There is America, for example, not always regarded by Ibsen with a kindly eye—it was here Peer Gynt made his fortune, traffick-

"The World of Ibsen" by Stephen Whicher. From *The Commonweal*, LXIV, 17 (July 27, 1956), 417-419. Copyright © 1956 by *The Commonweal*. Reprinted by permission of *The Commonweal*.

ing in slaves and idols. But Lona Hessel blows into *Pillars of Society* like a breath from the prairies to "let in some fresh air" on Bernick's living lie, and Dina Dorf escapes to a new freedom in the New World. Or we have an equally mythical Paris in *Ghosts*: "Over there the mere fact of being alive is considered a matter for exultant happiness." Peer answered for a part of his author when Kari asked him, "Will you travel far?" "To the sea." "So far?" "And farther still."

Yet here, remembering that Peer nearly annihilated himself by going "roundabout," we meet the counterforce. Though Ibsen chose exile on grounds of the highest principle, it is striking how few of his characters follow his example. With the steadfastness of Hawthorne's Hester Prynne, they face their lot where fate has cast it. Exile was a necessity for Ibsen, but he paid a heavy price for it. "Up here, by the fjords, is my native land. But—but—but! Where am I to find my homeland?"

Nothing is more unlike the Ibsen of the plays than the frock-coated, be-lilaced caricature of respectability which glares from his statues and pictures. His violently conflicting emotions would have torn him apart if he had not been able to discharge them into his plays. A fierce revolt and protest lies at their heart, a savage demand for freedom at all costs— matched by an iron conscience that told him all revolt must be paid for. The closing-in, opening-out character of Ibsen's landscapes mirrors his inner country.

His world opens not only outward but downward and upward. Downward lie the mines, where the ore sings to the hammerblows of the miner who will leave light and life behind to seek it out. Downward, too, are the depths of the sea where the maimed and broken can lie hidden in the weeds and everything that gnaws and rankles can find peace. But the heights drew Ibsen most. They seemed to impose a stern Either/Or which his Scandinavian soul could not resist: either love or greatness; either joy or one's calling; either humanity or freedom. His will to freedom is expressed in the early poem, "On the Vidde," in which a young lover, hunting on the upland moors, learns from a stranger "with eyes like glacial pools" to look down on the burning of his mother's house and the wedding of his bride to another man with detachment, as spectacles. Having "grieved my heart free," he is fitted for life on the heights.

> Now am I steelset; I follow the call
> That bids me roam the heights!
> I have lived out my lowland life;
> Here, up on the *vidde,* are freedom and God—
> The rest grope down below.

The same ambiguous call to the heights is the subject of *Brand,* Ibsen's challenge to his nation. To Brand the spirit of trimming and compromise is the deadly enemy; his motto is, Nothing—or All. He sets out single-handed to make his little flock of poor fishermen into supermen. One can understand the appeal of the Brand image to Ibsen, since in such a priest-hero he could imagine a union of the freedom he craved and the responsibility he could not surrender. Already in *Brand,* however, he showed his extraordinary power to stand aside and judge his own characters. Sacrifice is a lodestone-rock to Brand: his motto seems to mean, not *Win* all or nothing, but *Give* all or nothing. He is a fanatic of the Will; with tears and suffering, for he is not unfeeling, he denies his mother the last rites of the church and drives his son, his wife, and finally himself to a fruitless death. In the end he realizes that his heroic God has lacked *caritas.*

The same violent rebellion at man's damnable littleness lies at the heart of Ibsen's first "modern" plays: *Pillars of Society, A Doll's House, Ghosts,* and *An Enemy of the People.* All are blows against the petty forces in society that hinder man from obeying the motto taught in *Peer Gynt:* Be Thyself. Nora's challenge to society, for instance, is still Brand's, transferred from a Herculean figure to the least likely of persons, as if to stress its necessity to all men. When she ceases to be her husband's doll and sets out to be herself, she also must sacrifice children, reputation, all she has of value. She must give all or nothing. So Fru Alving, "Nora twenty years older," does not dare to give all—and her reward is nothing. Dr. Stockmann's great discovery is the same; "The strongest man in the world is he who stands most alone."

This genial nihilist, with his "All who live by lies ought to be exterminated," well illustrates the berserk, go-for-broke quality of Ibsen's challenge in these plays. His rebels do not announce a program; they do not even seriously pose questions; they simply explode. That explosions are destructive Ibsen knew as well as we do. Already the question is gathering under the surface: What gain can justify this havoc?

With *The Wild Duck* the undertone becomes the theme. The counter-image to Brand, the man of will, namely Peer, the dreamer and *digter,* comes to the fore again, this time not so indulgently treated. The idealist, too, is now clearly destructive, however well-meaning. Urge the dreamer to act, the play suggests, and the result is disaster. The last word is the doctor's: "Life would be all right if we could only get rid of these damned fools who keep dunning poor people like us with their 'claim of the ideal.' "

The same pessimistic skepticism controls the next three plays, varied as they are. *The Lady from the Sea,* the most "positive" and the slightest of the three, reads like a companion piece to *A Doll's House.* Wisely released by her husband, Ellida sees the folly of a desperate plunge like Nora's into the unknown, and freely chooses home and responsibility. In *Rosmersholm* the ruthless woman of action Fru Alving wished to be is broken by the ghost of the past as much as is the innocent idealist and dreamer; the dead wife claims them both. The divine discontent of Brand and the young Peer dwindles in *Hedda Gabler* to a sick restlessness, purely aimless and destructive. The cold dissection of the human animal in that most mirthless of comedies finds its spokesman in Hetman, the Brendel of the first draft of *Rosmersholm*: "The Master forgot to give us wings. Both outer and inner ones. So let us crawl on the earth as long as we can. There is nothing else to be done."

The hard detachment of *Hedda Gabler* masked Ibsen's own deep involvement. As the acid of skepticism ate inward, past the "Christian" condemnation of Brand and the general verdict on mankind of these later plays, it revealed the true pattern etched on the plate: Ibsen's personal guilt. He had charity for Peer, none for himself. He held Doomsday over himself in the four introspective plays of his old age, beginning with *The Master Builder.* What had the great work amounted to, each play asks over again, to which he had sacrificed so much? "Nothing, nothing! The whole is nothing." And the price! Happiness, love, life itself, and not his only but that of others as well.

Solness feels the thought of what he has done to those who loved him as "a great raw place here on my breast" that will never heal. The lure of the heights, as Allmers discovered, is the lure of death; and Borkman and Rubek finally discover that they *are* dead, self-slain.

The last plays have been called dramas of redemption, but surely no bubble of hope was ever more fragile than the castles in the air that the heroes of these plays dream of. The dominant image in them, one might well say in all Ibsen's drama, is the wide eyes of the dead children—all the sacrificed lives, including his own. "It is not true," Rita tells Allmers after the drowning of little Eyolf, "that he was swept away at once. They say they saw him lying on the bottom. Deep down in the clear water. They say he lay on his back. Quite still. With great open eyes. . . ." "And now we shall never, never see him again." "Day and night I shall see him before me as he lay there. With great open eyes."

To an American, Ibsen's terrible sense of responsibility is a tonic and a shock, since our literature, by and large, is a plea of Not Guilty. We are repelled, and rightly, as he was in the end, by the monstrous gigantism of Brand, the cult of Will that was Ibsen's demon. By contrast, the writers of our heroic age in literature, men like Emerson, Thoreau and Whitman, show a flexible receptivity, a reliance on sources of power larger than themselves, which is much richer and more human. But the relentless self-judgment with which Ibsen faced the upshot of his life and concluded, "I have what I have deserved," is something which, in the twilight of our Age of Innocence, we are not accustomed to find in our authors. It may be that as time goes on the great Norwegian dramatist will have more to say to us.

Ibsen the Romantic

by E. M. Forster

"My book is poetry, and if it is not poetry, then it will be."—Ibsen to Björnson.

Ibsen was a poet during the earlier part of his life. He began as a lyricist, and his first plays are either in verse or are inspired by an imaginative contemplation of the past. When he was about forty, a change occurred, the importance of which has been differently estimated. Certain critics, both friendly and hostile, regard it as a fundamental change. They argue that with *The League of Youth* the real or realistic Ibsen begins to emerge, the singer dies, the social castigator is born, the scene clarifies and darkens, and ideas come to the front which do not necessarily contradict previous ideas, but which are given a prominence that entirely alters the dramatic emphasis. We pass from the epic to the domestic. Peer Gynt becomes Hjalmar Ekdal, and Brand as Gregers Werle tears the spectacles of illusion from his eyes, and they work out their tragedy, not among forests and fjords, but in a photographic studio opening into a sort of aviary. The aviary contains a few dead Christmas trees, also a water trough, some rabbits but no bears, one wild duck and that a damaged one. We could not be further from romance, the critics say, and turn, if we are friendly, to the character drawing, the technique, and the moral and social issues; if they are hostile, to the squalor. "Somewhere in the course of the battle of his life Ibsen had a lyric Pegasus killed under him," writes Brandes. "Novel and perilous nonsense," wrote the *Daily Telegraph*. The critics agree in thinking that the poetry, if ever there was any, has gone.

Has it gone? Can the habits of forty years be set aside? Of twenty years—yes; most people are romantic at twenty, owing to lack of experience. As they grow older life offers various alternatives, such as world-

"Ibsen the Romantic" by E. M. Forster. From *Abinger Harvest* by E. M. Forster. Copyright 1936, © 1964 by E. M. Forster. Reprinted by permission of Harcourt, Brace & World, Inc. and Edward Arnold, Ltd., London.

liness or philosophy or the sense of humor, and they usually accept one of these. If, in spite of more solid temptations, they still cling to poetry, it is because a deep preference has to be satisfied. Ibsen was a poet at forty because he had that preference. He was a poet at sixty also. His continued interest in avalanches, water, trees, fire, mines, high places, traveling, was not accidental. Not only was he born a poet—he died one, and as soon as we try to understand him instead of asking him to teach us, the point becomes clearer.

He is, of course, not easy to understand. Two obstacles may be noted. In the first place although he is not a teacher he has the air of being one, there is something in his method that implies a message, though the message really rested on passing irritabilities, and not on any permanent view of conduct or the universe. In the second place, he further throws us off the scent by taking a harsh or a depressing view of human relationships. As a rule, if a writer has a romantic temperament, he will find human relationships beautiful. His characters may hate one another or be unhappy together, but they will generate nobility or charm, they will never be squalid, whatever their other defects. And the crux in Ibsen is that, though he had the romantic temperament, he found personal intercourse sordid. Sooner or later his characters draw their little knives, they rip up the present and the past, and the closer their intimacy the better their opportunities for exchanging pain. Oswald Alving knows how to hurt his mother, Rosmer his mistress, and married couples are even more favorably placed. The Helmers, the Tesmans, the Wangels, Solnesses, Allmers, Borkmans, Rubeks—what a procession, equally incapable of comradeship and ecstasy! If they were heroic or happy once, it was before the curtain rose, and only survives as decay. And if they attain reconciliation, like the Rentheim sisters, the curtain has to fall. Their intercourse is worse than unfriendly, it is petty; moral ugliness trespasses into the aesthetic. And when a play is full of such characters and evolves round their fortunes, how can it possibly be a romantic play? Poetry might perhaps be achieved if Ibsen's indignation was of the straight-hitting sort, like Dante's. But for all its sincerity there is something automatic about it, he reminds us too often of father at the breakfast table after a bad night, sensitive to the defects of society as revealed by a chance glance at the newspaper, and apt to blame all parties for them indiscriminately. Now it is the position of women that upsets father, now the lies people tell, now their inability to lie, now the drains, now the newspaper itself, which he crumples up, but his helpers and servers have to retrieve it, for bad as are all political parties he must really see who got in at Rosmersholm. Seldom can a great genius have had so large a dose of domestic irritability. He was cross with his enemies and friends, with theater-managers, professors, and students, and so cross with his countrymen for not volunteering to help the Danes in 1864 that he had to go to Italy to say so. He might have volunteered in person—he was in the prime of life at the time—but this did not occur to him; he preferred instead to write a scathing little satire about a Norwegian mother whose son was safe at the front. And it is (if one may adopt the phrase) precisely the volunteer spirit that is absent from his conception of human relationships. He put everything into them except the strength of his arm.

"Not a great writer . . . almost great, but marred by this lack of generosity." How readily the phrases rise to the lips! How false they are! For this nagging quality, this habitual bitterness—they are essential in his greatness, because they beckon to the poetry in him, and carry it with them under the ground. Underground. Into the depths of the sea, the depths of the sea. Had he been of heroic build and turned to the light and the sun, his gifts would have evaporated. But he was—thank heaven—subterranean, he loved narrow passages and darkness, and his later plays have a romantic intensity which not only rivals the romantic expansion of their predecessors, but is absolutely unique in literature. The trees in old Ekdal's aviary are as numerous as a forest because they are countless, the water in the chickens' trough includes all the waves on which the Vikings could sail. To his impassioned vision dead and damaged things, however contemptible socially, dwell for ever in the land of romance, and this is the secret of his so-called symbolism: a connection is found between objects that lead different types of existence; they reinforce one another and each lives more intensely than before. Consequently his stage throbs with a mysteriousness for which no obvious preparation has been made, with beckonings, tremblings, sudden compressions of the air, and his characters as they wrangle among the oval tables and stoves are watched by an unseen power which slips between their words.

A weaker dramatist who had this peculiar gift would try to get his effect by patches of fine writing, but with Ibsen as with Beethoven the beauty comes not from the tunes, but from the way they are used and are worked into the joints of the action. *The Master Builder* contains superb examples of this. The plot unfolds logically, the diction is flat and austere, the scene is a villa close to which another villa is being erected, the chief characters are an elderly couple and a young woman who is determined to get a thrill out of her visit, even if it entails breaking her host's neck.

Hilda is a minx, and though her restlessness is not so vulgar as Hedda Gabler's it is quite as pernicious and lacks the saving gesture of suicide. That is one side of Hilda. But on the other side she touches Gerd and the Rat-Wife and the Button-molder, she is a lure and an assessor, she comes from the non-human and asks for her kingdom and for castles in the air that shall rest on solid masonry, and from the moment she knocks at the door poetry filters into the play. Solness, when he listened to her, was neither a dead man nor an old fool. No prose memorial can be raised to him, and consequently Ibsen himself can say nothing when he falls from the scaffolding, and Bernard Shaw does not know that there is any-thing to say. But Hilda hears harps and voices in the air, and though her own voice may be that of a sadistic schoolgirl the sound has never-theless gone out into the dramatist's universe, the avalanches in *Brand* and *When We Dead Awaken* echo it, so does the metal in John Gabriel Borkman's mine. And it has all been done so competently. The symbolism never holds up the action, because it is part of the action, and because Ibsen was a poet, to whom creation and craftsmanship were one. It is the same with the white horses in *Rosmersholm,* the fire of life in *Ghosts,* the gnawing pains in *Little Eyolf,* the sea in *The Lady from the Sea,* where Hilda's own stepmother voices more openly than usual the malaise that connects the forces of nature and the fortunes of men. Everything rings true and echoes far because it is in the exact place which its sur-roundings require.

The source of Ibsen's poetry is indefinable; presumably it comes from the same place as his view of human nature, otherwise they would not harmonize as they do in his art. The vehicle in which poetry reached him —that can easily be defined; it was, of course, the scenery of western and south-western Norway. At some date previous to his Italian journey he must have had experiences of passionate intensity among the moun-tains, comparable to the early experiences of Wordsworth in the English lakes. All his life they kept returning to him, clothed in streams, trees, precipices, and hallowing his characters while they recriminated. In *Brand* and *Peer Gynt* they filled the stage; subsequently they shrank and concentrated; in the two last plays they again fill the stage and hasten the catastrophes by a shroud of snow. To compare Ibsen with Words-worth is to scandalize the faithful in either camp, yet they had one im-portant point in common: they were both of them haunted until the end of their lives by the romantic possibilities of scenery. Wordsworth fell into the residential fallacy; he continued to look at his gods direct, and to pin with decreasing success his precepts to the flanks of Helvellyn.

Ibsen, wiser and greater, sank and smashed the Dovrëfjeld in the depths of the sea, the depths of the sea. He knew that he should find it again. Neither his satire nor his character drawing dwelt as deep; neither the problems he found in human conduct nor the tentative solutions he propounded lay at the roots of his extraordinary heart. There, in that strange gnarled region, a primeval romanticism lurked, frozen or twisted or exuding slime, there was the nest of the Great Boyg. The Great Boyg did not strive, did not die, lay beneath good and evil, did not say one thing more than another:

> Forward or back, and it's just as far;
> Out or in, and it's just as strait.

What do the words mean, and, apart from their meaning, are they meant to be right? And if right, are the prayers of Solveig, which silence them for a moment, wrong? It is proper that we should ask such questions as these when focusing on the moral and social aspect of his work, and they have been brilliantly asked and answered by Bernard Shaw. But as soon as we shift the focus the questions go dim, the reformer becomes a dramatist, we shift again and the dramatist becomes a lyric poet, listening from first to last for the movements of the trolls. Ibsen is at bottom Peer Gynt. Side whiskers and all, he is a boy bewitched:

> The boy has been sitting on his mother's lap.
> They two have been playing all the life-day long.

And though the brow that bends over him can scarcely be described as maternal, it will assuredly preserve him from the melting ladle as long as books are read or plays seen.

Chronology of Important Dates

1828 *March 20*   Born in Skien, Norway, second of six children of Knut and Marichen Ibsen. His older brother dies a month after Henrik's birth, leaving him the eldest.

1836   His father's bankruptcy brings poverty and social ostracism.

1844   Ibsen leaves Skien for Grimstad and enters apprenticeship to an apothecary.

1846   Has illegitimate son by a servant girl ten years his senior; assumes partial support of this child for fifteen years.

1850   First play, *Catiline,* privately printed. Arrives in Christiania (Oslo) to attend university with intent of becoming a physician. Second play, *The Warrior's Barrow,* staged at Christiania Theater.

1851   Receives appointment, through Ole Bull, to Bergen Theater as dramatic poet and stage manager.

1853   Performance in Bergen of *Midsummer Eve,* reflecting brief theater studies in Copenhagen and Dresden.

1855   Performance in Bergen of *Lady Inger of Östraat.*

1856   *The Feast at Solhaug,* first success in the theater.

1857   *Olaf Liljekrans.* Becomes artistic director of the Norwegian Theater in Christiania.

1858   Marries Suzannah Thoresen. Stages *The Vikings at Helgeland* at Norwegian Theater.

1859   His son Sigurd is born. Major poem, "Paa Vidderne" ("On the Heights").

1862   Awarded university grant to gather folk songs and tales; travels widely in Norway. Norwegian Theater bankrupt. *Love's Comedy* published.

1863   Deeply in debt. Petition for aid passed over. *The Pretenders* published.

1864   Leaves Norway, settles in Rome. Danish-Prussian War.

1866   *Brand* appears. Norwegian government votes Ibsen annual stipend of 400 specie-dollars.

1867   *Peer Gynt* published (first performed, with Grieg's music, 1876).

1868   Moves to Dresden.

1869   *League of Youth* published and performed. Ibsen sent as Norway's delegate to opening of Suez Canal.

1871   Publishes his *Poems*.

1873   *Emperor and Galilean* appears.

1874   Summer visit to Norway.

1875   Settles in Munich.

1877   Honorary doctor's degree from University of Uppsala, Sweden. *The Pillars of Society*.

1879   Publication and production of *A Doll House*, written during stay in Rome and Amalfi.

1880   Moves to Rome.

1881   *Ghosts* appears. Storm of opposition.

1882   Ibsen answers with *An Enemy of the People*.

1884   *The Wild Duck*.

1885   Summer visit to Norway. Returns to live in Munich.

1886   *Rosmersholm*. Meiningen Players produce *Ghosts*.

1888   *The Lady from the Sea*. Meeting with Emilie Bardach.

1890   *Hedda Gabler*.

1891   Returns to Norway, settles in Christiania.

1892   Sigurd Ibsen marries Björnson's daughter, Bergliot. *The Master Builder*.

1894   *Little Eyolf*.

1896   *John Gabriel Borkman*.

1898   Extensive seventieth birthday celebrations. First volumes of Copenhagen edition of his collected works.

1899   Sigurd appointed head of Norwegian Foreign Office. Opening of new National Theater in Christiania. *When We Dead Awaken*.

1901   Partially incapacitated by stroke.

1906 *May 23*   Ibsen dies in Christiania.

Notes on the Editor and Authors

ROLF FJELDE, editor of this volume, is the translator of a number of Ibsen plays, including *A Doll House, The Wild Duck, Hedda Gabler,* and *The Master Builder* in prose, as well as a verse translation of *Peer Gynt.* He is an Associate Professor in the English Department at Pratt Institute.

ERIC BENTLEY'S many notable books, such as *The Playwright as Thinker, In Search of Theater,* and *The Life of the Drama,* are basic guides to the modern stage. He is Brander Matthews Professor of Dramatic Literature at Columbia University.

IRVING DEER, Chairman of the Division of Literature and Languages at Dickinson State College, is a frequent contributor to such journals as *Modern Drama, The Explicator, Educational Theater Journal,* and *Studies in the Mass Media.*

FRANCIS FERGUSSON, widely influential critic and analyst of the forms of drama, teaches at Rutgers University. Besides a study of Dante's *Purgatorio,* he is the author of *The Idea of a Theater* and *The Human Image in Dramatic Literature.*

E. M. FORSTER, famed for his novels *A Passage to India, Howard's End,* and *A Room with a View,* has augmented his reputation with the essays collected in *Abinger Harvest* and *Two Cheers for Democracy.*

GEORG GRODDECK (1866-1934), German psychotherapist, was a pioneer in the field of psychosomatic medicine. Among his provocative writings are *The Book of the It, The World of Man,* and *The Unknown Self.*

HALVDAN KOHT, former Foreign Minister of Norway and leading Norwegian man of letters, has written extensively on literary, social, and political subjects. Professor of History at the University of Oslo, he is author of the standard *Life of Ibsen* and co-editor of the monumental *Hundreaarsutgave* of Ibsen's collected works.

F. W. KAUFMANN, for many years Chairman of the Department of German and Russian at Oberlin College, has published studies of *Schiller* and *German Dramatists of the 19th Century.* He is currently preparing a book which will examine literature as an introduction to philosophical thinking.

LEO LOWENTHAL, Professor of Sociology at the University of California (Berkeley), is noted for his many perceptive books and articles on the sociology of literature, his most recent publication being *Literature, Popular Culture and Society.*

CAROLINE W. MAYERSON, educated at Wellesley College and Tulane University, is on the faculty of the Department of English, Newcomb College, in New Orleans.

JOHN NORTHAM, Lecturer in the English Faculty at Cambridge University, has written several articles on Ibsen and is best known for his penetrating study, *Ibsen's Dramatic Method*.

ROBERT RAPHAEL teaches German, Scandinavian, and comparative literature at Queens College of the City University of New York and has published studies of Strindberg and Wagner.

RICHARD SCHECHNER, whose writing, teaching, and directing castigate the American theater toward a fuller realization of its potentials, is the author of a book on Eugene Ionesco. He is editor of the *Tulane Drama Review*.

PAULUS SVENDSEN, Professor in the Institute for Philosophy and the History of Ideas at the University of Oslo, has lectured in Sweden, Denmark, Germany, Italy, and the United States. He is Secretary General of the Norwegian Academy of Science and Letters.

P. F. D. TENNANT, author of *Ibsen's Dramatic Technique*, served for many years in the British Foreign Service in Stockholm, Paris, and Berlin. He is presently Deputy Director-General of the Federation of British Industries.

STEPHEN WHICHER, whose death in 1961 cut short a career of great promise, was Professor of English at Cornell University, specializing in American literature and modern drama. He was the author of *Freedom and Fate: An Inner Life of Ralph Waldo Emerson* and co-editor of the anthology, *Twelve American Poets*.

Selected Bibliography

I. *Biography*

Ibsen, Bergliot. *The Three Ibsens.* New York: American-Scandinavian Foundation, 1952.

Koht, Halvdan. *Life of Ibsen,* 2 vols. New York: W. W. Norton & Company, 1931.

Zucker, A. E. *Ibsen the Master Builder.* New York: Henry Holt & Company, 1929.

II. *Books*

Bradbrook, M. C. *Ibsen, the Norwegian: A Revaluation.* New York: The Macmillan Company, 1948.

Downs, Brian W. *Ibsen: The Intellectual Background.* New York: The Macmillan Company, 1947.

————. *A Study of Six Plays by Ibsen.* New York: Cambridge University Press, 1950.

Jorgenson, Theodore. *Henrik Ibsen: A Study in Art and Personality.* Northfield, Minnesota: St. Olaf College Press, 1945.

Knight, G. Wilson. *Henrik Ibsen.* New York: Grove Press, 1962.

Lucas, F. L. *The Drama of Ibsen and Strindberg.* New York: The Macmillan Company, 1962.

Northam, John. *Ibsen's Dramatic Method.* London: Faber and Faber, Ltd., 1953.

Shaw, G. B. *The Quintessence of Ibsenism.* New York: Hill and Wang, 1957.

Tennant, P. F. D. *Ibsen's Dramatic Technique.* Cambridge: Bowes and Bowes, 1948.

Valency, Maurice. *The Flower and the Castle: An Introduction to the Modern Drama: Ibsen and Strindberg.* New York: The Macmillan Company, 1963.

Weigand, Hermann J. *The Modern Ibsen.* New York: E. P. Dutton and Company, 1960.

III. *Articles and Parts of Books*

Anderson, Andrew R. "Ibsen and the Classic World," *Classic Journal*, XL, 4 (January 1916), 216-225.

Anderssen, Odd-Stein. "Before the Centenary of *Peer Gynt,*" *World Theater*, XII, 4 (1963-64), 281-300.

Arestad, Sverre. "Ibsen's Concept of Tragedy," *PMLA*, LXXIV, 3 (June 1959), 285-297.

Arup, Jens. "On *Hedda Gabler,*" *Orbis Litterarum*, XII, 1 (1957), 4-37.

Bentley, Eric. "Wagner and Ibsen: A Contrast," *The Playwright as Thinker.* New York: Meridian Books, 1957.

———. "Ibsen, Pro and Con," *In Search of Theater.* New York: Vintage Books, 1959.

Brustein, Robert. "Henrik Ibsen," *The Theatre of Revolt.* Boston: Little, Brown and Company, 1964.

Engelstad, C. F. "Henrik Ibsen and the Modern Theater," *World Theater*, VI, 1 (1957), 5-26.

Hurrell, John D. "*Rosmersholm,* The Existentialist Drama and the Dilemma of Modern Tragedy," *Educational Theater Journal*, XV, 2 (May 1963), 118-124.

James, Henry. "*Hedda Gabler,*" "*The Master Builder,*" "*Little Eyolf,*" "*John Gabriel Borkman,*" *The Scenic Art,* ed. Allan Wade. New York: Hill and Wang, 1957.

Joyce, James. "Ibsen's New Drama" [*When We Dead Awaken*], *The Critical Writings of James Joyce,* ed. Ellsworth Mason and Richard Ellmann. New York: The Viking Press, 1959.

McFarlane, James Walter. "Henrik Ibsen," *Ibsen and the Temper of Norwegian Literature.* London: Oxford University Press, 1960.

Reinert, Otto. "Sight Imagery in *The Wild Duck,*" *Journal of English and Germanic Philology*, LV, 3 (July 1956), 457-462.

Thompson, Alan Reynolds. "Ibsen as Psychoanatomist," *Educational Theater Journal*, III, 1 (March 1951), 34-39.

IV. *Bibliography*

Pettersen, Hjalmar. *Henrik Ibsen 1828-1928.* Oslo: Cammermeyer, 1928.

Tedford, Ingrid. *Ibsen Bibliography 1928-1957.* Oslo: Oslo University Press, 1961.